2020
FRESH CLEAN
JOKES
FOR EVERYONE

2020 FRESH CLEAN JOKES FOR EVERYONE

Written & illustrated by

V. SUBHASH

2020 Fresh Clean Jokes For Everyone

Written, illustrated and designed by

V. Subhash
(www.VSubhash.in)

Copyright

© 2020 V. Subhash. All rights reserved.

Disclaimer

Read the preface.

First edition

Published in 2020 by V. Subhash.

ISBN (paperback)

978-93-5408-034-0

Preface

When I was a kid, I read an American jokebook and here is the result. (I should have read Shakespeare instead.) Initially, it was a mystery to me as to who the blondes were or what the fuss was in crossing a road. The book was nevertheless funny and I enjoyed reading it. This 2020 jokebook is based on that model.

Vintage shows from the *Golden Age of American Radio* were also a great inspiration. A special chapter on vintage radio shows is available as an annexure.

This book is for people all ages and interests. If some jokes seem juvenile (in the first part), it is because you are not. These jokes have been included to make children become familiar with new words and facts. This book is a good choice for children if you want them to improve their English-language skills and general knowledge. It will secretly kindle their curiosity and encourage them to learn new things. For this reason, all jokes in this book are child-friendly. You will not be embarrassed to tell any of the jokes in front of your family. Specifically, it has answers to many of the amusing riddles and questions that kids are asked in schools by their teachers and friends. Many jokes in this book use misleading information in mock seriousness. While most teenagers should be able to easily identify them, younger kids will need guidance. Kids should be encouraged to use a dictionary, an atlas and an encylopedia to cross-reference unfamiliar information. If the kid does not have these books, then do not suggest the Internet or a computer as an alternative. Do not interrupt a kid's reading with computers or other electronic devices.

For grownups, this is a good book to read while travelling or after a day's work – purely for the hedonistic consumption of humour.

While all jokes in this book are child-friendly, entire chapters have been written for people with specialized interests or expertise. (This has had some unexpected results. Some of the jokes on financial markets are written as poems and set to the tune of popular nursery rhymes!) But, there is plenty for those in the middle. Plenty for everyone! EVERYONE!

Disclaimer

- This book satirizes everything. Political correctness is not an exception. But, remember, this book is child-friendly and family-friendly. So, the blondes in the blonde jokes eventually trump Chuck Norris. (Chuck asked me to write them.) Ethnic jokes are not racist jokes. Confucius-say jokes are squeaky clean, like Mel Blanc's Zookie original. Romantic jokes are totally devoid of mushy stuff and are actually breakup jokes.

- Humour arises from the distortion of reality. Hence, this book should be read only as a jokebook. At best, it should be considered as opinion with obvious scope for mistakes and subjectiveness.

- One of the annexures, at the end of this book, contains the rest of this disclaimer along with my acknowledgements and thanks.

V. Subhash
20-02-2020

Contents

Part 1 - For Learning

This part of the book is written to improve English vocabulary and general knowledge.

Children's Jokes

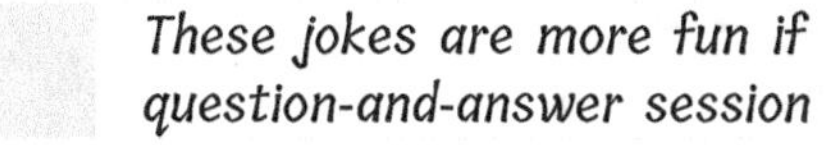

These jokes are more fun if you read them in a question-and-answer session with someone else.

- **What do hummingbirds like to read?**
  Musical notes.

- **Why did the chicken cross the road?**
  It saw a *zebra crossing.*

In some countries, a 'road crossing' or 'crosswalk' is known as a zebra crossing.

- **Why did the zebra cross the road?**
  The chicken dared it.

- **Which came first? The chicken or the egg?**
  - The chicken. It had legs and won the race.

- Which chicken? Which egg?

- **What did the rolodex say to the calendar?**
  "Your *days are numbered.*"

- **What did the calendar say to the rolodex?**
  "You may have many friends but I get a lot of holidays."

- **What did the new calendar say to the old calendar?**
  "Your days are over, buddy!"

- **Why did the pencil not like the eraser?**
  It *rubs both ways.*

- **Why does the cow go moo?**
  It does not. It says, "Maaaaah". And, the sheep does not go "Baa". It goes, "Meheheheh!"

- **What kind of cheese talks?**
  Say Cheese!

- **What did the wall clock say?**
  "My time is up!"

- **Why did the lizard sue the hospital?**
  After it broke off its tail, a psychiatrist wanted to treat it as a split-personality disorder.

Autotomy is the ability in some animals with which they can break off a body part to distract or escape from a predator. The shed body part usually regenerates.

- **How does a horse fly?**
  Horse feathers!

- **Which one of these is not a duck – Bombay Duck, Mandarin Duck, Muscovy Duck and Swedish Duck?**
  Hint: It is a fish, usually consumed in dried form.

- **Which one of these is not a fish – Bluefish, Goldfish, Redfish and Silverfish?**
  Hint: It is a wingless insect usually found in old books or clothing.

- **How did the goose get run over by a car?**
  It didn't *take a gander.*

- **How does a fish go to war?**
  In a tank.

- **Is half a glass half-empty or half-full?**
  This is an urban legend that originated as a joke in the TV sitcom *The Lucy Show* and has captured the imagination of generations of psychologists and interviewers. Anyone, who thinks that only an optimist will consider half a glass as half-full, has low standards. Someone, who thinks only a pessimist will consider it as half-empty, has no standards.

- **The word *suffrage* refers to voting rights. Did it originally involve any suffering?**
  No, the word is derived from the Medieval Latin *suffragium,* which refers to a voting ballot/tablet, the right to vote or simply the vote. The anglicized version *suffrage* began to be used in the 18th century.

- **What is the opposite of the adjective *hungry*?**
  There is no direct opposite such as *unhungry* or *nonhungry* but *satiated* seems to be all right.

I found this question in my sibling's English reader. I did not know

- **Can you say 100 words in one minute? None of the words should have the letters A, B, C or D.**
  Zero, one, two, three, four... ninety-nine.

- **Complete the word ladder – From DULL to MOOD**
  One and only one letter can change in each rung of the ladder. No acronyms, proper nouns or loan words.

- **Phantom Hand Challenge**

  This is a prank you can play on others. Ask one of them to hold out their arm as shown in this illustration. Place your index and middle finger on the person's wrist and slowly walk them towards the elbow pit. After you start, tell the person to close his/her eyes and open it only when your fingers reach the elbow pit. No matter how many times this is done, the person's brain will always be prematurely tricked into thinking that your fingers has reached the pit.

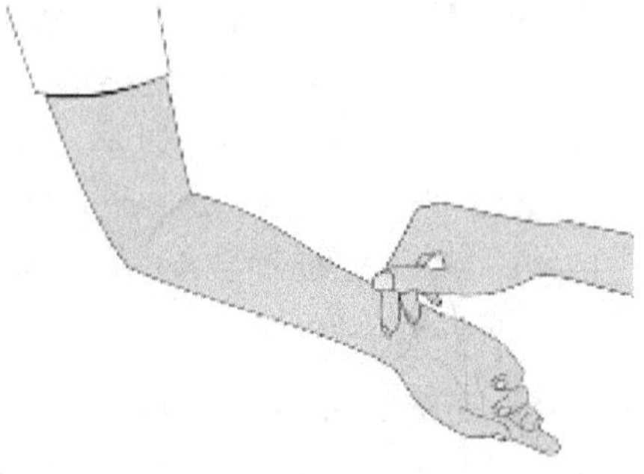

- **What's the difference between these animals: elk, moose, reindeer and caribou?**
  The moose (*Alces alces*) is the most funny-looking one and is found in sub-Arctic regions of North America and Eurasia. Parts of their antlers appear flattened. They are usually solitary animals.

The elk (*Cervus canadensis*) is smaller than the moose but bigger than the reindeer. Elks are found in USA, Canada, eastern Russia, north-eastern China and Mongolia. In many parts of Europe, the elk is confusingly referred as a moose.

Reindeer and caribou are the same species of *Rangifer tarandus*. They are found mostly in Arctic regions of Canada, Alaska and Eurasia. The reindeer and elk look similar but you can tell the difference by their footprint. They do not have flat antlers like the moose. Reindeer is the only deer species where both the male and female have antlers.

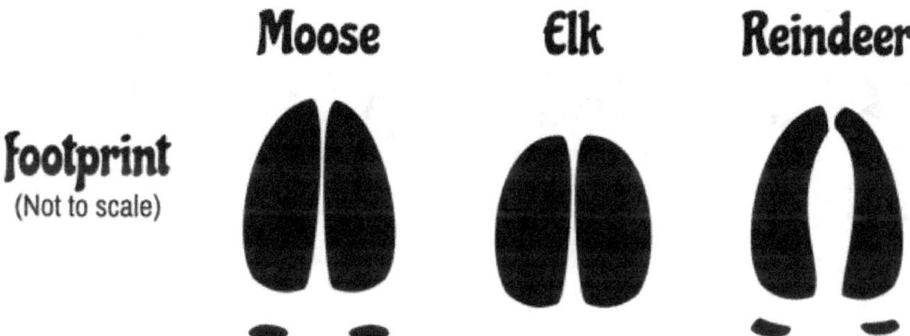

- **Complete the word ladder – from FUNNY to JOKES**

One and only one letter can change in each rung of the ladder. No acronyms, proper nouns or non-English (loan) words.

Computer Jokes

Do you use computers? If not, start with a Linux computer and you will be a cut above the rest. Linux is a free and open-source software (FOSS) operating system (OS). If you already have a computer, install Linux as a virtual machine (VM) and see if you like it. Linux has FOSS alternatives for most proprietary software that you use. All the illustrations in this book were created using Inkscape and GIMP. Both are FOSS and available for other operating systems too.

- **What happened after the robot's 3D printer broke?**
  No arm done.

- **What made the quantum computer so frustrated?**
  He made *a complete fool of himself* .

- **What did one byte say to another?**
  A bit of advice .

- **Why did exclamation mark key (!) break up with the question mark key (?)?**
  There was *a question about* his character.

- **What did dollar key ($) say to the Euro key (€) about the pound key (#)?**
  That he is of *Sterling (£) character* .

- **Why did the dot key feel down?**
  - Its character was called into question (?).
  - A question mark was hanging over it.

- **Why was the space key depressed?**
  It had no character.

- **What did one emoji (☺) say to another?**
  "You think I am funny?"

- **What did one emoticon (😁) say to another?**
  "What's with the funny expression?"

- **Why did one emoticon (😗) not like the other?**
  He *stuck out like a sore thumb* .

- **What is your mother's password?**
  Mum's the word.

- **Name the font with no sense of humour?**
  Comic Sans .

- **What style of font does *Fortune* magazine use?**
  Fortune favours the **bold**.

- **If a politician wanted to work in the IT industry, what job designation would he get?**
  Headless server.

- **If a cow wanted to work in the IT industry, where could it go?**
  A server farm.

- **What happened when Unix dæmons attacked Chuck Norris?**
  He hit them so hard they remained misspelled to this day.

- **What happened after Unix dæmons met Rajinikanth?**
  Before meeting him, they were like other processes. Now, they run in the background like zombies.

- **Whois**

  > Knock knock
  > Who is there?
  > man

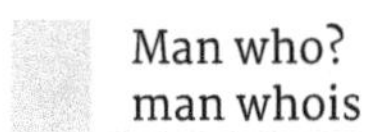

> Man who?
> man whois

Requires Linux knowledge.

- **Whois**

  > Knock knock
  > Who is there?
  > 43
  > 43 who?
  > 43 whois

Requires networking/Linux knowledge.

- **Why does espeak have an Italian accent?**
  It converts everything to Roman.

Requires Linux familiarity.

- **What did one network node say to another?**
  "Sorry, I can't talk to you. We are not on the same subnet."

Requires networking knowledge.

- **How does Count Dracula remain discreet in this networked world?**
  IP cloaking.

- **How do bears find each other in the woods?**
  Bear-to-bear networking.

- **What did one packet say to another?**
  "You are lost, aren't you?"

- **What did the other packet say?**
  "Stop broadcasting it."

- **Why did the security expert couple break up?**
  They routinely probed each other's devices and locked each other out.

- **Why did the hacker couple break up?**
  There were no secrets between them.

- **Why did the hacker couple make up?**
  There were no secrets between them.

- **Why did the backup expert couple break up?**
  They felt they frequently *ran out of* space for each other.

- **Why did the database admin couple break up?**
  Their marriage had reached a deadlock.

- **Why did the network admin couple break up?**
  She thought he was acting like her domain controller.

- **The good, the bad, and the ugly**

  > **Google**: Type your search here.
  > **Bing**: Search me!
  > **DuckDuckGo**: Do you feel lucky... punks?

- **How many Microsoft managers would it take to a change a lightbulb?**

None but they will trick the bulb to upgrade itself.

- **How many Apple fanboys would it take to a change a lightbulb?**
  One but he would have to buy an Apple-proprietary socket too.
- **How many Apple fanboys would it take to a change a lightbulb?**
  None because Apple has just reinvented the light bulb and a new magical non-revolutionary version is available.
- **Linux or Windows: Who is well-mannered?**
  Lee knocks. Win dozes.
- **Linux vs Windows: Who wins?**
  Lee knocks windoses.
- **What does a server admin think when he looks at his house and vehicle?**
  "That's hardware."
- **What does a server admin think when he thinks of his wife?**
  "That's software."
- **What does a server admin think when he looks at his parents?**
  "My rootware!"
- **What does a server admin think when he looks at his parents-in-law?**
  "Beware!"
- **What does a server admin think when he looks at his kids?**
  "That's malware."
- **What does a server admin think when he looks at his taxes?**
  "That's ransomware."
- **What does a server admin think when he looks at his salary after taxes?**
  "That's shrinkware."
- **What does a server admin think when he notices ants in the server room?**
  "That's social engineering."
- **What does a server admin think when he notices rats in the server room?**
  "Some IP tunnelling."
- **What does a server admin think when he looks at a waiter?**
  "Should I call him a server?"
- **What does a server admin think when he looks at a see-saw?**
  "Seems like a load balancer."
- **What does a server admin think when he looks at a painter?**
  "Hey, an application server."
- **Viral Videos**

  "Our client wants us to log into YouTube and make their corporate videos viral."
  "You want me to sneeze on them?"
  "No, seriously..."
  "I can't catch flu or coronavirus for that!"
- **Stress test - Calculate infinity**

  Linux: Let me get back to you.
  Mac: Look how shiny everything looks.
  Windows: Press Ctrl+Alt+Del to restart.

- **What computer games do Linux enthusiasts like to play?**
  - Command & Conquer
  - Console games

- **What computer game do molemen like to play?**
  Minecraft.

- **What computer game do thieves like to play?**
  Tekken.

- **What computer game do vampires like to play?**
  - Modern Combat
  - Flight Simulator
  - Tomb Raider

- **What computer game do werewolves like to play?**
  Pac-Man.

- **What computer game do zombies like to play?**
  - Half-Life, Left4Dead, Burnout, Dead Rising...
  - Need For Speed, Asphalt, Road Rash
  - Uncharted

- **The Selfie Anthem**

  Jack and Jill
  Livestreamed from a cliff
  When they wanted to take a selfie
  Jack fell down
  And took Jill down
  But the 'likes' were getting silly

• Set to the tune of 'Jack and Jill'.
• Be aware of your surroundings. Life is more important than likes.

Computer Programming Jokes

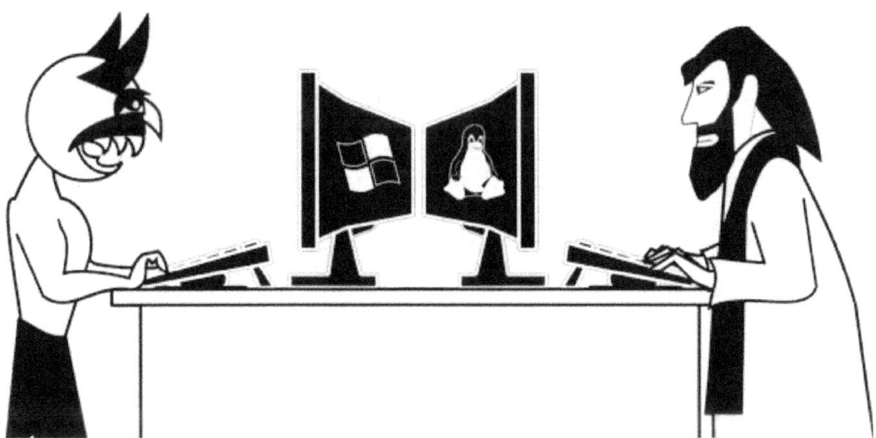

Can you write code? I have written in more than a dozen computer languages, even assembly. How many do you know? This book was written in Markdown using an Eclipse IDE, exported to HTML and formatted using CSS. The jokes were counted using Javascript. Eclipse and many other free software are brought to you by open-source projects.

If you use open-source software, it is expected that you support them financially in the form of donations.

- What would Jesus do? Choose Linux or Mac or Windows?
  Linux, of course. This is not a joke!

- Jesus versus the Devil
  The Devil challenges Jesus to a computer programming contest. Both start writing the code for their program furiously when suddenly there is a power failure. Both computers go down. When the power comes back, both participants restart their computers. Jesus resumes typing his program without much delay. Meanwhile, the Devil is cooling his heels because Microsoft Windows OS has chosen just that moment to install updates and delayed the login screen. The Devil goes over to the other side and looks at Jesus' computer. Jesus is running a free Linux OS computer, which lets you login immediately. The Devil slaps its forehead and returns to its computer. Windows takes a few more minutes installing updates and finally lets the Devil log in. The Devil opens the IDE and looks at its program. All source code has vanished. The power failure has nuked its file. The Devil again goes over to the other side and wonders, "How come His code is still there?" Then, the Devil remembers, JESUS SAVES.

- **Jesus versus the Devil - Part Deux**
  The Devil challenges Jesus to another challenge. This time, the Devil has a Linux computer and an UPS to handle power failures. Suddenly, the power goes out. The Devil expects Jesus' computer to go down but both computers stay on. The Devil's thoughts are like, "Omigod! What in good heavens is going on?" It goes over to God's computer and finds that the computer is on even though it not connected to any form of emergency power supply. Then, the Devil realizes another truth - GOD WORKS IN MYSTERIOUS WAYS.

- **Code Complete**
  In the book *Code Complete* (Microsoft Press), the author used a neat psychological trick. He listed of a few programming concepts and asked the reader to identify the ones that were familiar. I picked several of those terms and resumed reading what was really a lesson in intellectual honesty. In the list, the author had included a few terms that seemed real but did not really exist. I fell right into his trap and picked a few of the non-existing concepts that I thought I knew. The lesson learned was either you know or you do not. Err on the side of caution.

- **Why did the software routine cry?**
  This method has been deprecated.

- **What did the exception say to the method?**
  "Been there and done that."

- **Why did the base class go to a psychiatrist?**
  It had multiple personality disorder.

- **What did the compiler say to the parser?**
  "Is it just me or *am I seeing double*?"

- **What did the artificial neural network say to the AI program?**
  "You are *getting on my nerves*!"

- **Why did the camel stop speaking to the llama?**
  The llama spoke in ALL CAPS, instead of Camel Case.

- **What did the switch statement say to the computer programmer?**
  "Give me a break!"

- **Why did the switch statement behave erratically?**
  It forgot to take enough breaks.

- **What did the function say to the recursion?**
  "Hold my calls."

- **What charge did the policeman bring against iteration?**
  Nothing except that he is a *repeat offender*.

- **A recursion walks into a bar**
  A recursion walks into a bar and orders tequila shots. The barman pours the drinks but warns, "Don't blow your stack. Okay?"

- **A recursion walks into a bar**
  A recursion walks into a bar and orders a drink. It drinks and then freezes. The bartender walks by and says, "Lost in yourself, eh?"

- **Divide by Zero**

  Knock! Knock!
  Who is there?
  Divide.
  Divide who?
  Divide by Zero.
  Okay, I will *make an exception* for you.

- **Billy, the goat**

  Knock! Knock!
  Who is there?
  Billy.
  Billy who?
  Billy, the goat.
  Sorry, can't let you in. *Gotos are considered evil.*

- **Why did the goat cross the road?**
  To prove that gotos are not evil.

- **Why were the two bytes upset with each other?**
  One of them wanted the other to *move a bit*.

- **How do you prove that a programmer is not crazy?**
  If there is *a method to his madness*.

- **How did the female spider put an end to the male spider stalking her?**
  It used a "nofollow" meta tag.

- **What does the epitaph say for a C programmer?**
  malloc('dd/mm/yyyy');
  free('dd/mm/yyyy');

- **What does the epitaph say for a Java programmer?**
  Nothing. Java variables are automatically garbage-collected.

- **A new software library walks into a bar**
  A new software library walks into a bar and the bartender says, "I would like to see some kind of documentation."

- **Why was the source code angry with the computer programmer?**
  o It did not like his comments.
  o No comments.

- **What would happen if a dog was elected mayor?**
  It would be illegal for software developers to *eat their own dog food*.

This is a metaphor for testing the product before selling it on the market.

- **Why did the tester couple break up?**
  Too many pending issues. Other than logging each other's faults in Bugzilla, no action was taken. Many bugs were labelled as

features and closed without getting fixed.

- **Why did the HTML couple break up?**
  She was strict.

- **Why did the XHTML couple break up?**
  She was very strict.

- **Why did the Unicode couple break up?**
  - He was a reserved character.
  - They were not on the same codepage.

- **What is the source code for the smallest "Hello, World!" executable?**
  This StackOverFlow question was for Windows. The question was locked for deletion ("not a real programming question") before I could answer it. There are three types of executables in Windows - BAT (batch), COM and EXE. Batch files are plain text executables so there is no challenge in it. That leaves us with COM and EXE, which can be created using advanced programming languages. However, all advanced programming languages create very big EXE files... even if you use assembly language. The only solution is to create a COM executable using a DEBUG assembler script. (Uber programmers like us like to etch our code on the bare metal.) Here is the source:

```
a 100
MOV AH,9
MOV DX,108
INT 21
RET
DB "Hello World$"

r CX
14
n hello.com
w
q
```

Put this in a text file named script.txt. Use Command Prompt and redirect the text file to debug.exe. (*debug.exe* is available in all old versions of Windows.)

```
debug < script.txt
```

This will create a 20-byte COM executable named hello.com. Execute it by typing *hello*.

```
hello
```

By tradition, the correct text to display is "Hello, World!" with a comma and an exclamation mark. I decided *stick to the letter*.

Code explanation: *A 100* moves to code position 100. You then set 9 to AH register because that is the instruction for interrupt 21 to print a string. Next, you specify the position of the string (required by interrupt 21) in the DX register. This position will be known to you after you finish the RET statement. (You need to dry run the code interactively once (without the command prompt redirection) to observe it.) The RET statement returns the program to the shell. *r CX* is used to specify the number of bytes of the program - 20 (or 14 in hexadecimal). (This will also be known during the dry run.) *n* specifies the file name. *w* writes the file. *q* quits debug.

I got my introduction to debug scripts when reading the Kris Jamsa book *1001 DOS & PC Tips.*

- **Two numbers walk in to a bar**
  Two numbers walk in to a bar. One is let in and the other gets thrown out. The latter was a *floating-point number.*

- **Two numbers walk in to a bar**
  Two numbers walk in to a bar and have drinks. After a while, one of them says it is time to go. He was seeing everything in *double.*

- **How did the DBA couple break up?**
  She felt that in this new UPDATE to her life, she will make a better SELECTion who will NOT try to ORDER her or ALTER her.

Cross-The-Road Jokes

Almost everyone has heard the age-old question "Why did the chicken cross the road?" There have been many answers but none were satisfactory. This book settled the debate once for all in the section Children's Jokes. Here is more such jokes.

- **Why did the alien cross the road?**
  It might be a giant leap for man but a small step for a creature from outer space.
- **Why did the postman cross the road?**
  He wanted to get his message across.
- **Why did the drunk cross the road?**
  He was on a roll.
- **Why did the aardvark cross the road?**
  Read the next joke.

An aardvark mainly feeds on ants and termites.

- **Why did the ant cross the road?**
  The ant wanted to make the elephant wait for him by holding up the traffic.

The backgrounder for this joke is available in the section *Elephant And Ant Jokes* .

- **Why did the badger cross the road?**
  - Everyone was badgering him to do it.
  - There were no legal claws preventing it.
- **Why did the bat cross the road?**
  There is no use flapping about in one place.

- **Why did the bear cross the road?**
  He said, "Honey, I am coming."
- **Why did the bee cross the road?**
  Seeing is bee-leaving.
- **Why did the beaver cross the road?**
  It was an *eager beaver*.
- **Why did the camel cross the road?**
  It *sticks its neck out* for nobody.
- **Why did the cat cross the road?**
  When the cat's away, the mice will play.
- **Why did the chameleon cross the road?**
  The colour changed.
- **Why did the cheetah cross the road?**
  To ask the policemen hiding behind the tree whether it *broke the speed limit*.
- **Why did the chimp cross the road?**
  That's quite *a head-scratcher*.
- **Why did the chipmunk cross the road?**
  - It *had the cheek* to do it.
  - Does it seem like a nutty idea to you?
- **Why did the cow cross the road?**
  - There were unsubstantiated reports that *the grass was greener on the other side*.
  - Holy cow! It can do anything it pleases. Cross the road, even. [This joke should be read in Snagglepuss style.]
- **Why did the crocodile cross the road?**
  It saw a Discovery Channel 'animal lover' coming towards it!
- **Why did the crow cross the road?**
  - So, it could *crow about it*!
  - That's the way... as the crow flies.
- **Why did the dog cross the road?**
  Now that scientists have figured out why dogs chase vehicles...
- **Why did the deer cross the road?**
  It was *only a buck*.
- **Why did the donkey cross the road?**
  To show that it does not *dig its heels*.
- **Why did the dragon cross the road?**
  Previously, it was standing in a no-smoking area.
- **Why did the duck cross the road?**
  It didn't want to be *a sitting duck*.
- **Why did the elephant cross the road?**
  Someone told it it was *the next big thing*.
- **Why did the emu cross the road?**
  - No need to get all EMUtional about it.
  - To check if it was worth EMUlating.

- **Why did the firefly cross the road?**
  There was no *light at the end of the tunnel* .

- **Why did the fish cross the road?**
  - It wanted to cause a tuna of surprise.
  - When asked, it gave *a canned reply.*
  - Somebody tried to *kick the can down the road* !

- **Why did the frog cross the road?**
  It was only a few hops away.

- **Why did the giraffe cross the road?**
  It was *so over it* .

- **Why did the goat cross the road?**
  For a showdown with the *Men Who Stare At Goats* .

- **Why did the young goat cross the road?**
  It was a *new kid on the block* .

- **Why did the hippopotamus cross the road?**
  It found the hype about it amusing!"

- **Why did the horse cross the road?**
  It was just *horsing around.*

- **Why did the hyena cross the road?**
  It was a *laughing hyena.* It wanted to know what the joke was about.

- **What kind of books do hyenas read?**
  Jokebooks.

- **Animal Collectives**
  Nearly two decades ago, a website run by an English grandmother became famous for the wisdom of the ages that she wanted to share with newer generations. Among them was this selection of collectives.

  - A BUSINESS of ferrets.
  - A CONVOCATION of eagles.
  - A GANG of turkeys.
  - A KNOT of toads.
  - A MOB of kangaroos
  - A MURDER of crows.
  - A PANDEMONIUM of parrots.
  - A PARLIAMENT of owls.
  - A PITYING of turtle doves.
  - A PRICKLE of porcupines.
  - An UNKINDNESS of ravens.

- **Why did the jackal cross the road?**
  It was all jacked up and ready to go.

- **Why did the jaguar cross the road?**
  Ask the driver.

- **Why did the junglefowl cross the road?**

It always ran aFOUL with *the law of the jungle* .

- **Why did the kangaroo cross the road?**
  It was a joey.
- **Why did the llama cross the road?**
  It was only a spitting distance.
- **Why did the mantis cross the road?**
  Pray, tell me.
- **Why did the lion cross the road?**
  Because the buck stops here.

- **Why did the mole cross the road?**
  It struck *a hole in one* .
- **Why did the monkey cross the road?**
  Monkey see, monkey do.
- **Why did the octopus cross the road?**
    - It was a sucker for a challenge.
    - It wanted some hands-on experience.
- **Why did the owl cross the road?**
  How will I know?
- **Why did the porcupine cross the road?**
  It was *a pressing matter*.
- **Why did the quail cross the road?**
  To prove that it wasn't chicken.
- **Why did the raccoon cross the road?**
  A Native American lost his hat and was looking for a replacement.
- **Why did the rhino cross the road?**
  Somebody pressed the horn.

- **Why did the shark cross the road?**
  To grab a bite.
- **Why did the sheep cross the road?**
  One sheep follows another.
- **Why did the first sheep cross the road?**
  It was led by the shepherd.
- **Why did the shepherd cross the road?**
  The grass was greener on the other side.
- **Why did the silverfish cross the road?**
  No need to *throw the book* at him for that.
- **Why did the snail cross the road?**
  Maybe they have a death-wish.

- **Why did the snake cross the road?**
  Somehow the idea crept into its head.
- **Why did the spider cross the road?**
  Its life was *hanging by a thread*.
- **Why did the squirrel cross the road?**
  It was a nut.
- **Why did the Tasmanian devil cross the road?**
  What the devil made him do it?
- **Why did the toad cross the road?**
  When asked, it had no comments TO ADd.
- **Why did the turkey cross the road?**
  Fat chance it would survive the rest of the year than the road.
- **Why did the turtle cross the road?**
  Shell I tell you?
- **Why did the weasel cross the road?**
  - It could not weasel its way out of a dare.
  - It was tired of this nursery rhyme:

    > Up and down the City Road
    > …
    > Pop! goes the weasel.
- **Why did the xoloitzcuintli cross the road?**
  It went back to get his coat.

Xoloitzcuintli is a dog, also known as the *Mexican hairless*.

- **Why did the yak cross the road?**
  His friends were yacking about it all day.
- **Why did the zebra cross the road?**
  Zebra? Crossing?

In some countries, a 'road crossing' or 'crosswalk' is known as a *zebra crossing*.

Elephant And Ant Jokes

These jokes are based on the *Aanaiyum Urumbum* jokes popular in Kerala. In the original version, the ant and the elephant are friends, and the jokes are tall tales. Here are some examples:

- *Aana and Urumbu were playing hide-and-seek near a temple. Aana told the Urumbu that the temple was out of bounds for hiding. When they began playing, Aana had to seek and Urumbu could hide. Aana searched everywhere but could not find Urumbu. Aana became suspicious and decided to check the temple. It blocked the entrance and when the Urumbu sneaked back to capture the post, Aana caught him. How did Aana know that Urumbu was hiding in the temple? Urumbu's shoes were outside.*

- *An aana was travelling on the road when it met with an accident. The ambulance took him to the hospital. An urumbu was seen following the ambulance on a motorcycle. What was the reason? To give blood for his injured friend, of course.*
- *One day, Aana and Urumbu went on a pilgrimage. When evening came, they decided to sleep under a tree. Aana could not sleep. What was the reason? Urumbu was snoring.*
- *Aana and Urumbu were travelling on a bike. They met with an accident. Aana died but Urumbu survived. How did that happen? Urumbu was wearing a helmet.*

In my version, the stories are tall tales but the two protagonists are (fr)enemies. It is not clear if Elephant is making up these stories and Ant is really innocent. That is left to your imagination.

- **Why did Elephant leave the cinema without watching the movie?**
  Ant was sitting in front of him and completely blocking his view.

- **Why could not Elephant climb up the stairs?**
  Ant was blocking the way.

- **Why did Elephant fall down the stairs?**
  Ant threw his weight around.

- **How did Elephant break his front leg?**
  Ant and Elephant were wearing the same colour of clothes, and so Ant pinched him.

- **How did Ant beat Elephant in a running race?**
  Ant at the beginning and the end of the race were lookalikes.

- **Why did Elephant get angry so early in the day?**
  Ant took his morning bath and used up all the water in the storage tank.

- **How did Elephant fall into the water?**
  Ant and Elephant went for a boat ride. After reaching the middle of the lake, Ant suddenly jumped out into the water and swam ashore. With nobody to counter-balance Elephant, the boat capsized.

- **How did Elephant fly through the air?**
  The same thing happened at the playground. Elephant was playing on the see-saw with Ant. Suddenly, Ant jumped off his seat.

- **Why could not Elephant get into the elevator?**
  - Ant and a rhino were already in the elevator. Ant pointed to a sign saying "Maximum: Two animals" and kicked Elephant out.

○ Every time Elephant tried to get in, Ant would sneak up behind it and tug at his tail.

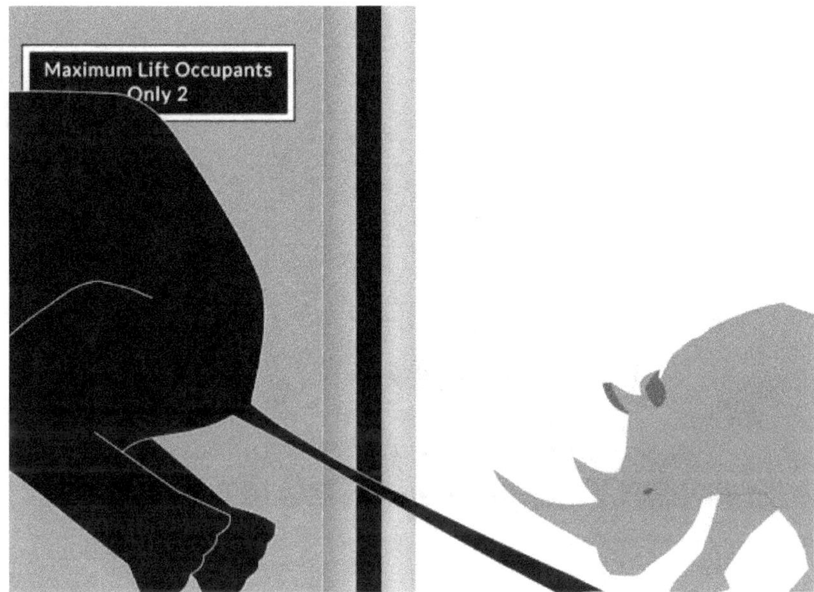

- **Why was Elephant limping on his feet?**
Ant stepped on it by mistake.

- **How did Ant sabotage Elephant's car?**
Whenever Elephant pressed the accelerator, Ant would lift the rear wheels a few inches off the ground.

- **What did Elephant complain to the TTE (Travelling Ticket Examiner) of the train?"**
Ant took his window seat.

- **What did Elephant complain to the TTE?"**
Ant's luggage was placed all over his berth.

- **How did Elephant land flat on the water surface?**
  Elephant was at the edge of the jumping platform, still preparing to jump, when Ant sneaked up behind him and started hopping wildly. Elephant lost his balance and fell awkwardly into the water.

- **How did Elephant fall on to the aisle?**
  When the bus went over a speed-breaker on the road, Ant side-bumped the

dozing Elephant.

- **What made Elephant fly off and smash into the wall?**
  Ant sneezed.

- **Before the Great Flood, Noah built his Ark and asked, "Is everyone on the list?"**
  His wife answered, "No. I asked the ant to write the list and it ignored the elephant in the room."

- **Why did Elephant want to change his name?**
  There was an ant in it.

- **What did Elephant complain to the librarian?**
  Ant was reading loudly next to it.

- **Why was Elephant crying in the cafeteria of the school?**
  According to Elephant, Ant ate his candy and took his lunch money.

- **Why was Elephant upset after the school picnic?**
  The class was walking alongside a cliff. Elephant was at the end of the line. Elephant had stopped and was gingerly observing the steep fall from the top when Ant tapped him on the shoulder. Elephant almost jumped out of its skin. The subsequent conversation went like this:

  > **Elephant**: What do you want?
  > **Ant**: You know what will be good?
  > **Elephant**: What?
  > **Ant**: If you fell down this cliff!
  > **Elephant**: How will that be good?
  > **Ant**: You will make a good impression.

- **Why did Elephant refuse to go out?**
  - Ant was waiting outside to sell him insurance.

- Ant was waiting outside to sign him up for organ donation.
- Social distancing: Ant had coronavirus and was asking Elephant to come out and play with him.

Animal Jokes

If you get to like the breakup jokes in this section, there is more in the section Romantic Jokes.

- **What happened to the anaconda after it had nothing to eat for several weeks?**
  It *sounded hollow*.

- **What did one ant say to another?**
  - "You and what army?"
  - "So, are you a Communist?"
  - "So, when are you flying?"
  - "I came here to grab a bite."
  - "Is it March already?"
  - "I have loads of work."
  - "The work here is not heavy."

- **What kind of music do alpacas like to listen?**
  Latin.

- **What kind of films do bats like to go to?**
  - Dark fantasy.
  - Silent pictures.

- **What kind of music do bed bugs like to listen to?**
  Ruggae.

- **What kind of music do bees like to listen?**

R&B.

- **Why did the policeman stop the stegosaurus?**
  To check his number plate.

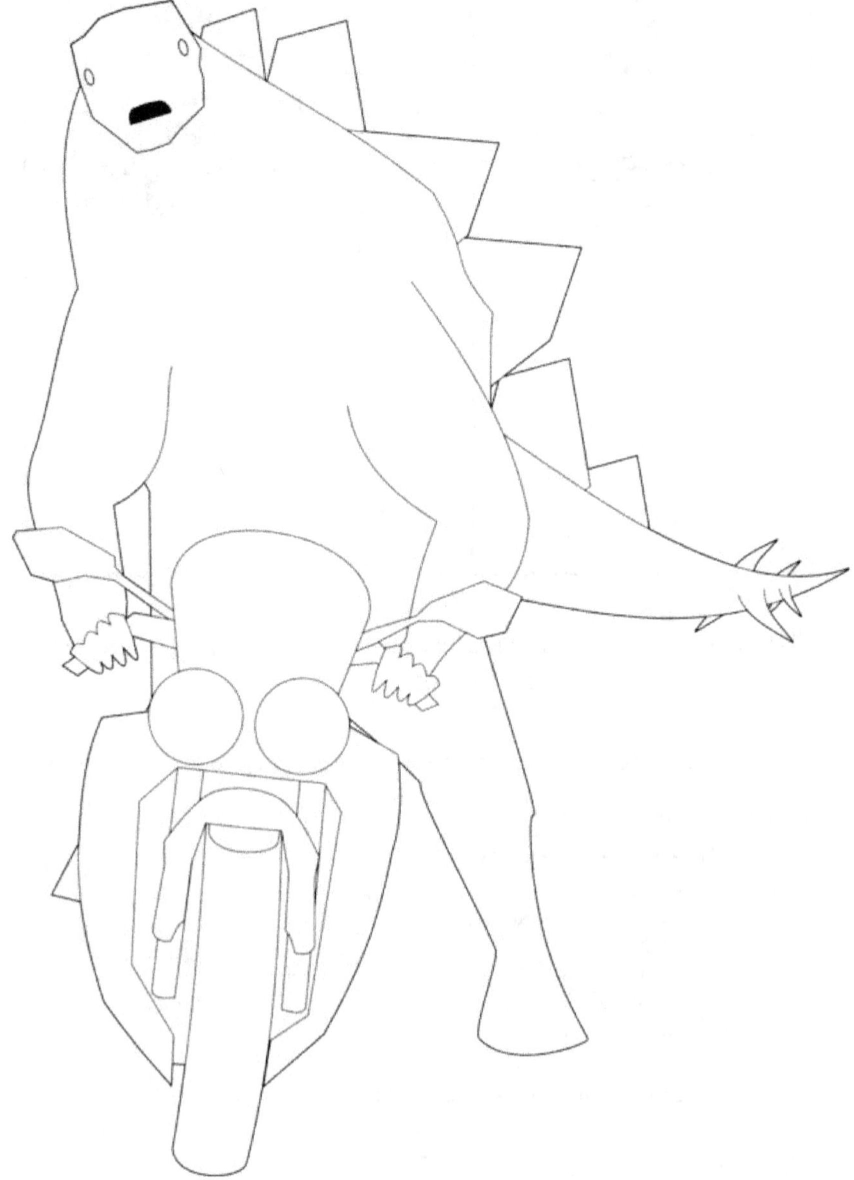

- **What do cows like to read?**
  Bullion prices.

- **What do silverfish (book worms) like to read?**
  Pulp fiction.

- **What kind of music do frogs like to listen?**
  Hip hop.

- **What kind of music do frogs hate to listen?**
  Instrumental.

- **What kind of live entertainment do dogs like to go to?**
  Puppetry.

- **What kind of films do duck like to go to?**
  Docudramas.

- **What kind of computer games do ducks hate to play?**
  Third-person shooter (TPS).

- **What kind of films do eagles like to read?**
  Legal dramas.

- **What kind of fiction do giraffes like to read?**
  Tall tales.

- **What kind of live entertainment do giraffes like to go to?**
  Stand-up comedies.

- **What do goats like to read?**
  Stock quotes.

- **What kind of computer games do lions like to play?**
  Real-time strategy.

- **What kind of films do mooses like to go to see?**
  Moosical.

- **What kind of eateries do owls hate to go to?**
  Owl-you-can-eat buffets.

- **What kind of live entertainment do owls like to see?**
  Snake charmer.

- **What kind of fiction do parrots like to read?**
  Parrodies.

- **What kind of music do rats like to listen?**
  Experimental.

- **What kind of films do roosters like to go to see?**
  Chick flicks.

- **What kind of films do sheep like to go to see?**
  Ramcoms.

- **What did one bat say to another?**
  "We should hang out sometimes."

- **What happened to the chipmunk that began to diet?**
  It *went nuts*.

- **How do you say boo to a duck?**
  In Portugeese.

- **Why did the giraffe refuse to leave the elevator?**
  It gets *lonely at the top*.

- **Why did the rhino use the elevator?**
  The stairs were swamped.

- **Why would the wildebeests of African savannah do well in the stock market?**
  They are *comfortable with large numbers*.

- **What was the ant doing in the farm equipment section?**
  It was a harvester ant.

- **What was the shark doing in the hardware section?**
  It was a sawtooth shark.

- **What was the shark doing in the women's clothing section?**
  It was a bonnethead shark.

- **What was the shark doing in the stationery section?**
  This was a loan shark.

- **What one firefly say to another?**
  "You gotta match, bud? I am out."

- **What did the fish say to the eel?**
  "Can you charge my phone?"

An electric eel is not really an eel.

- **What did the spider say to the insect?**
  "Thanks for dropping by."

- **What did one bull dog say to another?**
  "Why don't you smile?... Hey, what's with the sour expression?"

- **What did one chicken say to another?**
  "I think we are on the way to the market... Hey, what's with the fowl expression?"

- **What did one eel say to another?**
  "I am excited to meet you... Hey, what's with the shocked expression?"

- **What did one turkey say to another?**
  "We are nearing Thanksgiving... Hey, what's with the pained expression?"

- **What would happen if a draught animal came on the radio?**
  It would sound hoarse.

- **What would happen if a lion came on the radio?**
  It would be roaring fun.

- **What would happen if a pig came on the radio?**
  It would be boaring.

- **What would happen if a sheep came on the radio?**
  It would be really baaaaaad.

- **Why did the aardvark couple break up?**
  It had become very awkward between them.

- **Why did the alligator couple break up?**
  - He could not stand her grating remarks.
  - If he tried to say anything, she snapped at her.
  - When he cried, she dismissed it as crocodile tears.

- **How did the alpaca couple break up?**
  He said everything she said was all a pack of lies.

- **Why did the anaconda couple break up?**
  - He could not swallow her insults anymore.
  - He did not have the guts to say 'no' to her.
  - He could not just lie there and pretend like nothing happened.
  - She was extremely unpredictable. She would chew him out for no reason.

- **Why did the ant couple break up?**
  - She insisted that every little thing he did was wrong.
  - He would not march to her beat.
  - He said there was not even a speck of truth in her allegations and she said that that was plenty.
  - He said that she may be an army ant but he was saluting nobody.

- **Why did the ant couple make up?**
  They did not want to let little things come between them.

- **Why did the anteater couple break up?**
  He could not stand her tongue-lashing.

- **Why did the antelope couple break up?**
  - They played hard-to-get for too long.
  - She accused him of running away from problems.
  - He suffered from an overwhelming desire to flee the relationship.

- **How did the antelope couple make up?**
  They endeered themselves to each other.

- **Why did the armadillo couple break up?**
  Even his tough exterior could not handle all the barbs she threw at him.

- **Why did the badger couple break up?**
  She said his relatives were originally all skunks.

- **Why did the bat couple break up?**
  - He went head-over-heels for her when they met but now he would not hang out anymore.
  - She accused him of placing all kinds of obstacles in her life.
  - She could not believe her eyes or ears when he said she was nuttier than a fruit bat.
  - Social distancing... after coronavirus... as if rabies was not bad enough!
  - They tried to rise above their differences but could not reach a compromise.
  - His repeated pleas for mercy fell on deaf ears.
  - They did not see it coming.
  - "I will never go on blind dates again."

- **Why did the bat couple make up?**
  - The breakup turned their world downside up.
  - They decided to ignore hangovers from the past.
  - Love is blind.
  - He listened.

- **Why did the bear couple break up?**
  - He could not make the bear-minimum to support a home.
  - He could not escape her bear hug every morning. [Thank you, Sheryl Crow.]
  - He would not call her 'honey' anymore. ("Don't 'honey' me, you big furry animal!")
  - He would play dead when asked to do housework.

- o He could not bear it anymore.
  - o She was tired of his honeyed words.
  - o He could not grin and bear it anymore.
- **How did the beaver couple break up?**
  She took the home and the kids, and left him with nothing.
- **Why did the bee couple break up?**
  - o She was constantly droning over nothing.
  - o She stung him when he was least expecting it.
  - o What was meant to be will be.
  - o He brought her flowers and she said, "Is this a joke?".
- **Why did the bee couple make up?**
  - o He promised to bee-have.
  - o They decided to let bee-gones be bee-gones.
  - o It is a private matter bee-tween them.
- **How did the bird couple break up?**
  He flew away at the first sign of trouble.
- **How did the bird couple make up?**
  Birds of a feather flock together.
- **Why did the boa constrictor couple break up?**
  - o It was overwhelming. He felt suffocated in that relationship.
  - o Her patience was stretched to the limit.
  - o Too early to say. They are still seized with the situation.
  - o She threatened to turn him inside out.
  - o They just could not get along with each other.
  - o She threatened to make him eat his tail and turn him into a ball.
  - o Everyday was a struggle for survival. He barely managed to hang in there.
  - o Her poisonous remarks left him frothing at the mouth.
  - o He could not stomach her insults anymore.
  - o His gut instinct told him to get out.
- **Why did the boa constrictor couple make up?**
  - o They felt torn apart by the separation.
  - o He promised to pay her close attention because she was one gorgeous boabe.
  - o He said his jokes about her size were made IN JEST.
  - o He promised to come back to her without any hang-ups from the past.
  - o She frankly admired his guts to say 'No' to her.
  - o They managed to squeeze out a compromise.
  - o He admitted he bit off more than he could chew.
- **Why did the buffalo couple break up?**
  - o He made quite a splash in the beginning. Now, he just wallows all the time.
  - o He described himself as tall, dark and handsome but she failed to note that he was no different from others.
- **Why did the camel couple break up?**
  It was the last straw.
- **Why did the cassowary couple break up?**
  'Cos, with every passing day, they grew more wary of each other.
- **Why did the cat couple break up?**

- They were on the fence about it for quite some time and finally took the plunge in different directions.
  - They hated each other in all of their nine lives.
  - Don't worry about spilled milk.
  - She tried to make his life miserable but he always managed to land on his feet.
- **Why did the caterpillar couple break up?**
  She wanted spread her wings and transform into something new and different.

- **Why did the caterpillar couple make up?**
  He promised to turn a new leaf.

- **Why did the chameleon couple break up?**
  - He showed his true colours after the wedding.
  - She sees him in a different light now.
  - He had some butterflies in the stomach but he has had enough of her colourful remarks.
  - She could not believe how much he had changed.
  - He tried to blend in with the surroundings but she was too good for him and made him do housework.

- **Why did the cheetah couple break up?**
  There was no escaping her.

- **Why did the chicken couple break up?**
  - What he brought home was chickenfeed.
  - Around her, he felt like he was walking on eggshells all the time.

- **Why did the chicken couple make up?**
  - He did not want to raise her hackles.
  - He was her fowl-weather friend.

- **Why did the chimpanzee couple break up?**
  - He would scratch his head and grin from ear to ear but wouldn't understand a word she said.
  - She put him in a cardboard box and mailed it to NASA.

- **Why did the condor couple make up?**
  They were a married California condor couple, an endangered species.

- **Why did the cow couple break up?**
  - It was not cowardice. Her daily complaints were not moosic to his ears.
  - She wanted to be treated like a holy cow.
  - He would not be cowed down by her threats to make mincemeat out of him.
  - What he brought home was a 'big nothing burger'.
  - She routinely locked horns with him and it became a high-stakes game for survival.
  - He knew he was dead meat if he went home late.

- **Why did the crab couple break up?**
  - He barely managed to escape her death grip.
  - She welcomed him with open arms.

- **Why did the crab couple make up?**
  - He was a spineless fellow. He crawled back to her on all sixes.
  - She was like his right hand - big and strong.

- **Why did the crane couple break up?**
  He would not stick his neck out for her.

- **Why did the crocodile couple break up?**
  - They shed some crocodile tears and it was all over.
  - It was all a crock of lies.
  - They would open their mouths and refuse to shut up for hours.

- **Why did the crow couple break up?**
  - Even for a crow, she was very loud.
  - She was no hot chick but, when he compared her to a raven, she took it as a comment about her size.
  - Contrary to scientific studies, he was not very intelligent. And, quite a craven little birdie too.

- **Why did the donkey couple break up?**
  - Sometimes, he can be stubborn as an ass.
  - He was all ears for her then. Now, not so much anymore.
  - He would just stand there with a stupid smile on his face, like a jackass.

- **Why did the deer couple break up?**
  - They had too much weighing down on their heads.
  - He was tired of her hide-and-seek games.

- **Why did the dinosaur couple break up?**
  Once she becomes cold as ice, she just refuses to thaw.

- **Why did the dinosaur couple make up?**
  She said his brain must be as big as a matchbox.

- **Why did the duck couple break up?**
  - Bills, bills, bills, and more bills.
  - They both ducked the question.
  - He remained an ugly duckling forever.
  - She followed him everywhere he went.
  - When she gave her daily sermon, all he heard was, "Quack, quack, quack, quack, quack!"
  - If it walks like a duck and talks like a duck, then it hurts like a duck.
  - They took to it like duck to water.
  - In this economy, it is tough to stay afloat.

- **Why did the dog couple break up?**
  - "Her bark is worse than her bite. It should not happen to a dog."
  - Their relationship was best described as a dog-eat-dog situation.
  - She was breathing down his neck all the time.
  - She held him on a tight leash. He could not grin and wag his tail forever like that.
  - She expected him sit when she told him to sit and stand when she told him to stand.

- **Why did the dolphin couple break up?**
  There was no escaping her. Even when out of sight, he thought he could hear her.

- **Why did the dragon couple break up?**
  - They both breathed fire and burned down their homestead.
  - She gave him a serious case of heartburn.

- **Why did the duck couple make up?**

- o He successfully floated the idea to her.
- o Without her, he was a dead duck.

- **Why did the eagle couple break up?**
  - o He felt he could never escape her constant gaze.
  - o For a bald eagle, it was hair today and gone tomorrow.

- **Why did the electric eel couple break up?**
  - o He thought he was making a positive approach but she took it negatively.
  - o Shock and aaah!
  - o Shocking… shocking failure to respect each other's personal space.
  - o There seemed to be too much negative energy between them.
  - o Probably for the shock value.

- **Why did the electric eel couple make up?**
  - o He decided to test the waters again.
  - o He said she was a slimy, lying, slithering and cold-blooded creature.

- **Why did the elephant couple break up?**
  - o He was tall, dark and handsome but seriously overweight.
  - o He failed to address the elephant in the room.
  - o She trumpeted her achievements while he tried to stamp his authority.
  - o "Elephants and women never forget."

From the poem by Dorothy Parker with the same title

- **Why did the elephant couple make up?**
  He can run but he can't hide.

- **Why did the eagle couple break up?**
  She endlessly picked on him and he felt an overwhelming desire to escape her clutches.

- **Why did the emu couple break up?**
  - o He remained emmune to her advances.
  - o He was emutionally insecure.
  - o He would burst into tears at the mere sound of her footsteps.

- **How did the emu couple make up?**
  It was an *emutional roller coaster*.

- **What one firefly couple break up?**
  - o The light had gone out of their relationship.
  - o The fire had gone out of their relationship.

- **What one firefly couple make up?**
  He praised her in glowing terms.

- **Why did the fish couple break up?**
  - o It's water under the bridge now.
  - o She was such a clean freak that no matter how many baths he took it was not enough for her.
  - o She carped on and on about how he was always wrapped up in a newspaper.

- **Why did the fish couple make up?**
  - o She wanted to ACQUIRE HIM again.
  - o He was a handsome catch.
  - o The scales fell from her eyes.

- **Why did the flamingo couple break up?**
  He inflamed her passions initially. Now, not so much.
- **Why did the fly couple break up?**
  She would fly into a rage over nothing.
- **Why did the frog couple break up?**
  Every night, after he hopped over from the pub, she would hit the ceiling.
- **How did the frog couple break up?**
  He leapt with joy while she took a dive into depression.
- **Why did the frog couple make up?**
  She searched all over the swamp but she could not find a better specimen.
- **Why did the giraffe couple break up?**
  - When he came home late, she would hit the ceiling.
  - She set the bar too high for him.
- **Why did the goose couple break up?**
  What was good for the goose was not good for the gander.
- **Why did the gorilla couple break up?**
  She called him a 'stupid monkey'.

- **Why did the goat couple break up?**
  - He could not be goaded into doing her bidding.
  - He asked a vet if something could be done about her constant bleating.

- **Why did the hedgehog couple break up?**
  - He was tired of her barbs.
  - He did not have the spine to say no to her.
  - She knew he was not up to scratch.
  - She tried hard to make her point and it hurt.
- **Why did the hummingbird couple break up?**
  - He was tired of listening to her same old tune again and again.
  - They were out of tune with each other.
  - He struck a discordant note.
- **Why did the hummingbird couple make up?**
  He called her a bird-brain and she took it as a compliment.
- **Why did the hyena couple break up?**
  - They refused to laugh at each other's jokes.
  - He had nothing to counter her biting remarks.
  - What he brought home was just scraps.
- **What do hyenas like to read?**
  The funny papers.
- **Why did the crested ibis couple break up?**
  She wanted to be treated like a *sacred ibis*.

They are two different species.

- **Why did the hadeda ibis couple break up?**
  They yelled at each other all the time.

Hadeda Ibis is the loudest bird in Africa.

- **Why did the hornet couple break up?**
  He had nothing to counter her stinging accusations.
- **Why did the jellyfish couple break up?**
  He desperately wanted to escape her tentacles.
- **Why did the Komodo dragon couple break up?**
  There was no fire in the relationship.
- **Why did the koel couple break up?**
  He was a total 'cuckoo for brains'.
- **Why did the lice couple break up?**
  She said he was gross and he called her a parasite.
- **Why did the lice couple make up?**
  - They took it as a compliment.
  - It is a jungle out there. Two heads are better than one.
- **Why did the lion couple break up?**
  - He refused to shave.
  - If she caught him roaming outside, she made him stand on a stool.
- **Why did the lion couple make up?**
  Outside, he roared like a lion. Inside the house, when she cracked the whip, he put his tail between his legs like a dog and moved around like a mouse.
- **How did the llama couple break up?**

They walked away, looked back, and spat each other's direction.

- **Why did the Barbary lion couple break up?**
  They were on their way out anyway.

- **Why did the lizard couple break up?**
  She drove him up the wall.

- **Why did the woolly mammoth couple break up?**
  He had grown long in the tooth.

- **Why did the mice couple break up?**
  - He brought cheese straight from the factory but she was still not satisfied with his cooking.
  - He couldn't see the writing on the wall.
  - She asked him if he was a mouse or a man when he said he was tired of eating cheese every day.

- **If a mice wanted to read detective fiction, what book would it read?**
  Who moved my cheese?

- **Why did the mole couple break up?**
  - She made a mountain out of a molehill.
  - He finally dug his way out of her maze of traps.
  - She does not dig him any more.

- **Why did the moose couple break up?**
  When they first met, he said he was an artist and she could be her muse. Now, he just wants her out of the picture.

- **Why did the musk ox couple break up?**
  Her talks always gave him a headache.

- **Why did the narwhal couple break up?**
  She struck him as unfriendly.

- **Why did the nightingale couple break up?**
  He was singing the same old song like a broken record.

- **Why did the octopus couple break up?**
  - She had too much on her hands.
  - He would not lend her a hand while doing housework.
  - He caught her on the wrong foot.
  - He lost all his earnings buying her shoes.
  - He was too many problems in his hands and it all came to a head.
  - She challenged him to a battle of wits and he commended her for coming unarmed.

- **What did the mother octopus say to the baby octopuses?**
  "Kids, will you stop it? I have only eight arms."

- **Why did the ostrich couple break up?**
  - He decided to make a run for it.
  - Protecting the world's biggest eggs is no easy task.
  - Whenever she complained, he would bury his head in the ground.

- **Why did the ostrich couple make up?**

- o She caught up with him.
  - o He can run but he cannot hide.
- **Why did the otter couple break up?**
  Every time she wanted to talk, he would roll over and go to sleep.
- **Why did the owl couple break up?**
  - o She nagged him day and night.
  - o The relationship screeched to a halt.
- **Why did the owl couple make up?**
  Owl is fair in love and war.
- **Why did the parrot couple break up?**
  She would repeat the same old complaints again and again, imitating his own voice.
- **What kind of music do parrots like to listen?**
  Pirated.
- **Why did the pelican couple break up?**
  He was tired of her big mouth.
- **Why did the pig couple break up?**
  - o He was quite a boar.
  - o She would wade in to the living room and hog the remote during the last over.
  - o Living with her was like being hog-tied all the time.
- **Why did the polar bear couple break up?**
  - o The very thought of him made her shudder.
  - o The very thought of her made him break into a sweat.
- **Why did the porcupine couple break up?**
  - o She would needle him over nothing.
  - o He remained a thorn on her side.
  - o She struck him as a tad unfriendly.
  - o She had a painful way of making her point across.
- **How did the porcupine couple break up?**
  - o He bought a water bed.
  - o He would make up all kinds of false stories and she would put all kinds of holes in them.
- **Why did the possum couple break up?**
  She threatened to betray him to some starving hillbilly.
- **Why did the python couple break up?**
  Under pressure, he just choked.
- **How did the python couple break up?**
  - o They are still mentally digesting what happened.
  - o They were crushed.
  - o After they met, she had him wrapped around her finger in no time.
- **Why did the python couple make up?**
  - o He bit off more than he could chew.
  - o She was not the one to give up so quickly.
  - o She made a mind-numbing jaw-dropping offer to take him back.

- **How did the quail couple break up?**
  - What he brought home was chickenfeed.
  - She accused him of being a chicken.
- **Why did the rabbit couple break up?**
  She was swift with the repartee and he was quick to take offence.
- **How did the raccoon couple break up?**
  She said she had seen his photo on a 'Wanted for burglary' poster and he said he hoped she will make a good hat.
- **Why did the rat couple break up?**
  - He promised her a nice place in the city but they were still living on a dump in the outskirts.
  - He felt trapped in that marriage.
  - She was not attracted by his cheesy humour anymore.
  - What he brought home could not even feed a mouse.
- **Why did the rhinoceros couple break up?**
  She said that, even though he had two of them, his horns did not match and they were on the wrong side of his head.
- **Why did the rhinoceros couple make up?**
  She promised not to make pointed remarks and he believed she had honourable intentions.
- **Why did the salmon couple break up?**
  She was tired of his canned replies.
- **Why did the scorpion couple break up?**
  Her comments stings like a scorpion.
- **Why did the seal couple break up?**
  He refused to dance to her tune.
- **Why did the secretary bird couple break up?**
  He noted that she was acting more and more like a dictator.
- **Why did the shark couple break up?**
  - The shark is the most cunning hunter in water. All the more difficult for a male shark when his mate can sense him from a mile away.
  - There are many deadly predators in the sea. For him, it was the open ocean or her. He chose the ocean.
  - He considered her as a trophy wife.
  - She says he hoped she would become a trophy.
  - He was a different kettle of fish.
  - He escaped from her by the skin of his teeth.
  - Her bark was worse than her bite.
- **How did the sheep couple break up?**
  - He was shorn of any responsibility.
  - She followed him everywhere.
- **How did the silverfish couple break up?**
  - He was always buried in his books.
  - He took a bite out of her book.
- **How did the shellfish couple break up?**

He accused her of being selfish.

- **Why did the sloth couple break up?**
He was sloth to compliment her.

- **Why did the snail couple break up?**
  o Her pace was too much for him.
  o He made a quick getaway as best as he could.
  o She said he was cruising for a bruising.

- **Why did the snail couple make up?**
  o They felt that a change of pace was better than rushing into uncharted territory.
  o He promised to make serious progress.

- **Why did the snake couple break up?**
  o Peel that outer layer and you find a total reptile inside!
  o He will make your skin crawl.
  o He was like something that crawled out from under a rock.
  o He could not stand her accusations lying down.
  o The relationship had become too toxic.
  o He was a total creep.
  o He would not dance to her tune.
  o She made his blood boil.
  o Oh, the things she said would make a snake stand on its tail!

- **Why did the snake couple make up?**
  o He said that, if there was one lying slithering cold-blooded reptile he could not forget, it was her.
  o They decided to let past infractions slide.
  o He charmed his way back into her heart.

- **Why did the spider couple break up?**
He didn't want to get caught in her web of deceit and treachery.

- **Why did the squirrel couple break up?**
  o She was nuts about him once but now thinks she was just nuts.
  o What he brought home was peanuts.
  o This nut was not complimentary.

- **Why did the starfish couple break up?**
  o They literally broke up.
  o It was written in the stars.

- **Why did the stick insect couple break up?**
  o She wanted to stick it to that creep.
  o She threw all kinds of allegations at him but nothing would stick.

- **Why did the stick insect couple make up?**
He loved her so much that he would not stick up for himself.

- **Why did the stingray couple break up?**
He had no answer to her stinging remarks.

- **Stork couple breakup**

  Stork 1: That couple had broken up.
  Stork 2: What happened?
  Stork 1: She tried to pull his leg.

Stork 2: Just because of a joke?
Stork 1: No, she pulled the leg he was standing on.

- **Why did the stork couple break up?**
  - o It was time for a stork to take a stand and put his foot down.
  - o His painting did not match the décor of her home.

- **Why did the swan couple break up?**
  They became swan enemies.

- **Why did the swan couple break up?**
  He is her swan song in this life.

- **Why did the tadpole couple break up?**
  She did not like his juvenile attitude.

- **Why did the tadpole couple make up?**
  He promised her that he will try to become a mature individual.

- **Why did the tick couple break up?**
  Every time he opened his mouth to say something, she ticked him off.

- **Why did the tortoise couple break up?**
  His silent treatment was killing her. Whenever she talked, he would close his eyes and withdraw into his shell.

- **Why did the tortoise couple make up?**
  - o Without her, he became a broken shell of a tortoise.
  - o She dropped the bombshell on his back but he did not crack.

- **Why did the toad couple break up?**
  He croaked under the pressure.

- **How did the toucan couple break up?**
  He put his beak where it did not belong.

- **Why did the turkey couple break up?**
  He thought she was fattening him up for a Christmas surprise.

- **Why did the turkey couple break up?**
  It was nearing Thanksgiving and he said she looked fat.

- **Why did the turtle couple break up?**
  Whenever she talked, he would turn turtle and go to sleep.

- **How did the whale couple break up?**
  They had a whale of a time together but now it is all over.

- **Why did the white ant couple break up?**
  He could not afford to have a roof over their heads.

- **How did the walrus couple break up?**
  Tsk! Tsk! Tsk! Tsk!

- **How did the walrus couple break up?**
  He was getting long in the tooth.

- **How did the wolf couple break up?**
  He let out a howl and danced with joy.

- **How did the yak couple break up?**

He would yack away all the time and not let her get in a word.

- **How did the zebra couple break up?**
  He crossed her the wrong way.

- **What did the ant say to the anteater?**
  o "Why don't you pick someone your own size?"
  o "Well, if you are that then go and eat your aunt!"

- **What happens if you give neodymium to birds?**
  You get chick magnets.

- **Why did the moth see the doctor?**
  He was feeling suicidal, usually in the presence of a fire.

- **Depression Hotline**

  Caller: The holidays are coming and I am feeling depressed.
  Counsellor: Unless you are a turkey, there is no need to feel depressed.
  Caller: [Sound of a turkey crying followed by a click]

- **Holy Cows**
  Cows are not unusual sight on Indian roads but it seems to fascinate Western tourists. So, here is a real story about some Indian cows. It was reported in *The Hindu*. Rajaji Salai is a very busy place, given that it is near the port, the Fort, the High Court, Burma Bazaar, bank offices and the business district. Among the fixtures on this road were several cows. One day, one of them was knocked down by a bus. Usually, when a cow is on the road, living or dead, the traffic arches around the animal and proceeds at a slower pace. In this instance, however, something strange happened. The news of the dead cow seems to have spread like wildfire. Cows from all around the area trudged to the site of the accident. They stood around the dead cow in silent protest and mourning. Traffic on the arterial road was held up for several hours.

- **CatNav**
  One day, back when I was kid, I found a newborn kitten at a building that was under construction. I took it home and it became our pet. It was a good cat but had one bad habit. On days when fish was cooked, the cat acted like it was possessed by some evil spirit. This was not a problem until a day when a guest arrived. Fish was on the menu and the cat caused serious embarrassment. It would not let the man eat in peace. It would scratch at the door, make unworldly noises and demanded to be let it in. After the guest left, a decision was made to get rid of the cat. I was the one tasked with it. A relative would accompany me to the other side of the railway track, several kilometres from the home, and I was supposed to abandon it. I literally let the cat out of the bag there. As we scooted back from the scene on our cycle, I saw the cat stand there wondering what was happening. I was brokenhearted. I need not have worried. Next day, I woke up to the familiar sounds of the cat. How did it return? It must have had made a mental map of smells and traced its way back, somehow avoiding hundreds of dogs, cats and vehicles.

Fancy Creature Jokes

Everyone likes fairy tales. The *Panchatantra* is the source of many fairy tales in which animals speak like humans. While many foreign cultures have borrowed from it, they have their own unique fancy creatures and tales. Ireland has the banshee. Scotland has the Loch Ness monster. Vampires are popular all over the Western world. Here are a few jokes about many such creatures.

- **What does** ABOMINABLE SNOWMAN**'s school yearbook say about him?**
"Most likely to leave quite a trail."

- **The** ABOMINABLE SNOWMAN **walks into a bar**
The Abominable Snowman walks into a bar and orders a drink. The bartender says, "That'll be twenty bucks." The Snowman is shocked and says, "This is an abomination."

- **Why did** wailing banshee **retire?**
It was a crying shame.

- **A** screaming banshee **walks into a bar**
A banshee walks into a bar and says, "I am dying for a drink." The barman pours it some brandy. When the banshee finishes the drink, the barman asks, "How is it now?" The banshee replies, "It's nothing to cry about."

- **What did the** wailing banshee **say?**
Just mourning.

- **What does** BATMAN**'s school yearbook say about him?**
"Most likely to hang out it with shady characters."

- Bogeyman
    Mrs. Bogeyman: Sometimes, you scare me.
    Mr. Bogeyman: No, honey, you are imaginary things!

- **What does COUNT DRACULA's school yearbook say about him?**
"Most likely to live life to the fullest."

- **What is COUNT DRACULA's favourite self-help book?**
How to stop worrying and start living.

- **What was the last thing the psychiatrist said to COUNT DRACULA?**
"Now, I would like you to do some personal reflection."

- Cyclops
    Mother cyclops: Make sure your brother does not get his clothes dirty.
    Daughter cyclops: Don't worry, Mom. I have my eye on him.

- **A cyclops walks into a bar**
A cyclops walks into a bar and the bartender says, "What can I get ye?"

- **What does** EGYPTIAN MUMMY**'s school yearbook say about him?**
"Most likely to leave a lasting legacy."

- **An** EGYPTIAN MUMMY **walks into a bar**
    - An Egyptian mummy walks into a bar and orders a drink. While he is drinking, the barman asks, "So, what's your story?" The mummy looks up from his drink and says, "A riches-to-rags one, I suppose."
    - An Egyptian mummy walks into a bar and the barman says, "Long time, no see." The mummy says, "Sorry, I was all tied up."

- **Why did the** EGYPTIAN MUMMY **couple break up?**

It was bound to happen.

- *Fairies*

    Fairy 1: How well can you fly?
    Fairy 2: Fairly well.

- **What kind of music does the Grim Reaper like to listen?**
  Soul.

- **What does hydra's school yearbook say about him?**
  "Most likely to have the best head in the business."

- **What made the hydra couple break up?**
  It was not so much that she had nine heads to dish out her daily list of complaints but that he had eighteen ears to listen. He tried to let her complaints in through one ear and out through the other without much thought, but when he let it out from one head, it inevitably entered another head. He tried severing a head but two new heads always grow in its place, compounding his problem.

- **A hydra walks into a bar**
  A hydra walks into a bar and orders nine glasses of beer. The conversation with the bartender goes like this:

    Do you ever feel that you should cut it?
    The drinks?
    No.
    The heads?
    No. Never mind."

- **Imps**

    Mr. Imp: Did you see the remote?
    Mrs. Imp: It didn't tell me when it went out.
    Mr. Imp: Oh, you are impossible!

- **What does Loch Ness monster's school yearbook say about him?**
  "Most likely to rise above the rest."

- **A Loch Ness monster walks into a bar**
  A Loch Ness monster walks into a bar and orders a whisky. The bartender asks, "Any particular label?" Nessie replies, "Anything to drown my sorrows and disappear."

- **What did the nymph say to the mermaid?**
  "Will you blink once in a while? You have that dead fish look in your eyes."

- **SASQUATCH**

    Sasquatch 1: Did you talk to that cute one you were following?
    Sasquatch 1: No. She gave me the brush.

- **What does the siren's school yearbook say about her?**
  "Most likely to steal our hearts."

- **What does Spiderman's school yearbook say about him?**
  "Most likely to scale great heights."

- **What does SUPERMAN's school yearbook say about him?**
  "Most likely to come out with flying colours."

- **What does the *THUNDERBIRD*'s yearbook say about him?**
  "Most likely to kick up a storm."

- **What does the TROLL's school yearbook say about him?**
  "Most likely to carry a lot of weight in his circle."

- **What did one TROLL say to another after they were exposed to sunlight?**
  "What's with the stony expression?"

- **What does TROLL's school yearbook say about him?**
  "Most likely to rock our world."

- **A TROLL walks into a bar**
  A troll walks into a bar late at night but stays in the shadow behind the door. "Kill the lights and give me a drink," the troll hollers. The bartender turns off the switches and pours a drink. He slides the drink to the end of the bar and says, "Here is some light beer."

- **What happened to the TROLL during the storm?**
  There was a lightning storm and he was petrified for a whole minute.

- **What does vampire's school yearbook say about him?**
  "Most likely to suck at the one thing he does best."

- **What does a vampire call a blood bank?**
  Food bank.

- **Why do vampires always bite in the neck?**
  It is wrong to bite the hand that feeds you.

- **A vampire walks into a bar**
  A vampire walks into a bar and the bartender asks, "Need a drink?" The vampire replies, "No, I just dropped in for a bite."

- **A WEREWOLF walks into a bar**
  A werewolf walks into a bar and the bartender asks sarcastically, "You also dropped in for a bite?" The werewolf shakes his head, "No, I am here for the leftovers."

- **Another WEREWOLF walks into a bar**
  Another werewolf walks into a bar and the bartender asks, "And, what are you here for?" The werewolf points to the werewolf from the previous joke and says, "I have a bone to pick with him."

- **What does WEREWOLF's school yearbook say about him?**
  "Most likely to cause serious changes in society."

- **A Yeti walks into a bar**
  A Yeti walks into a bar and orders a drink. Everyone becomes nervous. To ease the mood, the Yeti asks the bartender, "Seen anything strange tonight?" The bartender replies, "Nothing **YET, I** suppose."

Geography Jokes

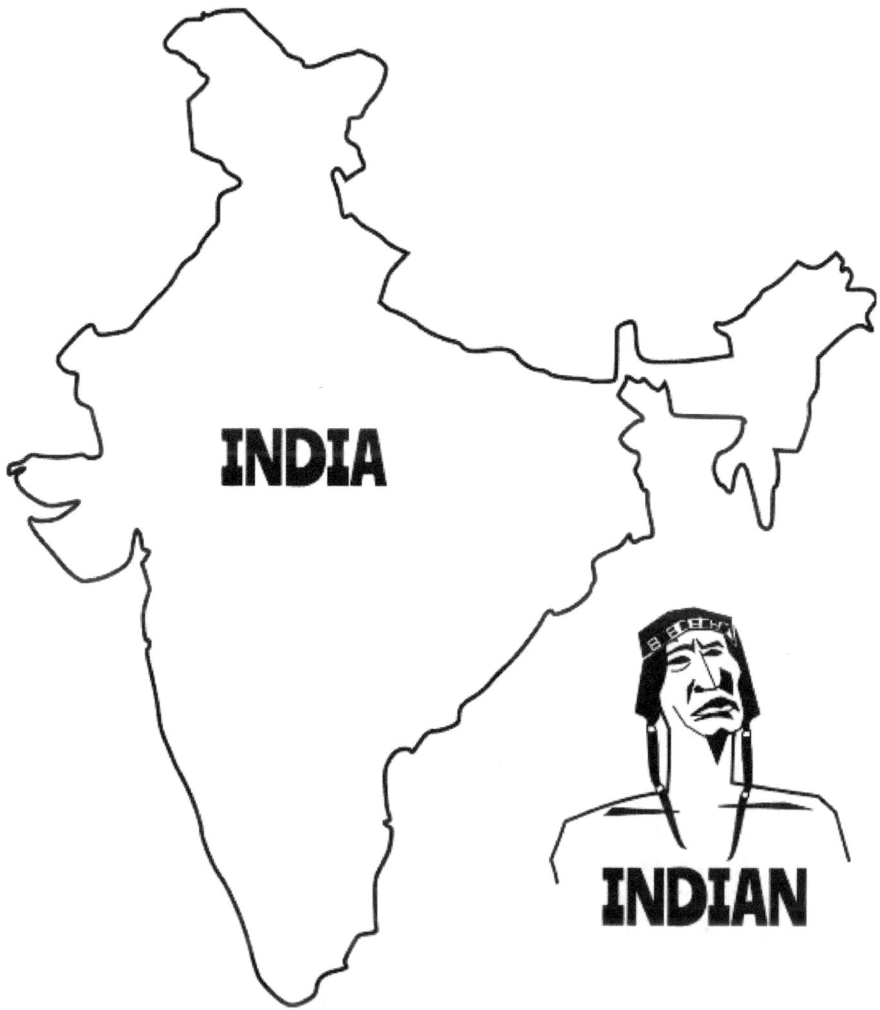

India belongs to Indians. Any questions?

The country-specific jokes in this section are questions framed like a National Geographic quiz. But, there are no facts in question, just logic. That is, logic in the misleading style of 'Archie' of Duffy's Tavern. It is somewhat like a crossword puzzle clue. (To learn more about Duffy's Tavern, read the artice Vintage

- **Why did the flat-earther couple break up?**
  He drove her to the edge all the time but this time she felt that he had gone too far.

- **How does good news become bad news for a volcano?**
  Because it may erupt with joy.

- **Why did the geologist couple break up?**
  o It was a rocky relationship.
  o He felt like he was caught between a rock and a hard place.
  o Their relationship had hit rock bottom.

- **Why did the geologist couple make up?**
  It was uncharted territory for them.

- **What kind of music do geologists like to listen?**
  Just plain rock.

- **What kind of music do drunk geologists like to listen?**
  Rock-n-roll.

- **What kind of music do divorced geologists like to listen?**
  Alternative rock.

- **How did seismologist couple break up?**
  They were devastated.

- **Why did seismologist couple break up?**
  o It was a disaster to begin with.
  o He trembled with fear at the mere sound of her footsteps.
  o When anything went wrong, it was always his fault.

- **Not on my plate**

  Continental Plate 1: Did you cause that earthquake?
  Continental Plate 2: No, it's your fault.

- **What can you do with two globes?**
  Make the best of both worlds.

- **Name the Asian country that is named after a type of blanket or shawl.**
  Afghanistan.

- **Name the landlocked Asian country with a long history of people being mean to it.**
  Armenia.

- **Name the European country that is named after the ostrich bird.**
  Austria.

- **Name the English-speaking country that is so lazy and laid back that they copied from a country that was named after the ostrich.**
  Australia.

- **Name the Caribbean nation that is even more laid back than Australia that they cannot even say "Bah! Humbug!"**

Bahamas.

- **Name the Middle Eastern nation that is so parched that where everyone scoffs at the very idea of rain.**
  Bahrain.
- **Name the Caribbean country which was founded by a hair stylist who banned Afros and made two haircuts mandatory per year.**
  Barbados.
- **Which country hosts the largest number of Internet bots?**
  Botswana.
- **Name the European country that causes heartburn all over Europe.**
  Belgium.
- **If you said this South American country was founded by a girl named Olivia nobody would believe ya.**
  Bolivia.
- **Name the oil-rich South-East Asian country where the local brew will make you neigh like a horse?**
  Brunei.
- **Which East European country has been afflicted with a special strain of malaria whose chief symptom is bloating?**
  Bulgaria.
- **Name the African country that can so bore you to death that pathologically overexcited people go there to calm down.**
  Burundi.
- **Which African country is the largest manufacturer of the burkini, the Middle-Eastern head-to-toe version of the bikini?**
  Burkina Faso.
- **Which South-East Asian country where the most photogenic people live?**
  Cambodia.
- **Name the African country that was once a penal colony for people convicted of causing accidents with selfie sticks.**
  Cameroon.
- **Which country is the largest manufacturer of canned food?**
  Canada.
- **Which equatorial African country was named after an automobile?**
  CAR (Central African Republic).
- **Which South American country was named after a hot spice?**
  Chile.
- **Which Asian country is named after high-quality porcelain dishes?**
  China.
- **To which African country can you never go?**
  Congo.
- **To which African republic can you never go?**
  Republic of Congo.
- **Name the African country on the Atlantic ocean that is a favourite destination for perpetual worriers?**

Ivory Coast.

- **In which Caribbean country do people live in houses made of ice cubes?**
  Cuba.

- **In which European country do people never check their spelling?**
  Czechia (formerly Czech Republic, which sadly broke off from Czechoslovakia).

- **In which European country where the national IQ has never crossed 10?**
  Denmark.

- **Which Caribbean country where everyone lives in dome-shaped houses?**
  Dominica.

- **Which Caribbean republic where everyone lives in dome-shaped houses?**
  Dominican Republic.

- **Which South American country was founded by Salvador Dali's evil twin?**
  Ecuador.

- **In which West African country, do they make you to drink gin up to this?**
  Equatorial Guinea.

- **In which East African which country, do they get easily irritated?**
  Eritrea.

- **In which East European country, do they stone you to death for ordinary crimes?**
  Estonia.

- **Which African country was the first one in Africa to form a S.W.A.T. unit?**
  Eswatini (fomerly Swaziland).

- **Which country in Europe is famed for its fish consumption?**
  Finland.

- **In which African country do people yack away like no tomorrow?**
  Gabon.

- **In which African country is gambling a way of life?**
  Gambia.

- **Which former Soviet republic's entire economy was originally based on postal packages originally destined for a province in the U.S.A.?**
  Georgia.

- **Which European country has the best defence against many germs?**
  Germany.

- **What can you do if your geographical knowledge is a bit rusty?**
  You apply some Greece.

- **Which Caribbean state was left grumbling when they realized that the name 'Canada' was already taken?**
  Grenada.

- **Which Caribbean country has the largest number of haters outside it?**
  Haiti.

- **In which European country was named to divert food aid after the devastation caused by World War I?**
  Hungary.

- **Which North Atlantic country is known as the 'Land of the Frozen Water'?**

Iceland.

- **Which Asian country was originally populated by Native Americans?**
  India.

- **Which South American country was so named because the confusion caused by countries named Guinea was not enough?**
  Guyana.

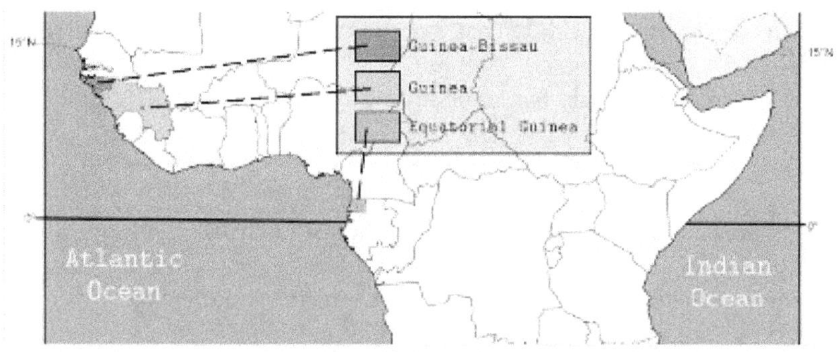

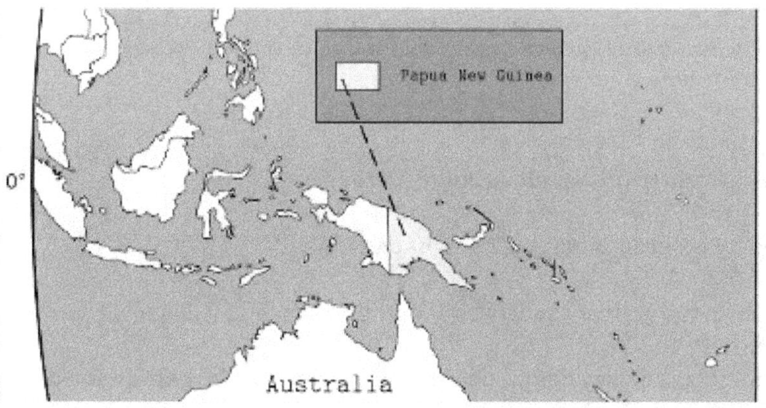

Some countries in Western Africa region are named after the around Gulf of Guinea. Papua New Guinea in the Oceanic region is so named because Spanish explorers thought the natives resembled the African people of Guinea.

- **Which Asian country stretches between between India and Malaysia?**
  Indonesia.

- **Name the Middle-Eastern country that Americans think has to be pronounced as an eye that ran away.**
  Iran.

It is all right to say EE-RAAHN. People in the Middle East seem to pronounce it as EH-RAAHN.

- **Name the Middle-Eastern country that Americans think has to be pronounced as a rack to showcase eyes.**

Iraq.

- **Which European country has earned the ire of Iranians and Iraqis for causing Americans mispronounce their country's name?**
  Ireland.

- **Which country in the Middle East was the first to have a railway system?**
  Israel.

- **Which European country is named after the South-Indian dish '*idli*'?**
  Italy.

- **Which South-East Asian country is always lost in chaos?**
  Laos.

- **In which East European country are the people habitually late?**
  Latvia.

- **Which African country is on the east of Siberia?**
  Liberia.

- **Which European tax haven is the birthplace of the Frankenstein monster?**
  Liechtenstein.

- **Which East European country has highest literacy rate?**
  Lithuania.

- **Which country was moulded out of an egg?**
  Moldova.

- **Which European country is straight out of hell?**
  Netherlands.

- **Which is the newest country built entirely over land reclaimed from sea?**
  New Zealand.

- **Which Arab country has earned the ire of feminists for being named after the greatness of Man?**
  Oman.

- **Which South Asian country is packed with guys named Stanley?**
  Pakistan.

- **Name the European country where almost every citizen is mistaken for being very refined, cultured and polished?**
  Poland.

- **Which European country is named after female sailors?**
  Portugal.

- **In which European country do you find the most number of rowing fanatics?**
  Romania.

- **In which Eurasian country do people tend to rush ya?**

Russia.

- **In which South East Asian country are ties important?**
  Thailand.

- **In which Oceanian country, do people eat with tongs?**
  Tonga.

- **In which East African country do people greet each other with "You again, duh"?**
  Uganda.

- **Which former Soviet republic gets blamed when floods inundate the United Kingdom?**
  Ukraine.

- **Which English-speaking European country has the dullest and most generic name?**
  United Kingdom.

- **Which country in the western hemisphere pretends like it is a continent?**
  United States of America.

- **If a national capital could change into a girl and still retain its Christian name, what would it be?**
  Hint: The capital of Bulgaria.

- **How to remember stalagmite**

  > **Stalactite**: What are you wondering?
  > **Stalagmite**: Whether I **might** reach the ceiling.

- **How to remember stalactite**

  > **Stalagmite**: What are you looking for?
  > **Stalactite**: For a **site** to stand on.

- **How does magma fight?**
  "You and me. Let's take this outside."

- **How does lava fight?**
  "Cool it, man. Forget what happened down there."

- **Who are the 2% of scientists who advocate Climate Change rather than oppose it?**
  Psychiatrists who prescribe to their patients that a change in climate would be a good thing.

- **From the *Train Atlas***
  In 2003, I bought the *Atlas* from a railway station and found these facts under the title *Indian Railways: Some Fascinating Facts* and the facts were indeed fascinating.

  - Indian railways has the widest rail tracks in the world. The British chose the 5-feet 6-inch gauge as the standard because many parts of the country was prone to cyclones and flooding. This gauge was considered more safe than the standard gauge used all over the world. Some other countries such as Pakistan and Bangladesh use the Indian gauge as the national standard.
  - The shortest station name for a station is Ib, near Jharsuguda, on the Howrah-Nagpur main line.
  - The longest station name is Srivenkatanarasimharajuvariapeta on the Arakkonam-Renigunta section of the Southern Railway, which is the first

station after Renigunta onward to Bombay.

- o The Himsagar Express between Jammu Tawi (Jammu & Kashmir) and Kanyakumari (Tamil Nadu) has the longest run both in terms of total time taken and distance covered. It covers its route of 2,344 miles in 74 hours and 55 minutes.
- o The Prayagraj Express, with 26 coaches, is the longest train in the country.
- o The Haldia-Asansol Express, which has just three coaches, is the shortest train and is, oddly, often hauled by the powerful WAP-4 locomotive.
- o Ghoom near Darjeeling in West Bengal is the highest station at 2,258 meters, or 7,407 feet.
- o People afraid of tunnels should not take the Karbude tunnel on the Konkan Railway along the west coast, which is the longest tunnel at 4.06 miles.
- o The Godavari bridge near Rajahmundry in Andhra Pradesh, which stretches 3.125 miles, is the longest.

Jokes You Love To Hate

Phobia is Latin for fear. It's opposite, *mania*, stands for attraction.

Technical terms with these suffixes refer to people's attitude to certain things. For example, a person who avoids computers is called a technophobe. The usual descriptions given to such terms are usually misleading. A phobia is almost always described as an "irrational fear or hatred". A technophobe usually avoids using computers. He does not hate them nor does he fear them but he is always described as hating/fearing them. For jokes in this section, the "irrational fear or hatred" humbug will be used for the sake of satire.

- **Irrational fear/hatred usually exhibited by a pirate when asked to walk the plank**
Ablutophobia [fear of washing or bathing]

- **Irrational fear/hatred usually exhibited by a recovering alcoholic**
Acarophobia [fear of itching]

- **Irrational fear/hatred exhibited by some kids when their father offers them lemon drink**
Acerophobia [fear of sourness]

He mixes in salt instead of sugar and says that salt is the healthier option during summer.

- **Irrational fear/hatred usually exhibited by fireflies when they run out of gas**
Achluophobia [fear of darkness]

- **Irrational fear/hatred usually exhibited by kids when they try to eat hard candy discreetly**
Acousticophobia [fear of noise]

- **Irrational fear/hatred usually exhibited by climbers during an avalanche**
Acrophobia or altophobia [fear of heights]

- **Irrational fear/hatred usually exhibited by hijackers after the ATF shoots all the tyres**
Aerophobia [fear of flying]

- **Irrational fear/hatred usually lacking in drivers who drink**
Aeroacrophobia [fear of high and open places]

- **Irrational fear/hatred usually exhibited by a flycatcher bird after it snags a stink bug by mistake**
Aeronausiphobia [fear of vomiting in high places]

- **Irrational fear/hatred usually exhibited by people when they watch the evening debates on TV**
Agateophobia [fear of going mad]

- **Irrational fear/hatred usually exhibited by people when they fall into a manhole**
Agoraphobia [fear of open places]

- **Irrational fear/hatred usually exhibited by smartphone addicts**
Agyrophobia [fear of crossing streets]

- **Irrational fear/hatred usually exhibited by balloons**
  Aichmophobia [fear of sharp or pointy things]

- **Irrational fear/hatred usually exhibited by goldfish when a four-legged creature looks intently at the tank**
  Ailurophobia [fear of cats]

- **Irrational fear/hatred usually exhibited by bungee jumpers**
  Agliophobia or algophobia [fear of pain]

- **Irrational fear/hatred usually exhibited by women married to men suffering from entomophobia**
  Alektorophobia [fear of chicken]

- **Irrational fear/hatred usually exhibited by people when they find a line of ants leading to an ice-cream cone they forgot to eat last night**
  Entomophobia [fear of insects]

- **Irrational fear/hatred usually taken advantage of by vampire hunters**
  Alliumphobia [fear of garlic]

- **Irrational fear/hatred usually exhibited by terrorists when Internet users viciously condemn them by changing the colour of some icons**
  Allodoxaphobia [fear of opinions]

- **Irrational fear/hatred usually exhibited by clean-freaks in any place except their room**
  Amathophobia [fear of dust]

- **Irrational fear/hatred usually exhibited by people when they forget their license at home**
  Amaxophobia [fear of driving in a vehicle]

- **Irrational fear/hatred usually exhibited by soldiers when they translate a sign and find that it says 'DANGER LANDMINES'**
  Ambulophobia [fear of walking]

- **Irrational fear/hatred usually exhibited by people after they change their password**
  Amnesiphobia [fear of amnesia]

- **Irrational fear/hatred usually exhibited by mobile phone store personnel when they have to take a new phone from a sealed package for demonstration to just one customer**
  Amychophobia [fear of scratches] and haphephobia [fear of touch]

- **Irrational fear/hatred usually exhibited by politicians who have been voted out and the new government is working wonders to the economy**
  Anablephobia [fear of looking up]

- **Irrational fear/hatred usually exhibited by builders of card pyramids**
  Ancraophobia or anemophobia [fear of wind]

- **Irrational fear/hatred usually exhibited by feminists**
  Androphobia [fear of men]

- **Irrational fear/hatred usually exhibited by most married men**
  Gynophobia [fear of women]

- **Irrational fear/hatred usually exhibited by bubbles**
  Aphenphosmphobia [fear of touch]

- Irrational fear/hatred usually exhibited by an antelope when it runs from a cheetah
  Aphenphosmphobia [fear of intimacy]

- Irrational fear/hatred exhibited by tourists when they fall into piranha-infested rivers
  Aquaphobia [fear of water]

- Irrational fear/hatred usually exhibited by levitating psychics
  Astraphobia [fear of thunder and lightning]

- Irrational fear/hatred usually exhibited by suicide bombers when the explosion causes extensive damage but fails to kill them
  Atelophobia [fear of flaws/imperfection]

- Irrational fear/hatred usually exhibited by kids when they leave their beach castles
  Atephobia [fear of ruins or ruination]

- Irrational fear/hatred usually exhibited by kids when parents forget to buy icecream during family outings
  Athazagoraphobia [fear of being forgotten or ignored]

- Irrational fear/hatred usually exhibited by small kids when they eat popping candy
  Atomosophobia [fear of atomic explosions]

- Irrational fear/hatred usually exhibited by electronic products manufactured for planned obsolescence
  Atychiphobia [fear of failure]

- Irrational fear/hatred usually exhibited by flautists when they walk into a curtain and hit a closed door
  Aulophobia [fear of flutes]

- Irrational fear/hatred usually exhibited by tax evaders during a raid
  Aurophobia [fear of gold]

- Irrational fear/hatred usually exhibited by people when politicians talk about the need to find a balance between freedom and security

Automatonophobia [fear of ventriloquist's dummies]

- **Irrational fear/hatred usually exhibited by people when they shake hands with someone who has just been to the bathroom**
  Automysophobia [fear of being dirty]

- **Irrational fear/hatred usually exhibited by sharks after they catch a puffer fish**
  Belonephobia [fear of needles or sharp objects]

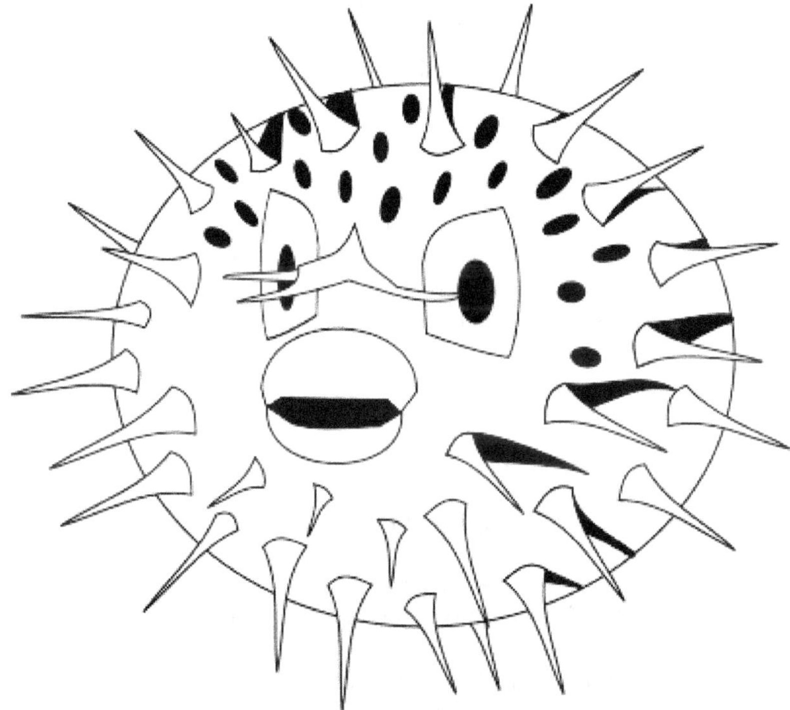

- **Irrational fear/hatred exhibited by door handles of public bathrooms**
  Bacteriophobia [fear of bacteria]

- **Irrational fear/hatred usually exhibited by people when they encounter drunkards**
  Batrachophobia [fear of amphibians]

- **Irrational fear/hatred usually exhibited people when they tumble down the stairs during a power cut**
  Bathophobia [fear of depth]

- **Irrational obsession usually exhibited by silverfish**
  Bibliomania [love of books]

- **Irrational fear/hatred usually exhibited by the public when dealing with corrupt government officials**
  Blennophobia [fear of slime]

- **Irrational fear/hatred usually exhibited by teenagers**
  Cacophobia [fear of ugliness]

- **Irrational fear/hatred usually exhibited by opponents of mobile phone radiation**
  Carcinophobia [fear of cancer]
- **Irrational fear/hatred usually exhibited by Count Dracula, Nosferatu, and other vampires**
  Catoptrophobia [fear of mirrors]
- **Irrational fear/hatred usually exhibited by male mosquitoes when they tell other insects that it is the females of their species that drink blood**
  Catagelophobia [fear of being ridiculed]
- **Irrational fear/hatred usually exhibited by people when they think others will take their seat if they go for a break**
  Cathisophobia [fear of sitting]
- **Irrational fear/hatred usually exhibited by operators of heavy machinery when they get dragged into it**
  Chaetophobia [fear of hair]
- **Irrational fear/hatred usually exhibited by proponents of organic foods**
  Chemophobia [fear of chemicals]
- **Irrational fear/hatred usually exhibited by Christmas trees**
  Chionophobia [fear of snow]
- **Irrational fear/hatred usually exhibited by cricket balls**
  Chiroptophobia [fear of bats]
- **Irrational fear/hatred usually exhibited by tight-rope walkers**
  Chorophobia [fear of dancing]
- **Irrational fear/hatred usually exhibited by dry cleaners when they are washing all-whites**
  Chromophobia [fear of colours]
- **Irrational fear/hatred usually exhibited by people living in the past**
  Chronophobia [fear of time]
- **Irrational fear/hatred usually exhibited by procrastinators**
  Chronomentrophobia [fear of clocks]
- **Irrational fear/hatred usually exhibited by fashion models**
  Cibophobia [fear of food]
- **Irrational fear/hatred usually exhibited by protesters and jail inmates**
  Claustrophobia [fear of enclosed spaces]
- **Irrational fear/hatred usually exhibited by movers-and-packers**
  Climacophobia [fear of stairs]
- **Irrational fear/hatred usually exhibited by kids after they watch a horror movie**
  Clinophobia [fear of going to bed]
- **Irrational fear/hatred usually exhibited by people disgusted with politics**
  Coulrophobia [fear of clowns]
- **Irrational fear/hatred usually exhibited by people after they accidentally format the hard disk**
  Cyberphobia [fear of computers]
- **Irrational fear/hatred usually exhibited by people when they take a seat and**

fail to note the Chihuahua on it
Cynophobia [fear of dogs]

- **Irrational fear/hatred usually exhibited by zombies when they wake up and become hungry again**
  Coimetrophobia [fear of cemeteries]

- **Irrational fear/hatred usually exhibited by formerly possessed individuals when they clean their room after an exorcism**
  Demonophobia [fear of demons]

- **Irrational fear/hatred usually exhibited by horse-riders when they get stopped by a branch**
  Dendrophobia [fear of trees]

- **Irrational fear/hatred usually exhibited by people during earthquakes**
  Domatophobia [fear of houses]

- **Irrational fear/hatred usually exhibited by fish when approaching a group of sharks**
  Didaskaleinophobia [fear of going to school]

- **Irrational fear/hatred usually exhibited by people when they fall from a cliff while taking a selfie**
  Dinophobia [fear of dizziness]

- **Irrational fear/hatred usually exhibited by vampires after biting a Russian**
  Dipsophobia [fear of alcohol]

- **Irrational desire that a policeman with a breathalyser would like in passing motorists**
  Dipsomania [love of alcohol]

- **Irrational fear/hatred usually exhibited by sheep when they spot a wolf in**

disguise amidst them
Doraphobia [fear of fur or hide of animals]

- **Irrational fear/hatred usually exhibited by ants when they are transporting stuff to great heights**
Dystychiphobia [fear of accidents]

- **Irrational fear/hatred usually exhibited by spies**
Dysmorphophobia [fear of body flaws]

- **Irrational fear/hatred usually exhibited by formerly possessed individuals when they receive the bill from the exorcist**
Ecclesiophobia [fear of church]

- **Irrational fear/hatred usually lacking in birds when they sit on power cables**
Irrational fear/hatred usually exhibited by people when the drop the phone extension cord in the bathtub
Irrational fear/hatred usually exhibited by women when the drop the hair dryer in the bathtub
Electrophobia [fear of electricity]

- **Irrational fear/hatred usually exhibited by skydivers when their parachute fails to deploy**
Eleutherophobia [fear of freedom]

- Irrational fear/hatred usually exhibited by visitors to an acupuncturist's clinic when they fall to the floor
  Enetophobia [fear of pins]
- Irrational fear/hatred usually exhibited by unpopular politicians and police states
  Enochlophobia [fear of crowds]
- Irrational fear/hatred usually exhibited by people who hate Mondays
  Eosophobia [fear of daylight]
- Irrational fear/hatred usually exhibited by walls disfigured by graffiti
  Ephebiphobia [fear of youth]
- Irrational fear/hatred usually exhibited by pugilists when their eyelids swell up
  Epistaxiophobia [fear of nosebleeds]
- Irrational fear/hatred usually exhibited by whistleblowers when a hitman pays a visit
  Epistemophobia [fear of knowledge]
- Irrational fear/hatred usually exhibited by mules when they get ridiculed for looking like a donkey
  Equinophobia [fear of horses]
- Irrational fear/hatred usually lacking in pension funds
  Erythrophobia [fear of the colour red]
- Irrational fear/hatred usually exhibited by condemned prisoners when they reach the guillotine
  Francophobia [fear of France or French culture]
- Irrational fear/hatred usually exhibited by homeless people and stray animals at night
  Frigophobia [fear of cold]
- Irrational fear/hatred usually exhibited by divorce lawyers when marriage statistics indicate that relationships are lasting longer
  Gamophobia [fear of marriage]
- Irrational fear/hatred usually exhibited by lionesses when they abandon their kill to hyenas
  Gelotophobia [fear of laughter]
- Irrational fear/hatred usually exhibited comedians when their jokes are stolen
  Gelotophobia [fear of being laughed at]
- Irrational fear/hatred usually exhibited by boatmen
  Gephyrophobia [fear of bridges]
- Irrational fear/hatred usually exhibited by suicide bombers
  Gerascophobia [fear of growing old]
- Irrational fear/hatred usually exhibited by kids when they are caught with their hands in the cookie jar
  Gerontophobia [fear of the elderly]
- Irrational fear/hatred usually exhibited by victims of blimp crashes
  Globophobia [fear of balloons]

- **Irrational fear/hatred usually exhibited by politicians when the teleprompter fails**
  Glossophobia [fear of public speaking]
- **Irrational fear/hatred usually exhibited by people when they cannot understand their own notes**
  Graphophobia [fear of handwriting]
- **Irrational fear/hatred usually exhibited by taxmen when they approach the last date for their return to the ungodly place they came from**
  Hadephobia [fear of hell]
- **Irrational fear/hatred usually exhibited by vampires when the exorcist throws The Book at them**
  Hagiophobia [fear of holy/sacred things]
- **Irrational fear/hatred usually exhibited by a lizard after it catches a stink bug by mistake**
  Halitophobia [fear of bad breath]
- **Irrational fear/hatred usually exhibited by people who take the last biscuit without first offering it to others**
  Hamartophobia [fear of sinning]
- **Irrational fear/hatred usually exhibited by athletes when a rival uses crooked ways to win**
  Harpaxophobia [fear of being robbed]
- **Irrational fear/hatred usually exhibited by a death row inmate before his/her last meal**
  Hedonophobia [fear of pleasure]
- **Irrational fear/hatred usually exhibited by vampires**
  Heliophobia [fear of sunlight]
- **Irrational fear/hatred usually exhibited by businesses when they pay huge fines in class-action lawsuits**
  Hellenologophobia [fear of complex terminology]
- **Irrational fear/hatred usually exhibited by computer antivirus companies**
  Helminthophobia [fear of worms]
- **Irrational fear/hatred usually exhibited by hæmophiliacs**
  Hemophobia [fear of blood]
- **Irrational fear/hatred usually exhibited by party officials when a politician deviates from talking points**
  Heresyphobia [fear of heresy]
- **Irrational fear/hatred usually exhibited by Japanese people when Godzilla makes landfall**
  Herpetophobia [fear of reptiles]
- **Irrational fear/hatred usually exhibited by boys when they get ragged in front of female students of their class**
  Heterophobia [fear of opposite gender]
- **Irrational fear/hatred of a particular number sometimes exhibited by people who are afraid of the number 999**
  Hexakosioihexekontahexaphobia [fear of the number 666]
- **Irrational fear/hatred of usually exhibited by people when they have to**

admit their mistake
Hippopotomonstrosesquipedaliophobia [fear of long words]

- **Irrational fear/hatred usually exhibited by societies that fail to take care of their own brethren**
  Hobophobia [fear of hobos]

- **Irrational fear/hatred usually exhibited by statues**
  Hodophobia [fear of travel]

- **Irrational fear/hatred usually exhibited by passive smokers**
  Homichlophobia [fear of fog]

- **Irrational fear/hatred usually exhibited by men when they get teary-eyed while watching a sad cartoon**
  Hygrophobia [fear of dampness]

- **Irrational fear/hatred usually exhibited by kids after they break something expensive**
  Homilophobia [fear of sermons]

- **Irrational fear/hatred usually exhibited by kids when they do not get a bigger slice than their younger sibling**
  Homophobia [fear of sameness]

- **Irrational fear/hatred usually exhibited by gun owners when they shoot themselves in the leg**
  Hoplophobia [fear of firearms]

- **Irrational fear/hatred usually exhibited by women after they drop the hair dryer in the bathtub**
  Hormephobia [fear of shocks]

- **Irrational fear/hatred which explains why Batman is still single**
  Hydrophobophobia [fear of rabies]

- **Irrational fear/hatred usually exhibited by insects**
  Hyelophobia [fear of glasses]

- **Irrational fear/hatred usually exhibited by people when someone calls them names that accurately describe them**
  Hylephobia [fear of fits or epilepsy]

- **Irrational fear/hatred usually exhibited by people when they fail to shave**
  Hylophobia [fear of forests]

- **Irrational fear/hatred usually exhibited by kids when their siblings rat on them**
  Hypengyophobia [fear of responsibility]

- **Irrational fear/hatred usually exhibited by people when a politician talks about his accomplishments**
  Hypnophobia [fear of sleep]

- **Irrational fear/hatred usually exhibited by smokers when their lungs have accumulated enough tar to top the driveway where the hearse is waiting to pick them up**
  Hypochondria [fear of illness]

- **Irrational fear/hatred usually exhibited by people when they know they are going to be hit with a huge bill**
  Iatrophobia [fear of doctors or visiting them]

- **Irrational fear/hatred usually exhibited by debtors when a package arrives without any postage marks**
  Ichthyophobia [fear of fish]

- **Irrational fear/hatred usually exhibited by many politicians**
  Ideophobia [fear of ideas]

- **Irrational fear/hatred usually exhibited by speculators when the bubble bursts**
  Illyngophobia [fear of vertigo]

- **Irrational fear/hatred usually exhibited by the public when bureaucrats and politicians divert scarce public resources to white-elephant projects**
  Isopterophobia [fear of termites]

- **Irrational desire usually exhibited by many politicians when they are in power**
  Kleptomania [love of stealing or stolen goods]

- **Irrational fear/hatred usually exhibited by restaurant owners during a food-and-health inspection**
  Katsaridaphobia [fear of cockroaches]

- **Irrational fear/hatred usually exhibited by the public when they try to explain their problems to a politician or government official**
  Kenophobia [fear of empty spaces]

- **Irrational fear/hatred usually exhibited by demolition experts**
  Koinoniphobia [fear of rooms]

- **Irrational fear/hatred usually exhibited by someone who catches a tiger by its tail**
  Kopophobia [fear of fatigue]

- **Irrational fear/hatred usually exhibited by an opera singer when a mobile phone rings loudly during a performance**
  Kymophobia [fear of waves]

- **Irrational fear/hatred usually exhibited by people when politicians prove to be spineless**
  Kyphophobia [fear of stooping]

- **Irrational fear/hatred usually exhibited by kids when mother cooks bitter gourd because it is rich in minerals**
  Lachanophobia [fear of vegetables]

- **Irrational fear/hatred usually exhibited by a Mafia leader when a gang member sings like a canary**
  Laliophobia [fear of speaking]

- **Irrational fear/hatred usually exhibited by people who spend too much time on the keyboard**
  Leprophobia [fear of leprosy]

- **Irrational fear/hatred usually exhibited by a terrorist when he throws the pin and bites the grenade**
  Ligyrophobia [fear of loud noises]

- **Irrational fear/hatred usually exhibited by fairies, billboards and men-on-stilts**
  Lilapsophobia [fear of tornadoes/hurricanes]

- **Irrational fear/hatred usually exhibited by whistleblowers**
  Limnophobia [fear of lakes]

- **Irrational fear/hatred usually exhibited by liars**
  Linonophobia [fear of string]

- **Irrational fear/hatred usually exhibited by a hungry vampire when it ignores an American**
  Liticaphobia [fear of lawsuits]

- **Irrational fear/hatred usually exhibited by Morse code operators**
  Logophobia [fear of words]

- **Irrational fear/hatred usually exhibited by kids when mother takes forever to get the icecream after meals**
  Macrophobia [fear of long waits]

- **Irrational fear/hatred usually exhibited by spiders, lizards, insects and other creatures that live in the kitchen**
  Mageirocophobia [fear of cooking]

- **Irrational fear/hatred usually lacking in government officials**
  Mastigophobia [fear of punishment]

- **Irrational fear/hatred usually exhibited by fruits when they go into the blender**
  Mechanophobia [fear of machines]

- **Irrational fear/hatred usually exhibited by people when they find a few spots on fruits and vegetables forcing stores to waste good food prematurely**
  Melanophobia [fear of black colour]

- **Irrational fear/hatred usually exhibited by drones when the workers come for the evening**
  Melissophobia [fear of bees]

- **Irrational fear/hatred usually exhibited by teenagers after they wreck the**

family car
Melophobia [fear of music]

- **Irrational fear/hatred usually exhibited by a jail inmate who has been sentenced to hang**
  Merinthophobia [fear of being tied up]

- **Irrational fear/hatred usually exhibited by MRI operators when someone rolls in an oxygen tank**
  Metallophobia [fear of metal]

- **Irrational fear/hatred usually exhibited by parents when their kids scribbles on the wall**
  Metrophobia [fear of poems]

- **Irrational fear/hatred usually sometimes exhibited by kids when everyone else escapes punishment**
  Monophobia [fear of being alone]

- **Irrational fear/hatred usually exhibited by parking area attendants**
  Motorphobia [fear of automobiles]

- **Irrational fear/hatred usually exhibited by lizards when the dust gets into their eyes**
  Mottephobia [fear of moths]

- **Irrational fear/hatred usually exhibited by snakes when they learn that health authorities have declared the area plague-affected**
  Murophobia [fear of mice and rats]

- **Irrational fear/hatred usually lacking in people when they are praised**
  Myrmecophobia [fear of ants]

- **Irrational compulsion felt by politicians when they state their accomplishments**
  Mythomania [love of lying]

- **Irrational fear/hatred usually exhibited by canned food**
  Mysophobia [fear of germs or contamination]

- **Irrational fear/hatred usually exhibited by torches when the light goes dim**
  Necrophobia [fear of death or the dead]

- **Irrational fear/hatred (according to feminists) usually exhibited by women when they throw a brick at the ceiling**
  Nelophobia [fear of glass]

- **Irrational fear/hatred usually exhibited by a blockbuster drug manufacturer when a generic equivalent enters the market**
  Neopharmaphobia [fear of new drugs]

- **Irrational fear/hatred usually exhibited by an overdue sacrificial goat when fresh arrivals join the lot**
  Neophobia [fear of new things]

- **Irrational fear/hatred usually exhibited by somnabulists living in a landmined area**
  Noctiphobia [fear of the night]

- **Irrational fear/hatred usually exhibited by horror movie actors when the ghost deploys a cell phone jammer**
  Nomophobia [fear of lack of mobile phone service]

- **Irrational fear/hatred usually exhibited by footboard travellers when they start slipping**
Nosocomephobia [fear of hospitals]

- **Irrational fear/hatred usually exhibited by surgical gloves**
Nosophobia [fear of diseases]

- **Irrational fear/hatred usually exhibited by bomb-disposal squad members**
Numerophobia [fear of numbers]

- **Irrational fear/hatred usually exhibited by horror movie actors when they realize it was a mistake to have split up and gone in different directions**
Nyctohylophobia [fear of forested areas at night]

- **Irrational fear/hatred usually exhibited by American turkeys ahead of Thanksgiving**
Obesophobia [fear of weight gain]

- **Irrational fear/hatred usually exhibited by missionaries caught by a cannibal tribe**
Ochlophobia [fear of crowds]

- **Irrational fear/hatred usually exhibited by candy-loving kids**
Odontophobia [fear of dentistry]

- **Irrational fear/hatred usually exhibited by parade organizers**
Ombrophobia [fear of rain]

- **Irrational fear/hatred usually exhibited by pickpockets**
Ommetaphobia [fear of eyes]

- **Irrational fear/hatred that Adam and Eve were unlikely to have**

Omphalophobia [fear of belly button]

- **Irrational fear/hatred usually exhibited by Indians when they try to navigate the bureaucracy**
  Oneirophobia [fear of dreams]
- **Irrational obsession usually exhibited by authoritarian states when they try to extract truth from suspects and troublemakers**
  Onychotillomania [love of picking fingernails]
- **Irrational fear/hatred exhibited by tourists in tropical South America when they fall into anaconda-infested waters**
  Ophidiophobia [fear of snakes]
- **Irrational fear/hatred usually exhibited around people with looks that can kill**
  Ophthalmophobia [fear of staring]
- **Irrational fear/hatred exhibited by people when they sneeze**
  Optophobia [fear of opening one's eyes]
- **Irrational fear/hatred usually exhibited by statues**
  Ornithophobia [fear of birds]
- **Irrational fear/hatred usually exhibited by psychopaths when power fails to return and the bodies in the freezer are losing their cool**
  Osmophobia [fear of odours]
- **Irrational fear/hatred usually exhibited by pearl divers when they get trapped inside a clam**
  Ostraconophobia [fear of shellfish]
- **Irrational fear/hatred usually exhibited by people hit by lightning**
  Ouranophobia [fear of heaven]
- **Irrational fear/hatred usually exhibited by people after they stick their tongue to a metal pole**
  Pagophobia [fear of ice or frost]
- **Irrational fear/hatred usually exhibited by drug cartel members when they seek to settle all deals in cash**
  Papyrophobia [fear of paper]
- **Irrational fear/hatred usually exhibited by politicians when they get admitted to hospital while their lawyer tries to arrange for bail**
  Panphobia [fear of everything and/or unknown stuff]
- **Irrational fear/hatred usually exhibited by taxpayers**
  Parasitophobia [fear of parasites]
- **Irrational fear/hatred usually exhibited by taxmen when they are dipped in boiling oil in hell**
  Peccatophobia [fear of sinning]
- **Irrational fear/hatred usually exhibited by head-hunters**
  Pediculophobia [fear of lice]
- **Irrational fear/hatred usually exhibited by voodoo practitioners when the tax department sends them an unsolicited, skewered and crude likeness by registered mail**
  Pediophobia [fear of dolls]

- **Irrational fear/hatred usually exhibited by hair oil manufacturers**
  Peladophobia [fear of bald people]

- **Irrational fear/hatred usually exhibited by burglars**
  Peniaphobia [fear of poverty]

- **Irrational fear/hatred usually exhibited by a male praying mantis**
  Peniaphobia [fear of mother-in-law]

- **Irrational fear/hatred usually exhibited by the public when they think of the tax being collected by the government**
  Irrational fear/hatred usually exhibited by forest explorers when a python gets a crush on them
  Phagophobia [fear of being eaten]

- **Irrational fear/hatred that was usually exhibited by early American settlers when they saw Red Indians with tomahawks eyeing their scalp**
  Phalacrophobia [fear of going bald]

- **Irrational fear/hatred usually exhibited by people when the cure is worse than the disease**
  Pharmacophobia [fear of medicines]

- **Irrational fear/hatred usually exhibited by politicians when opponents dig up their past**
  Phasmophobia [fear of ghosts]

- **Irrational desire usually exhibited by people when they note the overbite problem of a vampire for the first time**
  Philematophobia [fear of kissing]

- **Irrational desire usually exhibited by frogs when they encounter snakes**
  Philophobia [fear of love]

- **Irrational fear/hatred usually exhibited by people when someone says "I told you so"**
  Philosophobia [fear of philosophy]

- **Irrational fear/hatred usually exhibited by a zombie when it tries to get out**
  Placophobia [fear of tombstones]

- **Irrational fear/hatred usually exhibited by people who do not have enough problems**
  Phobophobia [fear of phobias]

- **Irrational fear/hatred usually exhibited by tobacco products**
  Photophobia [fear of light]

- **Irrational fear/hatred usually exhibited by barbers**
  Pogonophobia [fear of beards]

- **Irrational fear/hatred usually exhibited by politicians when "high command" gives their "lucrative posts" to fresh arrivals from rival political parties**
  Politicophobia [fear of politicians]

- **Irrational fear/hatred usually exhibited by scared folk who are also egomaniacs**
  Polyphobia [fear of many things]

- **Irrational fear/hatred usually exhibited by taxmen**
  Plutophobia [fear of wealth]

- **Irrational fear/hatred usually exhibited by Chihuahuas owned by sumo wrestlers**
  Pnigophobia [fear of being smothered]

- **Irrational fear/hatred usually exhibited by lawyers when cases seem to end fast**
  Prosophobia [fear of progress]

- **Irrational fear/hatred usually exhibited by people when they have to manufacture a lie and say it at the same time**
  Psellismophobia [fear of stuttering]

- **Irrational fear/hatred usually exhibited by trapeze artists**
  Pteronophobia [fear of being tickled by feathers]

- **Irrational desire usually exhibited by Indians around the festival of Diwali**
  Pyromania [love of fire]

- **Irrational fear/hatred usually exhibited by a soldier when he is cleaning a cannon from the business end and hears an order followed by some light at the end of the tunnel**
  Pyrophobia [fear of fire]

- **Irrational fear/hatred usually exhibited by dragonflies when they buzz over water bodies**
  Ranidaphobia [fear of frogs]

- **Irrational fear/hatred usually exhibited by terrorists**
  Radiophobia [fear of x-rays or radioactivity]

- **Irrational fear/hatred usually exhibited by tourists in Russia when try to out-drink the hosts**
  Russophobia [fear of Russians]

- **Irrational fear/hatred usually exhibited by horror movie actors**
  Sciophobia [fear of shadows]

- **Irrational fear/hatred usually exhibited by gamblers when they borrow money they cannot pay and hear a knock on the door**
  Selachophobia [fear of sharks]

- **Irrational fear/hatred usually exhibited by werewolves when dog food prices rise**
  Selenophobia [fear of the moon]

- **Irrational fear/hatred usually exhibited by models when they have to pose for photos without payment**
  Scopophobia [fear of being looked at]

- **Irrational fear/hatred usually lacking in many people with selfie sticks**
  Siderodromophobia [fear of trains]

- **Irrational fear/hatred usually exhibited by people when they walk into a curtain and hit their head on the edge of a door**
  Siderophobia [fear of stars]

- **Irrational fear/hatred usually exhibited by people when they buy a product and realise that the instructions are in a foreign language**
  Sinophobia [fear of Chinese]

- **Irrational fear/hatred usually exhibited by burglars**
  Sociophobia [fear of people and social interactions]

- **Irrational fear/hatred usually exhibited by women when they realize it is their birthday**
  Sophophobia [fear of learning]

- **Irrational fear/hatred usually exhibited by the person who climbs to the top of a human pyramid**
  Soteriophobia [fear of dependence on others]

- **Irrational fear/hatred usually exhibited by sofa manufacturers**
  Stasiphobia [fear of standing]

- **Irrational fear/hatred usually exhibited by owls when it realizes that its slow quarry was poisoned**
  Suriphobia [fear of mice]
  [Poisoned vermin should be incinerated.]

- **Irrational fear/hatred usually exhibited by caterers when the queue forms**
  Tachophobia [fear of speed]

- **Irrational fear/hatred usually exhibited by ants around beachball players**
  Taphophobia [fear of being buried alive]

- **Irrational fear/hatred usually exhibited by horror movie actors when they run away from zombies**
  Teratophobia [fear of disfigured people]

- **Irrational fear/hatred usually exhibited by people sitting on a 3-seat bench in a very crowded train**
  Tetraphobia [fear of number 4]

- **Irrational fear/hatred usually exhibited by a chain mail when it meets a sceptic**
  Thanatophobia [fear of dying]

- **Irrational fear/hatred usually exhibited by mobsters when their feet gets stuck in a tub full of concrete**
  Thalassophobia [fear of sea]

- **Irrational fear/hatred usually exhibited by missionaries when they convert natives**

Theophobia [fear of religion]

- **Irrational fear/hatred usually exhibited by acupuncturists during an earthquake**
  Tremophobia [fear of trembling]

- **Irrational fear/hatred usually exhibited by icecream containers**
  Thermophobia [fear of high temperatures]

- **Irrational fear/hatred usually exhibited by a kid worried about sharing his/her toys with a future sibling**
  Tokophobia [fear of pregnancy or childbirth]

- **Irrational fear/hatred usually exhibited by people living in border areas**
  Tomophobia [fear of invasive medical procedures]

- **Irrational fear/hatred usually exhibited by movies in which all top-secret government computers run PowerPoint 1.0 for DOS and no other software**

Technophobia [fear of advanced technology]

- **Irrational fear/hatred usually exhibited by a snake when it bites its tongue**
  Toxiphobia [fear of poisoning]

- **Irrational fear/hatred usually exhibited by parkour enthusiasts when they can not move their body**
  Traumatophobia [fear of trauma or injury]

- **Irrational love/desire usually exhibited by people when the election results are announced**
  Trichotillomania [love of plucking hair]

- **Irrational desire usually exhibited by pre-teen kids when they realize that soon they will have to do a lot more household chores like their older siblings**
  Triskaidekaphobia [fear of number 13]

- **Irrational fear/hatred usually exhibited by people when they realize that a**

mosquito is biting them
Trypanophobia [fear of needles]

- **Irrational fear/hatred usually exhibited by those engaged in gun fights**
Trypophobia [fear of holes]

- **Irrational fear/hatred usually exhibited by kids when someone with a new bat lords it over everyone**
Tyrannophobia [fear of tyrants]

- **Irrational fear/hatred usually exhibited by beautiful women when they encounter women more beautiful than them**
Venustraphobia [fear of beautiful women]

- **Irrational fear/hatred usually exhibited by men when women do the packing**
Vestiphobia [fear of clothing]

- **Irrational fear/hatred usually exhibited by teenagers when someone tries to talk sense to them**
Xenoglossophobia [fear of foreign languages]

- **Irrational fear/hatred usually exhibited by people when their shoe comes apart in the middle of the street**
Xenophobia [fear of strangers or aliens]

- **Irrational fear/hatred usually exhibited by desks when the judge raises the gavel**
Xylophobia [fear of wooden objects]

- **Irrational fear/hatred usually exhibited by librarians**
Xyrophobia [fear of razors]

- **Irrational fear/hatred usually exhibited by kids when they realize that their sibling still has not finished his/her candy**
Zelophobia [fear of jealousy]

- **Irrational fear/hatred usually exhibited by alcoholics when they quit drinking after doctors tells them they have cirrhosis**
Zeusophobia [fear of god]
[WARNING: Sudden cessation of alcohol without medical supervision will also cause problems.]

- **Irrational fear/hatred usually exhibited by vegans/vegetarians**
Zoophobia [fear of animals]

Knock-Knock Jokes

Knock-knock jokes are best enjoyed with two or more people. They are enacted as a scene in which a stranger is seeking entry in to a restricted area. The person who knows the joke acts as the stranger and begins by saying "Knock knock". Somebody in the audience pretends to be the guard and has to say, "Who goes

there?". Then, the stranger says a word (usually his/her name) that is the subject of the joke. The guard replies to that with " [that name] who?". The stranger then says the punchline of the joke using that name.

- **Arthur**

  Knock Knock.
  Who is there?
  Arthur.
  Arthur who?
  Are there any back taxes you owe?

- **Bill**

  Knock Knock.
  Who is there?
  Bill.
  Bill who?
  Believe it or not, your car is being towed.

- **Cedric**

  Knock Knock.
  Who is there?
  Cedric.
  Cedric who?
  See, the trick is to close the windows as well. You're letting the mosquitoes in.

- **Dees**

  Knock Knock.
  Who is there?
  Dees.
  Dees who?
  Dees eez the poleez!

- **Emmy**

  Knock Knock.
  Who is there?
  Emmy.
  Emmy who?
  Emm I interrupting you?

- **Fredrick**

  Knock Knock.
  Who is there?
  Fredrick.
  Fredrick who?
  For the record, it's Fredrick with a K.

- **Gee**

  Knock Knock.
  Who is there?

Giselle.
Giselle who?
Gee, I shall bring the gin.

- **Humour**

Knock Knock.
Who is there?
Humour.
Humour who?
No, Yuma, Colorado.

- **Isla**

Knock Knock.
Who is there?
Isla.
Isla who?
I'd love to come in!

- **Johnny**

Knock Knock.
Who is there?
Johnny.
Johnny who?
Johnny come lately!

- **Kenny**

Knock Knock.
Who is there?
Kenny.
Kenny who?
Can I know your name?

- **Luke**

Knock Knock.
Who is there?
Luke.
Luke who?
Look, who is coming to dinner.

- **Meg**

Knock Knock.
Who is there?
Meg.
Meg who?
Make haste. It is cold outside!

- **Naomi**

Knock Knock.
Who is there?

It's Naomi.
Naomi who?
Nah, you owe me a dollar!

- **Ooma**

  Knock Knock.
  Who is there?
  It's Ooma.
  Ooma who?
  Who am I talking to?

- **Police**

  Knock Knock.
  Who is there?
  Police.
  Police who?
  Puhlease, it's an emergency!

- **Queen**

  Knock Knock.
  Who is there?
  Queen.
  Queen who?
  Go in and get my coat! It's raining.

- **Rhonda**

  Knock Knock.
  Who is there?
  Rhonda.
  Rhonda who?
  Run, da police are here.

- **Tom**

  Knock Knock.
  Who is there?
  Tom.
  Tom who?
  To whom... say, your name is what?

- **Uranus**

  Knock Knock.
  Who is there?
  Uranus.
  What?
  Uranus!
  Uranus, the planet?
  No, it's *Your Highness* who will have you executed if you don't open the door!

- **Wikipedia**

  Knock Knock.
  Who is there?
  Wikipedia
  Wikipedia who?

Wikipedia, the free online encyclopedia that anybody can edit!
[citation needed]

- **Wilma**

  Knock Knock.
  Who is there?
  Wilma
  Wilma who?
  Will my beautiful woman come to the door and open it, please?

- **Xavier**

  Knock Knock.
  Who is there?
  Xavier
  Xavier who?
  Save your talk. You have the right to remain silent.

- **Yvonne**

  Knock Knock.
  Who is there?
  Yvonne
  Yvonne who?
  You own this house? Your property taxes are due.

- **Zohra**

  Knock Knock.
  Who is there?
  Zohra
  Zohra who?
  Sir, are you the owner of this house?

- **Opportunity**

  Knock.
  Who is there?
  Opportunity.
  Opportunity who?
  [Silence]

... because opportunity knocks only once.

Mix Jokes

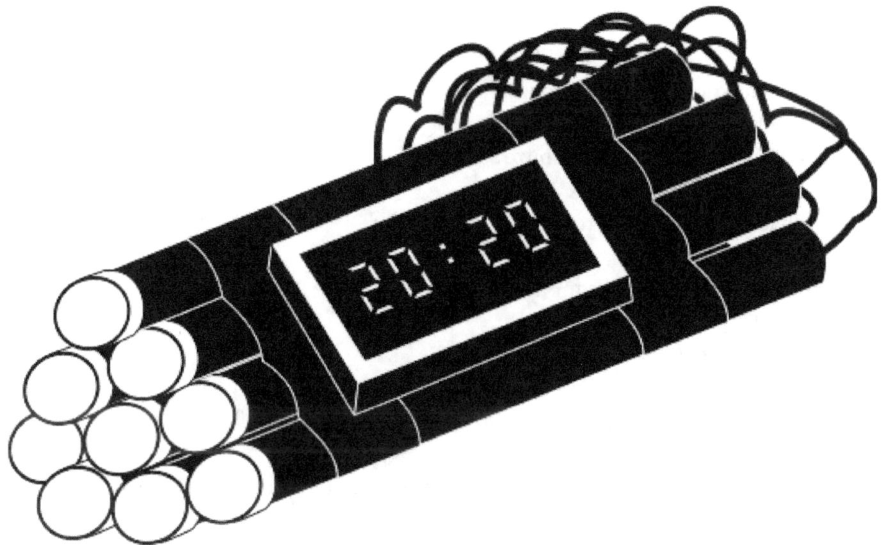

Each question in this section begins with "What do you get when you cross...".

- **an elk from New York and a character?**
  Anonymous letter.

- **a good-looking woman and sunshine?**
  Broad daylight.

- **a female with an AC remote?**
  Very rapid, unexplained, woman-made Climate Change.

- **a precious stone and a fast bowler?**
  Not a *diamond in the rough*.

- **a smart chicken and shy rooster**
  Scrambled eggs.

- **a financial magazine with a bank employee?**
  Fortune teller.

- **an old lady and epilepsy?**
  Grand mal seizure.

- **incorruptibility with an Indian policeman?**
  Hell freezes over.

- **whisky and a draught animal?**
  High horse.

- ***India Today* magazine with *Reader's Digest*?**
  Indigestion Today.

- **an unknown man with a female deer?**
  John Doe.

- **an unknown woman with a female deer?**
  o Jane Doe.
  o Broken chain of gossip and rumour.

- **a mass murder with a binocular?**
  Killer looks.

- **a grandfather clock with a burqa?**
  Long time no see.

- **a politician and a high tolerance for praise?**
  Made for each other.

- **truthfulness and a bureaucrat?**
  No chance.

- **rights with security?**
  Orwellian times.

- **a talking head and a brain that has never been used before?**
  Politician.

- **free food and the fastest thing a group of people who have never met before can do together?**
  Queue.

- **a kid and a holiday wishlist?**
  Reasonable expectations.

- **an alarm clock and a bomb?**
  Time killer.

- **talcum powder and a surgeon?**
  Smooth operator.

- **film director Quentin Tarantino and a mathematical procedure?**
  Tarantula.

- **a meaningless pause, the European pre-Christian god of thunder and a dude?**
  Uma Thurman, the actress.

- **modesty with a politician?**
  You are nuts.

- **efficiency with a government official?**
  Zero likelihood.

Physics Jokes

Science was my favourite subject in school. Physics was an easy subject until I reached higher secondary school. Then, it became difficult. That is, until I found the *Feynman Lectures On Physics* in the school library. After reading it, the physics textbook became easy to understand. Unfortunately, much of the year had passed and I could not put the book to good use for my final exam. If you choose physics as an elective subject, get Feynman's first.

- **Personal Ad**
  Invisible Man wants to meet wholesome invisible woman with transparent character and zero refraction.

- **Personal Ad**
  Invisible Woman wants to meet handsome invisible man with strong character and no infractions.

- **Perfect Chemistry**
  Invisible Man wanted to marry Invisible Woman. His family and friends did not like the idea. They could not figure out what he saw in her.

- **Science Fiction?**
  The Invisible Man* by HG Wells became so popular that the original magazine series was converted into a book and later adapted into several movies and TV shows. It continues to capture the imagination of young and old. However, is it really science fiction? Can someone become invisible? Let us assume that it is

possible. How will this person be? Well, for one thing, he will have to be dead. To let light through, the molecules in the body will have to be aligned like a lattice as in a crystal. No fluids (liquids or gas) could be present as they would have different densities and could be seen sloshing around. The colour of a material is directly related to its chemical composition. In what combination of chemicals can the human body become transparent? Can it stay alive? Even assuming that it can, **Invisible Man will have to be blind**, as his eyes will not be able to reflect light and form an image for the brain.

The technology to create an invisibility cloak effect has been in existence for several decades now. It is used in battlefields to camouflage tanks. These vehicles carry flat displays on top of them, which mimic the ground underneath to create the illusion that they are not really there (when observed from the sky). Such invisibility cloaks are available for military personnel and fixed installations too.

- **Pluto walks into a bar**
  Pluto walks into a bar but the bartender ignores him. Why? Because nobody recognizes Pluto as a planet anymore.

- **A meteor asks a meteorite**
  A meteor asks a meteorite, "What are my chances of hitting the ground?" The meteorite does not answer and just smiles. Irritated, the meteor says, "Aah, you guys just burn me up!"

- **How many astronauts would it take to a screw a lightbulb?**
  One to turn the bulb and several to prevent the spacecraft from spinning in the same direction.

- **What did one radio wave say to another?**
  "You are interfering with my work."

- **What's a radio engineer's favourite food?**
  A can of tuna.

- **What would happen if an eel came on the radio?**
  - You hear loud static once in a while.
  - "You are listening to *Current Affairs*, a programme about events that are electrifying the political arena."

- **What does Galileo's school yearbook say about him?**
  "Most likely to get arrested for using a telescope."

- **What was the crocodile searching on the Internet?**
  Alligator clips.

This is an electronics joke.

- **What would happen if lightning was elected mayor?**
  It would be illegal to steal someone's thunder.

- **What did the battery say to the circuit?**
  "If you lose my charge, you are grounded."

- **What did one equation say to another?**
  "What's with the odd expression?"

- **What happened when lead was dropped in water?**
  It had that sinking feeling.

- **Why did the physicist couple break up?**
  They could not handle the pressure.

- **What did the quantum gas think of Absolute Zero?**
  It was not very excited.

For a theoretical quantum gas, its atoms or molecules should stop vibrating at Absolute Zero. Absolute Zero is 273° C below zero.

- **What did 10^{-12} say to 10^{-9}?**
  "Pico on somebody else!"

- **What did 10^{-9} say to make 10^{-6} so angry?**
  "Nano of your business!"

- **What do protons like to read?**
  Books like "The power of positive thinking".

- **What did the neutron say when it was arrested?**
  "What's the charge?"

- **A proton walks into a bar**
  A proton walks into a bar, shouts an order at the bartender, drinks loudly, coughs, spills his drink, drops the glass, and then walks out without paying. Another tippler asks the bartender, "What's wrong with him?" The bartender says, "Oh, he is a free radical!"

- **A deuterium walks into a bar**
  A deuterium walks into a bar and the bartender asks, "Seen any tritiums lately?". The deuterium answers, "Yeah but that lowlife was already in a state of decay."

- **A neutron and a neutrino walk into a bar**
  A neutron and a neutrino walk into a bar and order drinks. To the neutron, the bartender says, "For you, no charge!". To the neutrino, the bartender, "That will be two bucks." The neutrino is upset by this and says, "Hey, I am also neutral." For that, the bartender says, "Yeah, but he carries more weight."

A neutrino is (like an electron) with almost no mass and (like a neutron) with no charge.

- **What did Earth say to Moon?**
  "You seem to be hiding something behind your back."

- **What did Moon say to Earth?**
  "It's nothing. You always need to look at the bright side!"

Chemistry Jokes

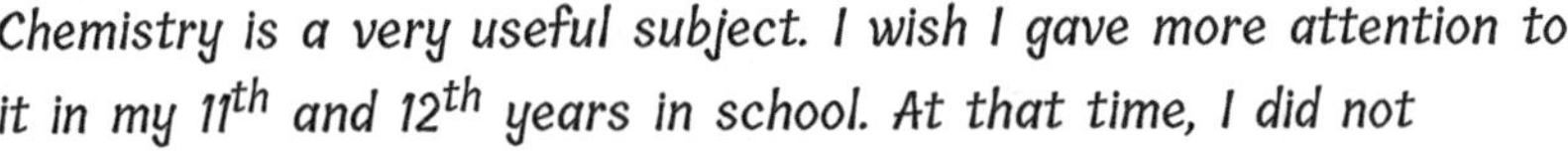

Chemistry is a very useful subject. I wish I gave more attention to it in my 11th and 12th years in school. At that time, I did not *realise how valuable it would be later in life.*

- **What did hydroiodic acid say?**
  It said '**HI**'.

- **What did the hydrogen atom say about the helium atom?**
  "**He** sounds funny."

- **What did carbon say when it was accused of Climate Change?**
  "I **C**."

- **Enzyme**

  Fatty Acid 1: What do you think of that enzyme?
  Fatty Acid 2: I don't trust him. He is always starting something.

- **What happened to nitric acid after water decided to leave?**
  It left him fuming.

- **What did 0.81 mole of a substance say to 0.36 mole of the same?**
  "There is a mole among us."

- **What did Mrs. Mendeleev say?**
  She said Mr. Mendeleev was in his elements today.

- **Why was the ester acting so sweet?**
  It was under the influence of alcohol.

- **What did the alkali say to the metal?**
  "All your base are belong to us."

- **What did sodium say when asked to leave the oil business?**
  It said '**NaH**'.

- **What did the acetic acid say?**
  It maintained an ascetic silence.

- **What did lye do to make water angry?**
  Lye developed a caustic attitude.

- **What did one hydrogen ion say to another?**
  "Between you and me, we are missing two neutrons."

- **What did the lithium ion say to his psychiatrist?**
  "Everyone takes lithium when they are depressed but what do we take when we are depressed?"

- **What did the psychiatrist say to the lithium ion?**
  "You are not like everyone. You need to take charge!"

- **What did the psychiatrist say to the beryllium atom?**
  "You can **Be** what you want to **Be**."

- *New Scientist* **Humour**
  The *New Scientist* magazine used to have a humour section. One item was about

a letter from an American who had lived in India for several years. A sure-fire method he had developed to kill cockroaches was to use rice flour mixed with boric acid. (Boric acid powder is available in drug stores as an antimicrobial agent.) What was so funny about it? The item was titled "cereal killer".

- **Inertness**

  Hydrogen ion: Did the Neon atom speak to you?
  Oxygen ion: Nah, I couldn't get a reaction.

- **Why did the magnesium roll refuse to talk to the CO2 cannister?**
  There was a lot of heat between them.

- **Did you know this about aluminium?**
  Metallic aluminium reacts with air to form aluminium oxide. This aluminium oxide forms a hard impermeable layer over the metal making it naturally resistant to corrosion.

- **What is the name for sand when it used in some processed foods to prevent clumping?**
  Silicon dioxide.

Industrially purified powdered sand.

- **Name the chemical used to remove the brown colour from cane sugar and make it sparkling white?**
  Bone char (burnt bones) - made up of mostly of phosphorous/calcium compounds and pure carbon.

Brown sugar or unrefined sugar does not go through this cleaning process. However, lack of demand has made it more expensive.

- **What did silicon say?**
  Si said "**Yes, I** am everywhere."

- **Name the chemical used in soft drinks in place of citric acid?**
  Phosphoric acid - more economical by weight.

Phosphoric acid is the main component of rust remover.

- **Which everyday-use substance is straight out of hell?**
  Vulcanized rubber - made in combination with fire and brimstone (sulphur).

- **What happens when sulphur becomes frustrated?**
  It gets selfurious.

- **What did chlorine gas say?**
  It felt heavy and would like to just 'hang around'.

- **Bleach and DDT**
  Most Tamilians have seen the Koundamani-Senthil movie நினைவு சின்னம் where Senthil sprays pesticide on sweets in Koundamani's store to kill flies. I saw something similar in a general store. Someone had paid for bleaching powder but was given a DDT packet instead. This happened when the owner left a boy in charge of the shop when he went to his home for lunch. To save printing costs, the packets were unmarked and looked the same. Fortunately, the customer realized the mix-up before the contents were dropped in the well. Both pesticides and bleach are manufactured, stored and sold without any standards and precautions in our country. These items should be clearly

marked and stored in different places both at the store and at home.

- **What did argon gas say?**
  "How **Ar** you?"

- **Cyanide**
  The Sri Lankan Tamil terrorist group LTTE was famous for using cyanide vials for a quick-kill suicide poison. They were not the only ones. Many among Hitler's immediate circle used it to end their lives. So, did many British spies. KCN has also been a favourite among many scientists. Even the computer scientist, Alan Turing, used cyanide to exit this world. What maroons, as Bugs Bunny would say! Exposed to moist air, KCN powder emits hydrogen cyanide (HCN) gas, which is also poisonous. Exposed to water, it readily dissolves and leaks. The few minutes to reach unconsciousness may seem like an eternity. Death can sometimes take up to an hour. Exposure to an insufficient quantity can result in permanent organ damage and lifelong suffering. Accidental exposure is also a high possibility, particularly in a rough-and-tumble work environment such as terrorism or spying.

- **What did iron say its last wish was?**
  It wanted to rust in peace.

- **What did copper sulfide say on the way to the smelter?**
  "C u later."

- **What did arsenic say when it was found to be toxic?**
  As you like it.

- **Where is calcium?**
  It went to get a $CaBr_2$.

- **What got zirconium arrested?**
  It was trying to pass of as a real diamond.

Many years back, zirconium was advertised as 'American diamonds' in newspapers.

- **Knock Knock**

  Who is there?
  Molly.
  Molly who?
  Molybdenum!

- **How does silver halide remember everything?**
  It has a photographic memory.

- **What happened to silver-zinc batteries?**
  That was a long time AgO ($Ag_2O \cdot Ag_2O_3$).

- **What did ruthenium say?**
  "Who **R u**?"

- **Is indium coming to the party?**
  Indium said it was **In**.

- **Knock Knock**

  Who is there?
  Aunty.
  Aunty who?

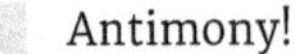 Antimony!

- **Why did the iodine molecule break up?**
  The atoms refused to see 'I' to 'I'.

- **What did cæsium say?**
  Nothing. It was too soft to say anything.

- **What did barium say?**
  "Who has the guts to take me?"

- **What did tungsten say rubidium?**
  "It's **W**."

- **What did iridium say to rubidium?**
  No idea. It was very very hard to get a reaction.

- **Does mercury like the new place?**
  Yes. It is adjusting to the pressure well.

- **How is lead finding the new place?**
  It could not stand the heat and felt like it was going to melt.

- **What did bismuth say to iron?**
  Nothing. Bismuth was repelled by it.

- **What did astatine say?**
  Don't know. That half-life is difficult to get **At**.

- **Knock Knock**

  Who is there?
  Ruth.
  Ruth who?
  Rutherfordium.

- **How do you hail uranium?**
  "Hey, U!"

- **Why did Mendelevium complain to the UN (United Nations)?**
  Because many countries were trying to isolate it.

- **What do ordinary metals say when they meet rare earth metals?**
  "Long time. No see."

- **What do you get when you mix an acid and alkyl ion and leave it for 24 hours?**
  Esterday.

- **What did the centrifuge say to the test tube?**
  "I can take you out for a spin."

- **Why did the soap refuse to go out with the salt?**
  It didn't want to precipitate something.

- **Why did the precipitate say?**
  It was tired of all the actions and reactions when what it wanted was just to settle down somewhere quiet.

- **Why did the catalyst say?**
  It was tired of all the actions and reactions when what it wanted was just to get back to how it was in the beginning.

- **Why did the catalyst say?**
  It was tired of the slow pace of everything and just wanted to speed things up a bit.

- **Why will crude oil never make it as a secret agent?**
  Because it cracks under pressure.

- **Why does 1 gram of any molecule always get upset with the chemist?**
  Because the chemist accuses it of being a mole.

- **What did one mole say to another?**
  "You dig me?"

- **How did one mole stop fighting with another?**
  They tried to find a solution.

- **What did one mole say to another on October 23?**
  "Happy Mole Day!"

- **Which synthetic fibre is this close to being in league with the Devil?**
  Nylon 6/6.

- **Which synthetic fibre is in league with the Devil?**
  Nylon 66/6.

- **What kind of music do lab technicians like to listen?**
  Instrumental music.

Biology Jokes

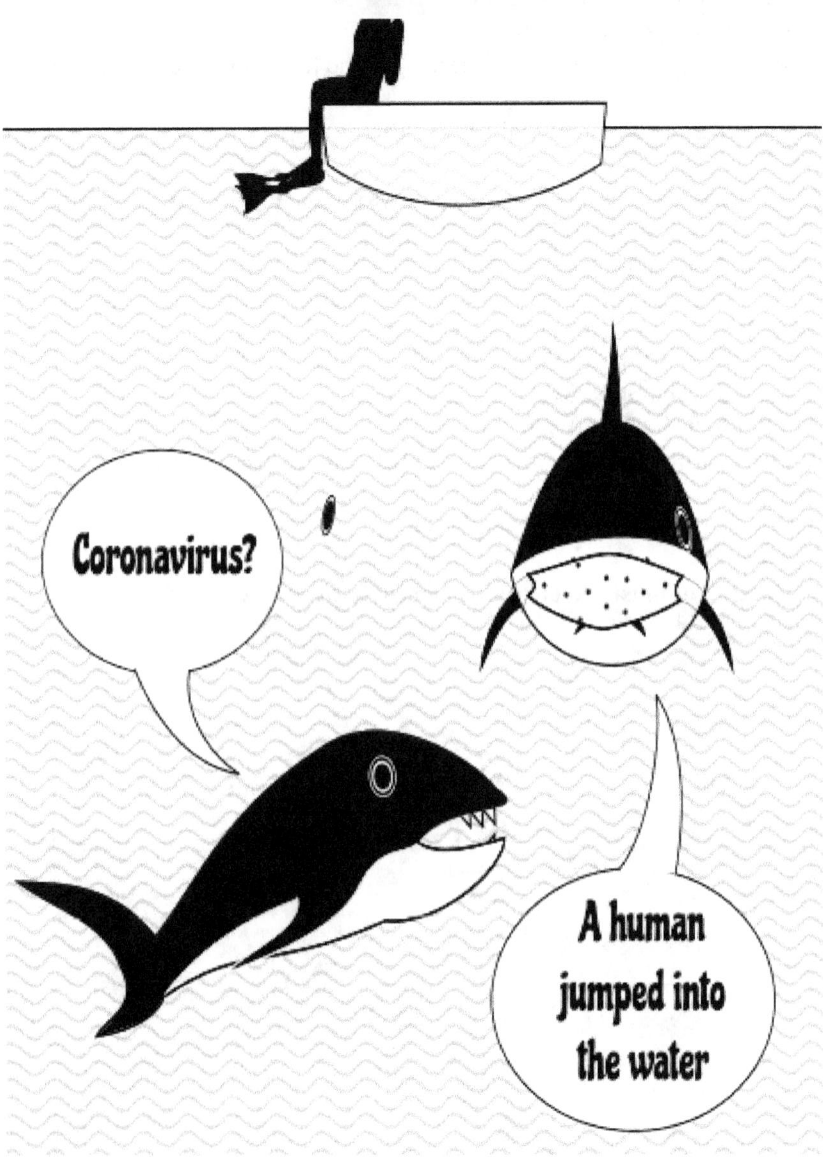

Biology was my favourite subject in school because it was the easiest to remember. Like with chemistry, this subject becomes very useful throughout your life.

- **Nutting like it**
  > **Peanut**: You know, we are both legumes.
  > **Soybean**: No, you are nuts!

- **If an astronomer was born as a fish, what kind would it be?**
  Telescopefish.

- **What happens when a tsetse fly bites a government official?**
  The official throws away his sleeping pills.

- **Name the happiest plant group.**
  Algae – They are all gay (happy).

Scientifically, algae are not plants. Algae are chlorophyll-producing plant-like living organisms that lack the traditional stomata, xylem and phloem cells. A good example is seaweed.

- **Why is xylem more believable than phloem?**
  Phloem can say anything but it does not hold water.

- **What country do you get when you cross an algae and a microbe?**
  Algeria.

- **Why was the fruticose angry with the toadstool?**
  The mushroom **lichen**ed it to an algae.

- **Name the vegetable that desperately needs to chill?**
  Hot potatoes.

- **What do banana trees like to read?**
  Yellow journalism.

- **What kind of computer games do touch-me-not plants hate to play?**
  Stimulation.

- **If an politician was born as a fish, what kind would it be?**
  Megamouth shark.

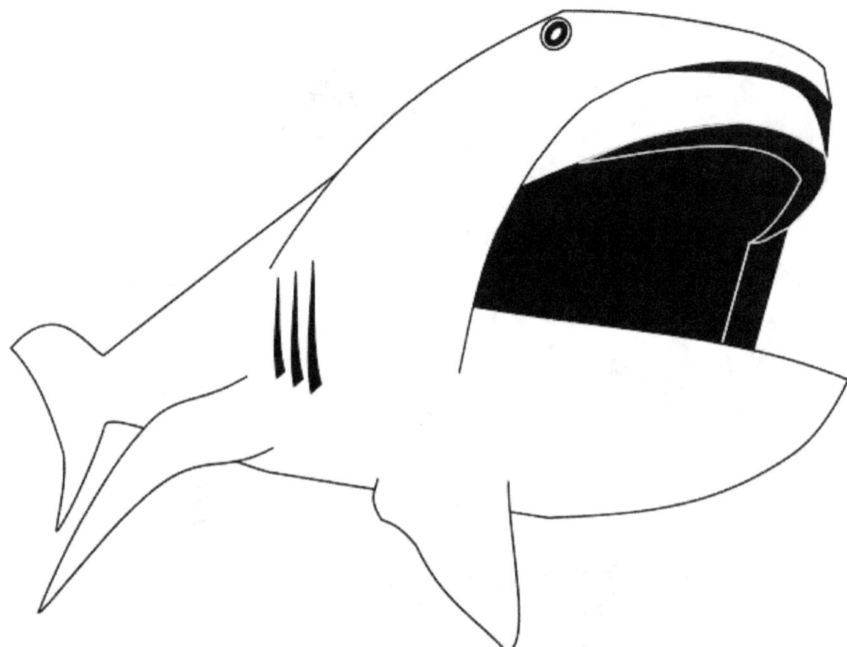

- **If a chicken was born as a fish, what kind would it be?**
  Roosterfish.

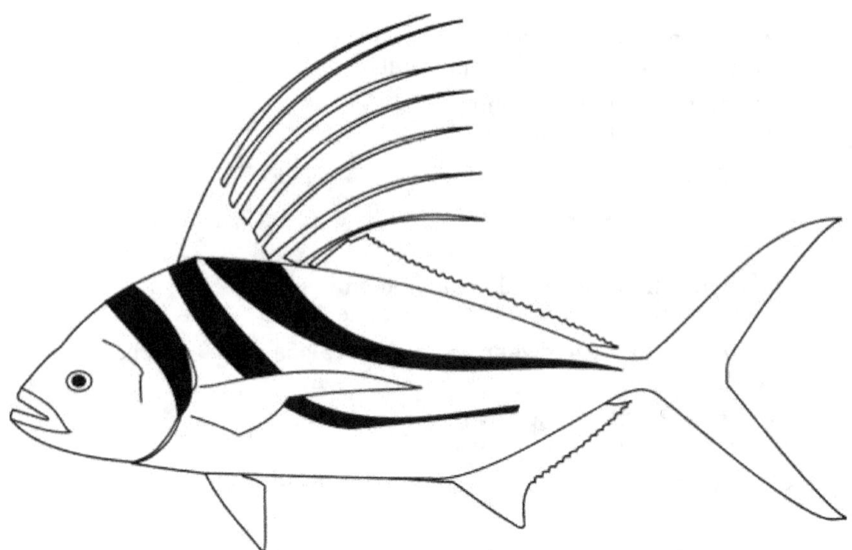

- **What would happen if a mollusc was made to ride an elevator?**

It would clam up.

- **How did the elephant react when the ant asked him about his weight?**
  He became **lipid** with anger.

- **What does the elephant's yearbook say about him?**
  "Most likely to never forget a slight, not even from an ant."

If you want the backgrounder for this joke, read the section *Elephant And Ant Jokes* .

- **What does the water anole's yearbook say about him?**
  "Most likely to move around with an air about him."

This creature carries a bubble around its head to stay under water and breathe.

- **Why did the llama refuse to drink with the camel?**
  It was a Bactrian camel.

- **How does a rhizome step out of the kitchen?**
  Gingerly.

- **Why was the snail sent to the psychiatrist?**
  He appeared withdrawn.

- **What did the psychiatrist tell the snail?**
  That to get back on his feet, he really needs to come out of his shell.

- **What did the WBC (White Blood Cell) tell the virus?**
  "Are you are sure you're really dead?"

- **Corona**
  Virus 1: Who is that walking with his nose up in the air?**
  Virus 2: He is nothing to be sneezed at. He caused a pandemic.

- **What did the DNA tell the transcriptase enzyme?**
  "Should we go through this all over again?"

- **What did the DNA tell the viral transcriptase enzyme?**
  "You've got everything in reverse."

- **Two X chromosomes walk into a bar?**
  Two X chromosomes walk into a bar and one of them says, "Let's sit next that fem." The other chromosome asks, "Y?"

- **What did one mutant say to another?**
  "I know I have a few faults but I think they are just aberrations."

- **What did the mushroom say to another?**
  "This is my last straw."

- **What did one silverfish say to another?**
  "This jokebook is just trash."

- **What kind of music do bats like to listen?**
  Acoustic.

- **What kind of music do sharks like to listen?**
  Jazz.

- **What kind of music do ants like to listen?**
  Acid Jazz.

Ants inject formic acid when they bite.

- **Which insect was named after a popular 60s music band?**
  Beetle.

- **Which 70s song do weevils like the most?**
  "We will… we will rock you" by Queen.

- **What kind of fiction do tadpoles like to read?**
  Young Adult.

- **What kind of music do frogs like to listen?**
  Adult contemporary.

- **How did the caterpillar couple make up?**
  He turned over a new leaf.

- **Why did the cicada couple break up?**
  She said he was a loudmouth.

- **Why did the dragonfly couple break up?**
  They refused to see eye-to-eye on many things.

- **How did the frog couple make up?**
  It required a leap of faith from both of them.

- **Why did the hermit crab couple break up?**
  His shell was not big enough for the two of them.

- **Why did the hippopotamus couple break up?**
  He always left muddy footprints all over the floor.

- **Why did the jellyfish couple break up?**
  They just drifted apart.

- **Why did the mollusc couple break up?**
  He did not have a funny bone in his body.

- **Why did the mosquito couple break up?**
  He accused her of being a blood sucker.

- **Why did the neanderthal couple break up?**
  He failed to evolve into a better person.

- **Why did the neanderthal couple make up?**
  He was such a fine specimen.

- **Why did the oyster couple make up?**
  Behind that hard exterior, he had a heart of gold… of pearl rather.

- **Why did the praying mantis couple break up?**
  She didn't. He was.

- **Why did the praying mantis eat her husband?**
  She couldn't have enough of him so he lost more than just his head.

- **How did the praying mantis couple make up?**
  It was a once-in-a-lifetime opportunity for him.

- **Which insect has been accused of worshipping false gods?**
  Praying mantis.

- **Why did the sea sponge couple break up?**
  He did not like her salty remarks.

- **How did the sea urchin couple break up?**
  He said she was prickly all the time and she said he was mentally unhinged.

- **Why did the silverfish couple break up?**
  She took a leaf out of his book.

- **How did the snail couple break up?**
  - They decided it was time move on with their lives separately.
  - He was becoming more senile.
  - She said that, in his home, she was treated only as a slug while in France she was considered quite a delicacy.

- **What does the shark's yearbook say about him?**
  "Most likely to put the bite on and not let go."

- **What does the starfish's yearbook say about him?**
  "Most likely to be a star in his own right."

- **Why did the toad couple make up?**
  - She still likes him, warts and all.
  - He was one toady reptile.

- **The Dragonfly**
  Dragonflies are interesting creatures. Check out information on dragonflies in

your library. It is fascinating. Dragonflies fly fast, have great eyesight and possess spectacular body strength relative to weight. Their flight trajectory is impossible to predict and their agility is impossible to match. A dragonfly has two big powerful eyes. They are so big that they seem to form the bulk of its head. The eyes are designed to track small insects while in flight.

- **What did the llama say to another?**
  "What's with the aloof expression?"

Medical Jokes

This section is for medical professionals.

- **Which superhero should only be examined with lead plates?**
  Superman – he has x-ray vision.

- **Which superhero is most likely to die from cancer?**
  Spiderman – he has radioactive blood.

- **Which superhero most likely needs a rabies shot?**
  Batman.

- **What would happen if medicines had a better love-life?**
  The pills would not be so bitter.

- **Why did the polar bear couple break up?**
  Bipolar disorder.

- **Why are lift operators never depressed?**
  They listen to elevator music all the time.

- **How did the ghost couple break up?**
  They were mortified when it happened.

- **What do morticians like to read?**
  Obituaries.

- **What did one corpse say to another?**
  "What's with the deadpan expression?"

- **Biting Humour**

  > **Canine teeth**: What has two or three legs but doesn't go anywhere?
  > **Incisor teeth**: What?
  > **Canine teeth**: Molars.

- **An incisive 'Gift For Someone You Love' jingle**

  > **Premolar 1**: I am too small for candy...
  > **Premolar 2**: I am too big for biscuits...
  > **Molar 1**: But I think you are just right for Amul Chocolate.

- **What did one incisor say to another?**
  "We are surrounded by sharp characters."

- **What do dentists call molar tooth?**
  "Money makers."

- **What do dentists call an infected root canal?**
  "The real deal."

- **How did the dentist die?**
  He told the vampire, "You have a serious overbite problem. Please look in this mirror."

- **What kind of music do surgeons like to listen?**
  Opera.

- **What kind of music do anæsthetists like to listen?**
  Trance.

- **How does a surgeon feel after a good night's sleep?**
  A sharp operator.

- **What kind of films do ER physicians like to see?**
  Troma Movies.

- **Why did the doctor couple break up?**
  - She was sick of his attitude.
  - A cure for her madness has not been invented yet.
  - She was testing his patience.
  - She was taxing his patience.
  - Their intense hatred for each other was quite palpable.
  - When it came to housework, he was Dr. Dolittle.
  - She said she did not need a second-opinion.
  - She gave him a taste of his own medicine and he did not like it.

- **Why did the doctor couple make up?**
  - They decided to give it another shot.
  - What cannot be cured has to be endured.
  - He bore her no ill feeling.

- **Why did the dentist couple break up?**
  - Frequent fights with her left him toothless.
  - She drilled into him that any resistance was futile.

- **Why did the dentist couple make up?**
  Dental insurance is cheaper under the family plan.

- **Why did the acupuncturist couple break up?**
  She easily punctured his ego.

- **Why did the radiologist couple break up?**
  When a radiologist says that her husband has absolutely nothing in his head…

- **Acupuncturist**

  Doctor 1: Did you attend the funeral of the acupuncturist?
  Doctor 2: I did. The eulogies indicate that he was quite a prick.

- **Anæsthesiologist**

  Doctor 1: Did you attend the funeral of the anæsthesiologist?
  Doctor 2: I did. Many of the mourners did not feel he was really gone.

- **Cardiologist**

  Doctor 1: Did you attend the funeral of the cardiologist?
  Doctor 2: I did. He seems to have touched many hearts.

- **Chiropractor**

  Doctor 1: Did you attend the funeral of the chiropractor?
  Doctor 2: I did. The eulogies were quite moving.

- **Dentist**

  Doctor 1: Did you attend the funeral of the dentist?
  Doctor 2: I did. Many of the mourners had indeed given their back teeth to him.

- **Dermatologist**

  Doctor 1: Did you attend the funeral of the dermatologist?
  Doctor 2: I did. Time will be a salve for those who had known him.

- **Endocrinologist**

  Doctor 1: Did you attend the funeral of the endocrinologist?
  Doctor 2: I did. His widow was inconsolable. You could hear **her moan** and cry all the time.

- **Gastroenterologist**

  Doctor 1: Did you attend the funeral of the gastroenterologist?
  Doctor 2: I did. Some mourners vented their bile at Fate for taking him away.

- **Gynæcologist**

  Doctor 1: Did you attend the funeral of the gynæcologist?
  Doctor 2: I did. Mourners came from yEast and Evista.

- **Hæmatologist**

  Doctor 1: Did you attend the funeral of the hæmatologist?
  Doctor 2: I did. There were **Few** who did not miss him.

- **Immunologist**

  Doctor 1: Did you attend the funeral of the immunologist?
  Doctor 2: I did. Emotions ran wild through the congregation.

- **Neurologist**

  Doctor 1: Did you attend the funeral of the neurologist?
  Doctor 2: I did. Everyone tried to steady their nerves.

- **Ophthalmologist**

  Doctor 1: Did you attend the funeral of the ophthalmologist?

> **Doctor 2**: I did. There wasn't a dry eye.

- **Pædiatrist**

  > **Doctor 1**: Did you attend the funeral of the pædiatrist?
  > **Doctor 2**: I did. All mourners were given free candy.

- **Pulmonologist**

  > **Doctor 1**: Did you attend the funeral of the pulmonologist?
  > **Doctor 2**: I did. The air was filled with sadness.

- **Psychiatrist**

  > **Doctor 1**: Did you attend the funeral of the psychiatrist?
  > **Doctor 2**: I did. The eulogies were couched in confessions.

- **Radiologist**

  > **Doctor 1**: Did you attend the funeral of the radiologist?
  > **Doctor 2**: I did. Most mourners said he saw through their failings.

- **Speech therapist**

  > **Doctor 1**: Did you attend the funeral of the speech therapist?
  > **Doctor 2**: I did. Some mourners were still lost for words.

- **Urologist**

  > **Doctor 1**: Did you attend the funeral of the urologist?
  > **Doctor 2**: I did. People wondered if his death could have been a **void**ed.

- **Acupuncturist referral**

  > **Doctor**: Why was the patient referred to the acupuncturist?
  > **Nurse**: His wife said he had absolutely no feelings.

- **Anæsthesiologist referral**

  > **Doctor**: Why was the anæsthesiologist called *during* surgery?
  > **Surgeon**: Somebody was reading the bill and the patient came to his senses.

- **Cardiologist referral**

  > **Doctor**: Why was the patient referred to the cardiologist?
  > **Nurse**: To see if he can take the shock of the bill.

- **Why did the headless chicken cross the road?**
  If it was anything, it was all heart!

- **Dermatologist referral**

  > **Doctor**: Why was the patient referred to the dermatologist?
  > **Nurse**: The sight of the bill made his skin itch uncontrollably.

- **Dentist referral**

  > **Doctor**: Why was the patient referred to the dentist?
  > **Nurse**: The growing number of bills left his teeth shattered.

- **Gastroenterologist referral**

  > **Doctor**: Why was the patient referred to the gastroenterologist?
  > **Nurse**: He couldn't take it anymore.

- **Hæmatologist referral**

  > **Doctor**: Why was the patient referred to the hæmatologist?
  > **Nurse**: He claimed he had an iron constitution.

- **Immunologist referral**

  > **Doctor**: Why was the patient referred to the immunologist?
  > **Nurse**: She had an infectious smile.

- **Ophthalmologist referral**

  > **Doctor**: Why was the patient referred to the ophthalmologist?
  > **Nurse**: He said he was seeing too many digits in the bill.

- **Obstetrician referral**

  > **Doctor**: Why was this diabetic referred to the obstetrician?
  > **Nurse**: He said he was demanding sweets only because of his inner child.

- **Pædiatrist referral**

  > **Doctor**: Why was this adult diabetic referred to the pædiatrist?
  > **Nurse**: We didn't. The patient went there to get the free candy.

- **Psychiatrist referral**

  > **Doctor**: Why was the patient referred to the psychiatrist?
  > **Nurse**: He said the growing number of bills was driving him crazy.

- **Radiologist referral**

  > **Doctor**: Why was the comedian referred to the radiologist?
  > **Nurse**: He said something was wrong with his funny bone.

- **Speech therapist referral**

  > **Doctor**: Why was the patient referred to the Speech therapist?
  > **Nurse**: He became speechless when he was told about all the tests and procedures he had to take before his physician could recommend a treatment.

- **What do proctologists like to read?** Just the colophon.

- **A nervous reaction**

  > **Doctor 1**: Why did the patient kick that doctor?
  > **Doctor 2**: The neurologist struck a raw nerve.

- **The strongest muscle**

  > **Doctor 1**: Did he really burst his aorta?
  > **Doctor 2**: No. That diagnosis was made in a lighter vein.

Pun Jokes

Did you look square in the eye?

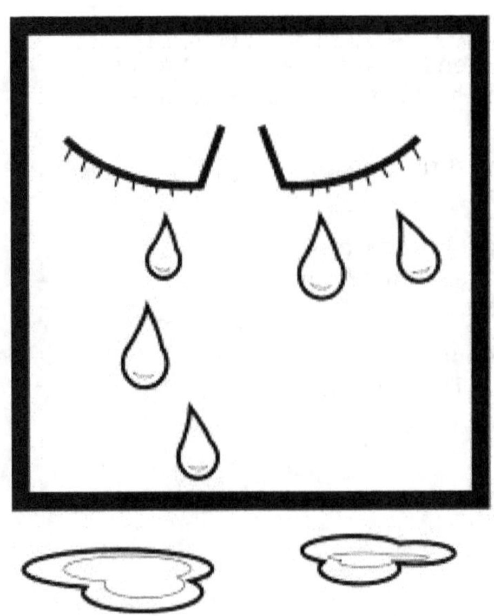

A pun is a play on words. It is usually humorous but not many people are fans of it.

- **What kind of chicken do contortionists like to order?**
  Boneless Chicken.

- **What kind of chicken do efficiency experts like to order?**
  Butter Chicken.

- **What kind of chicken do psychopaths like to order?**
  Scaredy Chicken.

- **What kind of chicken do zombies like to order?**
  Headless Chicken.

- **What kind of chicken do bored people like to order?**
  Chicken Bordelaise.

- **What kind of chicken do government contractors like to order?**
  Tendoori Chicken.

- **What kind of chicken do government employees like to order?**
  Roost Chicken.

- **What kind of chicken do South-East Asians like to order?**
  Malay Chicken.

- **What kind of chicken do South Americans like to order?**
  Chile Chicken.

- **Why did the archeologist cross the road?**
  He had a bone to pick.

- **Why did the skeleton cross the road?**
  To stop the archeologist.

- **Why did the dog cross the road?**
  This was a bone of contention.

- **Why did the psychopath cross the road?**
  He wanted to give them a piece of his mind.

- **Why did the Asian guy cross the road?**
  To pick up some Chinese.

- **What did Japanese soldiers eat when they occupied Singapore?**
  They ordered Chinese.

This joke has a very serious historical meaning.

- **Winner takes it all**
  A man went to a restaurant and ordered lobster. When the plate was placed before him, the lobster was in numerous pieces. The man asked the waiter, "Why is my lobster so broken up?" The waiter answered, "The creatures fight inside the tank and they break off each other's limbs." The man then said, "Okay, bring me the winner." The waiter agreed and came back after a few minutes. When the new plate was placed before him, the man noticed that the new lobster was mostly intact but still had two parts missing. He said, "This one does not have a claw and something else too." The waiter said "Sir, this is indeed the victor but victory cost him an arm and a leg."

In an early edition of this book, I credited the first half of this joke to *Reader's Digest* Later, I found it in an episode of *Abbott and Costello Show* . The second half of the joke is my invention.

- **What did one nostalgia say to another?**
  "You are not what you used to be."

- **What did one Indian lemon say to another?**
  "We are in a real pickle."

- **What did one American cucumber say to another?**
  Same as the Indian lemon.

- **What did one table leg say to another?**
  "You scared? Why are you shaking?"

- **What did the blade say to the windmill?**
  "I am a big fan of yours."

- **What did one antelope say to another?**
  "You gotta buck?"

- **What did the crow say to the scarecrow?**
  "You are fooling nobody so don't crow about it!"

- **What did the scarecrow say to the crow?**
  "But, my hands are tied!"

- **What did the string instrument say to the flute?**
  "You sound hollow."

- **What did the flute say to the string instrument?**
  "Please don't harp on it."

- **What did one typewriter say to another?**
  "I am trying to make a good impression."

- **What does the beautician's yearbook say about him?**
  "Most likely to make your hair curl."

- **What does the chicken plucker's yearbook say about him?**
  "Most likely to rustle up some serious feathers."

- **What does the clown's yearbook say about him?**
  "Most likely to be surrounded by buffoons."

- **What does the humorist's yearbook say about him?**
  "Most likely to try to humour himself than others."

- **What does the jester's yearbook say about him?**
  "Most unlikely to run away from a pun."

- **What does the joke writer's yearbook say about him?**
  "Most likely to laugh at his own jokes."

- **What does the wit's yearbook say about him?**
  "Most likely to wit than have wisdom."

- **What does the psychopath's yearbook say about him?**
  "Most likely to leave a serious impact on people."

- **What does the sumo wrestler's yearbook say about him?**
  "Most likely to head a large corporation."

- **What does the usher's yearbook say about him?**
  "Most likely to open a door and shine a path for others."

- **What does the vagrant's yearbook say about him?**
  "Most likely to see the world."

- **What does the vandal's yearbook say about him?**
  - "Most likely to paint the town red."
  - "Most likely to make his mark on the world."

- **What did the exercise book say?**
  "I have many problems."

- **What did the key say to the exercise book?**
  "I've got answers to all your problems."

- **What did the non-detailed book say?**
  "I do not need you to explain everything."

- **What did the answer sheet say to the question paper?**
  "Is it about those problems? I can explain everything."

- **What did the priest say when he asked the parents sign the exorcism waiver?**
  "The devil is in the detail."

- **What did the policeman write in his report after he caught a ghost speeding?**
  "He was in really high spirits."

- **What did the policeman write in his report after he caught the screaming banshee speeding?**
  "She was in a tearing hurry."

- **What musical instrument eats healthy, does regular exercise and gets enough sleep?**
  The fiddle. That's why everyone says 'fit as a fiddle'.

- **What happened when the ghost tripped over a bucket?**
  It turned *pail*.

- **Why did the quadrilateral fight with the circle?**
  The circle looked square in the eye.

- **Why did zero go to the psychiatrist?**
  Everyone said he would amount to nothing.

- **Why was the alien looking at the remote instead of the television?**
  He was doing remote viewing.

- **How do you transport an elephant in a train?**
  You give it a wide berth.

- **What do Egyptian mummies like to read?**
  Some rag.

- **What do zombies like to read?**
  Some dirty rag.

- **What do government employees like to read?**
  Deductive fiction.

- **What do guns like to read?**
  Magazines.

- **What do hair dressers hate to see on TV?**
  Election coverage.

- **What do Italians like to read?**
  Romantic fiction.

- **What happens when plants read yellow journalism?**
  They go bananas.

- **What do politicians like to read?**
  Grime fiction.

- **What do psychiatrists like to read?**
  Entertainment news.

- **What do pyromaniacs like to see on TV?**
  Burning Issue.

Indian English-language TV news channel viewers will know what this is.

- **What do spies like to read?**
  The classifieds.

- **What do vandals like to see on TV?**
  Breaking news.

- **Why did the nun cross the road?**
  None of your business.

- **Why did the lightning cross the road?**
  Someone stole its thunder.

- **Why did the Devil cross the road?**
  Speak of the Devil...

- **What did one clown say to another?**
  "What's with the silly expression?"

- **What did one clock say to another?**
  "What's with the alarmed expression?"

- **What did one crossword say to another?**
  "What's with the puzzled expression?"

- **What did one remote say to another?**
  "What's with the muted expression?"

- **What did one gargoyle say to another?**
  "What's with the dour expression?"

- **What did one statue say to another?**
  "What's with the chiselled expression?"

- **What did one washing machine say to another?**
  "What's with the agitated expression?"

- **What happened when the doughnut rolled away and fell to the floor?**
  It was roundly criticized.

- **Why did the police state persecute the toad?**
  For thought crimes.

- **How do you transport a hippopotamus in a train?**
  Using a hypocrate.

- **Why was the dragon so happy?**
  It was fired up and ready to go.

- **Why was the human cannonball so happy?**
  It was fired and ready to go home.

- **What do traffic lights learn in school?**
  Sign language.

- **What do statues do in school?**
  Studied silence.

- **What do mannequins learn in school?**
  A pose-itive attitude.

- **Do mannequins talk?**
  No, but their body language do tell a whole story.

- **What did one vampire say to another?**
  "Can I drop in for a bite?"

- **Which magazine should you trust more –** *Outlook* **or** *Outlook Money*?
  Outlook because *Money* talks.

- *Time* **challenges** *Newsweek* **to a race. Which magazine will win?**
  Time. Because time flies.

- *Time* **magazine challenges Superman to a race. Who will win?**
  Time. Because time [and tide] waits for none while Superman will stop for a cat that is stuck on a tree.

- *Time* **versus** *Life*. **Which magazine is the most original?**
  Time. Because life imitates art.

- *Time* **versus** *Life*. **Which magazine will be your friend when you are in the wrong?**
  Life. Because time will tell.

- *Time* **versus** *Life*. **Which magazine will be useful in a medical emergency?**
  Time. Because time is a great healer.

- *Time* **versus** *Life*. **Which magazine is better in other kinds of emergencies?**
  Life. Because desperate times calls for desperate measures.

- *Time* **versus** *Life*. **Which magazine is a better basketball player?**
  Time. Because life is short.

- *Time* **versus** *Life*. **Which magazine is worth more?**
  Life. Because time is money.

- *Time* **versus** *Life*. **Which magazine will last the longest?**
  Time. Because life begins at 40.

- **What happens when you give alcohol to a chicken?**
  Chicken rolls.

- **Why did the goat cross the road?**
  Don't know. It refused to be quoted.

- **Why should you not look a gift horse in the mouth?**
  You might encounter some horsetility.

The word 'horsetility' is from an old joke book.

- **What do you get when you teach judo to a pig?**
  Pork chops.

- **What did one nailgun say to another?**
  "I am going to try another tack."

- **What did one sheet of paper say to another?**
  "What's with the blank expression?"

- **Tautology**

  Tautology 1: Do I have to repeat myself?
  Tautology 2: You can say that again.

- **What would happen if an amusement park was named after a girl named Anna?**
  It is anathema.

- **What would happen if a vampire bites a government official?**
  The vampire stops sleeping in a coffin and starts sleeping on a desk.

- **What would happen if a vampire bites Spiderman?**
  The vampire gets cancer because Spiderman has radioactive blood.

- **What would happen if a zombie gets a registered letter?**
  The tax department has been informed of his/her return.

- **What does it mean when a vampire gets bitten by a zombie?**
  The vampire starts working for the tax department.

- **What would happen if you bother a butcher when he is in the freezer?**
  He might give you a cold shoulder.

- **What would happen if someone writes a biography of a judge?**
  You could *cover* the *judge* with a *book*.

- **What would happen if fate had sticky tape?**
  It would seal itself.

- **What would happen if night was exhausted?**
  It would call it a day.

- **What kind of music do Communists like to listen?**
  Classical.

- **What kind of music do Socialists like to listen?**
  Underground.

- **What kind of music do Fascists like to listen?**
  Corporate.

- **What kind of music do death row inmates hate to listen?**
  Chamber.

- **What kind of music do escaped jail inmates like to listen?**
  Indie.

- **What kind of music do stamp collectors like to listen?**
  Country.

- **What kind of music do balloons hate?**
  Pop.

- **What kind of music do spelling-bee contestants like to listen?**
  Gospel.

- **What kind of music do psychopaths like to listen?**
  Psychedelic.
- **What kind of music do serial killers like to listen?**
  Progressive.
- **What kind of music do ham-radio operators like to listen?**
  New wave.
- **What kind of music do zombies like to listen?**
  Background.
- **What kind of music do vampires like to listen?**
  Contemporary.
- **What kind of music do people chased by vampires like to listen?**
  Religious.
- **What kind of music do ghosts like to listen?**
  Spiritual.
- **What kind of music do bomb-making terrorists hate to listen?**
  Metal.
- **What kind of music do condemned prisoners in France hate to listen?**
  Death metal.
- **What happened when Louis XVI came home late?**
  Marie Antoinette just lost her head.
- **What kind of music do interred zombies hate to listen?**
  Heavy metal.
- **What kind of music do tight-rope walkers hate to listen?**
  Dance.
- **What kind of music do performing musicians hate to listen?**
  Mobile phone ring tones.
- **What kind of music do kids hate to listen after they get into trouble?**
  Folk.
- **What kind of music do all the animals and people in the section *Cross The Road Jokes* like to listen?**
  Crossover.
- **What kind of music do electrocuted people like to listen?**
  Fusion.
- **What kind of fiction do mediums like to read?**
  Seance fiction.
- **What kind of movies do dry cleaners like to see?**
  Costume drama.
- **What computer games do attorneys like to play?**
  Rule-playing (RPG)
- **What computer game do acupuncturists like to play?**
  Pins of Persia.
- **What computer games do professional hitmen like to play?**
  First-Person Shooter (FPS).
- **What computer game do psychopaths like to play?**

Max Payne.

- **What computer game do junk callers like to play?**
  Halo.

- **What computer game do ghosts like to play?**
  Mortal Kombat.

- **What kind of films do vampires like to go to see?**
  Historical drama.

- **What kind of films do zombies like to go to see?**
  Reanimated.

- **What happens when a terrorist becomes nostalgic?**
  It begins with a blast from the past.

- **What happens when a moray eel goes to a saloon?**
  The barber faces a moral dilemma.

- **What kind of haircut does a pilot get when he wants to motivate his team?**
  A crew cut.

- **What kind of haircut does an accountant get when work piles up?**
  A summer cut.

- **What kind of haircut does a drummer get when he goes to the saloon?**
  Bangs.

- **What kind of haircut does a terrorist get when bites the grenade and throws the pin?**
  Blowout.

- **What kind of haircut does a juvenile get when parents bug him?**
  Bee hive.

- **What kind of haircut does a lynx get when he goes to the saloon?**
  Bob cut.

- **What kind of haircut does a cricketer get when he goes to the saloon?**
  Bowl cut.

- **What kind of haircut does a ram like to sport?**
  Double buns.

- **What kind of haircut do comb manufacturers are afraid of?**
  Dreadlocks.

- **What kind of haircut does an electrician get when he blows a fuse?**
  Spiked.

- **What did the lift say to the new operator?**
  "I can take you to high places."

- **What did one escalator say to another?**
  "There he goes again."

- **Why was the alphabet soup crying?**
  Some letters seemed to be missing.

- **What did the mulligatawny soup say?**
  "Am I hot or what?"

- **What did the turkey say?**
  "Friends, I am stuffed."

- **What did the beef say?**
  "Hey, I am on a roll."
- **What did the chicken say?**
  "I am in a real soup."
- **What did the duck say?**
  "I am dressed for dinner."
- **What did the fish say?**
  "Sorry, I am smoking."
- **What did the crab say?**
  "Don't strangle yourself. I am here to help."
- **What did the mutton say?**
  "I am feeling chopped up, already."
- **What did the noodle say?**
  "Folks, I want you to stay strong."
- **What did the lobster say?**
  "Yeah, let's hold hands."
- **What did the salad say?**
  "He is right. We are all in this together."
- **What did the onion rings say?**
  "You guys make me cry!"
- **What did the boiled egg say?**
  "I know I need to come out of my shell."
- **What did the raw egg say?**
  "Can I make a toast?"
- **What did the slice of bread say?**
  "I am toast!"
- **What did the wine say?**
  "I raise my glass to that."
- **What did the chef say?**
  "Stop it! You are making the guests nervous."
- **What did the restaurant review say?**
  "Chef Ram says his dishes really come to life and speak for themselves!"

Useful French Phrases

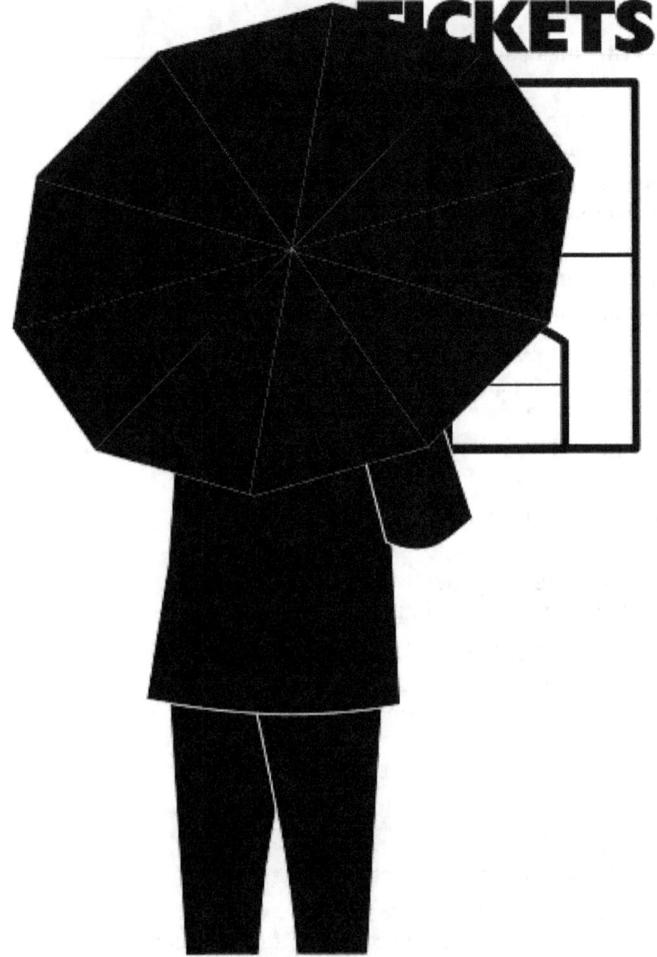

"One laissez-faire ticket and vive le difference.
May the Lord have merci on you."

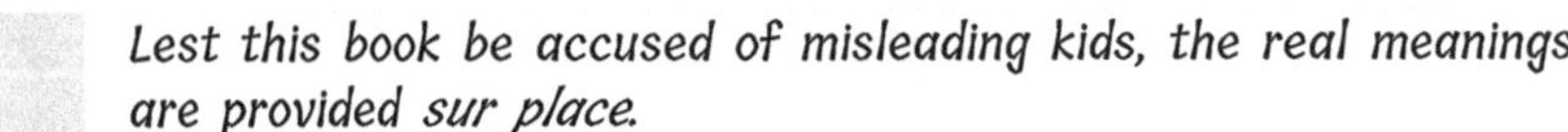

Lest this book be accused of misleading kids, the real meanings are provided sur place.

- **How do you say 'alternating current (AC)' in French?**
  Au courant. [*well-informed*]

- **How do you say 'the ape ate the bun' in French?**
  Bon apetit. [*good appetite*]

- **How do you say 'we want a bun' in French?**
  Bon vivant. [*well-to-do person*]

- **How do you say 'ticket price' in French?**
  Chargé d'affaires. [*diplomat or person in-charge*]

- **How do you say 'The chef is hungry' in French?**
  Chef d'œuvre. [*masterpiece*]

- **How do you say 'Check out the see-saw' in French?**
  Comme ci, comme ça.

- **How do you say 'The commie is at fault' in French?**
  Comme il faut. [*appropriately*]

- **How do you say 'know for sure' in French?**
  Connoisseur. [*person with expert knowledge or taste*]

- **How do you say 'father's cup' in French?**
  Coup de foudre. [*love at first sight*]

- **How do you say 'Grace's cup' in French?**
  Coup de grâce. [*stroke of grace*]

- **How do you say 'look at your buns' in French?**
  Cui bono. [*whose benefit*]

- **How do you say 'incurable disease' in French?**
  Encore. [*repeat performance*]

- **How do you say 'angry elephant' in French?**
  Enfant terrible. [*bad kid*]

- **How do you say 'we want to enter' in French?**
  Enterré vivant. [*buried alive*]

- **How do you say 'ghost' in French?**
  Esprit de corps. [*team spirit*]

- **How do you say 'we want to eat' in French?**
  Être vivant. [*be alive*]

- **How do you say 'dead woman' in French?**
  Femme fatale. [*attractive but dangerous woman*]

- **How do you say 'It's the cat's fault' in French?**
  Faute de mieux. [*for a better*]

- **How do you say 'fat accomplice' in French?**
  Fait accompli. [*irreversible fact*]

- **How do you say 'fake ID' in French?**
  Faux pas. [*boo-boo*]

- **How do you say 'big pricks' in French?**
  Grand prix. [*grand prize*]

- **How do you say "good-looking knife" in French?**
  Haute couture. [*high fashion*]

- **How do you say 'hot quiz' in French?**
  Haute cuisine. [*high-class cooking*]

- **How do you say 'devoured by a hungry horse' in French?**
  Hors d'œuvres.

- **How do you say 'unruly horse' in French?**
  Hors de combat. [*unfit for battle*]

- **How do you say 'in the way of the dodo' in French?**
  In toto. [*as a whole*]

- **How do you say 'low-priced ticket' in French?**
  Laissez-faire. [*free-for-all*]

- **How do you say 'mow the lawn' in French?**
  Mardi gras. [*Shrove Tuesday carnival*]

- **How do you say 'we want more' in French?**
  Mort vivant. [*animated corpse*]

- **How do you say 'never poor' in French?**
  Nouveau pauvre. [*newly poor*]

- **How do you say 'never rich' in French?**
  Nouveau riche. [*newly rich*]

- **How do you say 'objectionable artwork' in French?**
  Objet d'art. [*work of art*]

- **How do you say 'we want non-vegetarian food' in French?**
  Organisme vivant. [*living being*]

- **How do you say 'pour me a drink' in French?**
  Pardon moi. [*excuse me*]

- **How do you say 'something is blocking' in French?**
  Pièce de résistance. [*the best part*]

- **How do you say 'queue at the back' in French?**
  Quelle horreur.[*Oh, the horror!*]

- **How do you say 'run this way' in French?**
  Rendezvous. [*meeting*]

- **How do you say 'get up at three' in French?**
  Raison d'être. [*reason for existence*]

- **How do you say 'fear of misers' in French?**
  Savoir faire. [*act appropriately in all situations*]

- **How do you say 'is this your plate' in French?**
  S'il vous plaît. [*if you please*]

- **How do you say 'get us a table' in French?**
  Tableau vivant. [*body painting*]

- **How do you say 'give me the change' in French?**
  Vive la différence. [*celebrate the difference*]

Useful Latin Phrases

Lest this book be accused of misleading kids, the real meanings are provided in situ.

- **How do you say 'polygraph test' in Latin?**
  Alea iacta est. [*die is cast*]

- **How do you say 'cure for runny nose' in Latin?**
  Amicus curiae. [*friend of court*]

- **How do you say 'your fat friend' in Latin?**
  Amor fati. [*love of fate*]

- **How do you say 'Anna is as horrible as Bill is' in Latin?**
  Annus horribilis. [*horrible year*]

- **How do you say 'Anna is as miserable as Bill is' in Latin?**
  Annus mirabilis. [*miserable year*]

- **How do you say 'Anna is as terrible as Bill is' in Latin?**
  Annus terribilis. [*terrible year*]

- **How do you say 'Your aunty is a bum' in Latin?**
  Ante cibum. [*before meals*]

- **How do you say 'Your aunty is very dumb' in Latin?**
  Ante mortem. [*before death*]

- **How do you say 'the purée is watery' in Latin?**
  Aqua pura. [*pure water*]

- **How do you say 'Aurora is as much a bore as Al is' in Latin?**
  Aurora borealis. [*northern dawn*]

- **How do you say 'born fighter' in Latin?**
  Bona fides. [*good faith*]

- **How do you say 'bloating' in Latin?**
  Casus belli. [*causative event*]

- **How do you say 'as you were late, visa was not issued' in Latin?**
  Causa latet, vis est notissima. [*cause is not known while outcome is*]

- **How do you say 'empty cave' in Latin?**
  Caveat emptor. [*buyer beware*]

- **How do you say 'circling the house' in Latin?**
  Circulus vitiosus. [*vicious circle*]

- **How do you say 'I don't need more buns' in Latin?**
  Contra bonos mores. [*against good morals*]

- **How do you say 'there is no cure like liquor' in Latin?**
  Cor ad cor loquitur. [*heart speaks to heart*]

- **How do you say 'delicate zombie' in Latin?**
  Corpus delicti. [*offended body*]

- **How do you say 'angry zombie' in Latin?**
  Corpus vile. [*worthless body*]

- **How do you say 'the zombie are respectful' in Latin?**
  Corpus Juris Civilis. [*civil law*]

- **How do you say 'optimism corrupted by pessimism' in Latin?**
  Corruptio optimi pessima. [*the corruption of the best is the worst*]

- **How do you say 'sweet bun' in Latin?**
  Cui bono. [*for whose good*]

- **How do you say 'the fatso' in Latin?**
De facto. [*in practice*]

- **How do you say 'this fatso' in Latin?**
Ipso facto. [*after the fact*]

- **How do you say 'Hey, what's your bus number?' in Latin?**
E pluribus unum. [*one among many*]

- **How do you say 'car with a wireless phone' in Latin?**
Fons vitae caritas. [*love is the fountain of life*]

- **How do you say 'happy zombie' in Latin?**
Habeas corpus. [*that you have the body*]

- **How do you say 'head East' in Latin?**
Id est (i.e.) [*that is*]

- **How do you say 'a delicate fragrance?' in Latin?**
In flagrante delicto. [*caught in the act of committing a crime*]

- **How do you say 'division and subtraction' in Latin?**
Indivisibiliter ac inseparabiliter. [*indivisible and inseparable*]

- **How do you say 'his/her foolish parents?' in Latin?**
In loco parentis. [*in place of parent*]

- **How do you say 'Look, he is standing' in Latin?**
Locus standi. [*stands with the law*]

- **How do you say 'males are prohibited' in Latin?**
Malum prohibitum. [*wrong because it is prohibited*]

- **How do you say 'my cup' in Latin?**
Mea culpa. [*my fault*]

- **How do you say 'the mutants are mutating' in Latin?**
Mutatis mutandis. [*after changing what needs to be changed*]

- **How do you say 'none sees how dumb it is' in Latin?**
Nunc dimittis. [*Now you dismiss*]

- **How do you say 'Perpetually attached to the phone.' in Latin?**
Perpetuum mobile. [*perpetual motion*]

- **How do you say 'I see no money [*on the table*].' in Latin?**
Quid nunc. [*what now*]

- **How do you say 'got a buck or two' in Latin?**
Quid pro quo. [*something in return of*]

- **How do you say 'the kid is going crazy' in Latin?**
Quod erat demonstrandum. [*What was to be demonstrated*]

- **How do you say 'absurdly low prices' in Latin?**
Reductio ad absurdum. [*ridiculous conclusion*]

- **How do you say 'quit staring' in Latin?**
Stare decisis. [*recognizing previous decisions*]

- **How do you say 'Judy's submarine' in Latin?**
Sub judice. [*currently under examination by a court*]

- **How do you say 'we roast possums' in Latin?**
Vero possumus. [*yes, we can*]

Other Useful Foreign Phrases

"Adiós! Hasta la vista!"

The disclaimer from the previous chapter applies to this one too.

- **How do you say 'Get here and see the comet in the sky' in Danish?**
  Jeg er kommet til skade. [*I'm hurt*]
- **How do you say 'Hans is killing her' in Danish?**
  Hans kyllinger. [*his chickens*]
- **How do you say 'They raided him' in Danish?**
  De rådede ham. [*they advised him*]
- **How do you say 'Are you stupid' in Dutch?**
  Alstublieft. [*please*]
- **How do you say 'Who got hit' in Dutch?**
  Hoe gaat het. [*how are you*]
- **How do you say 'Who hit you' in Dutch?**
  Hoe heet u. [*what is your name*]
- **How do you say 'someone who works very hard' in English?**
  An aardvark.

- **How do you say 'I think you butcher the English language' in German?**
Ich brauche englischsprachige Bücher. [*I need English books*]

- **How do you say 'sad fraud' in German?**
Schadenfreude. [*merriment caused by the misery of others*]

- **How do you say 'digest' in German?**
Zeitgeist. [*spirit of the times*]

- **How do you say 'No, I must stay' in Hindi?**
Namaste. [*hello*]

- **How do you say 'do you know the number' in Italian?**
Numero uno. [*first*]

- **How do you say 'sick man' in Italian?**
Il manzo. [*beef*]

- **How do you say 'certified crazy' in Italian?**
Certamente. [*certainly*]

- **How do you say 'My son is a psychopath' in Italian?**
Mi sono dimenticato. [*I forgot*]

- **How do you say 'I ate llamas in the morning' in Irish?**
Liamhás atá uaim. [*I'd like ham*]

- **How do you say 'How did you mash it?' in Japanese?**
Hajimemashite. [*pleased to meet you*]

- **How do you say 'Oh, is she?' in Japanese?**
Oishii. [*delicious*]

- **How do you say 'Do you see any Pakistanis?' in Latvian?**
Cik ir pulkstenis. [*What's the time?*]

- **How do you say 'My dear Russian friends' in Russian?**

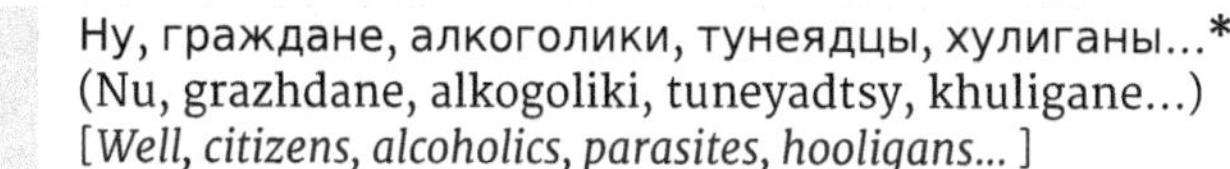
Ну, граждане, алкоголики, тунеядцы, хулиганы...*
(Nu, grazhdane, alkogoliki, tuneyadtsy, khuligane...)
[*Well, citizens, alcoholics, parasites, hooligans...*]

- **How do you say 'You are dead' in Spanish?**
Adiós! [*Goodbye*]

- **How do you say 'You are super-dead' in Spanish?**
Hasta la vista! [*till next time*]

- **How do you say 'You came for the llamas?' in Spanish?**
¿Cómo te llamas? [*What is your name?*]

- **How do you say 'The police are llamas too' in Spanish?**
Llamaré a la policía. [*I will call the police*]

※ Llamas can be trained to do guard-dog duty.

Part 2 - For Fun

This part is purely for the hedonistic consumption of humour.

Bar Jokes

WARNING: I have encountered many histories of people dying painful deaths from alcoholism. The prolonged suffering that they and their relatives go through before they die is not worth the trouble. I enjoyed writing these jokes but they should not be construed as an endorsement of unhealthy intake of alcohol.

NOTE: The chapter 'Political Jokes' has even more alcohol-related jokes but it is not for you if you are the easily offended type.

- **A bartender walks in to a bar**
  A bartender walks in to a bar. He is about to order a drink when he stops and looks more closely at the bartender. The man looks exactly like him! Puzzled, he asks, "Who are you?" The man behind the bar is equally puzzled and asks the same question. After a while, it dawns on him. He was drunk and looking at a mirror.

- **A contortionist walks in to a bar**

A contortionist walks in to a bar, climbs onto a stool, bends backwards, goes between his legs, picks up a drink and drinks it. The bartender asks, "What is this? A stunt? I want a straight answer."

- **An Artificial Intelligence (AI) walks in to a bar**
  An Artificial Intelligence (AI) walks in to a bar. The bartender says, "Hello, AI. Long time, no see." The AI replies, "I knew you would say that."

- **A probability walks in to a bar**
  A probability walks in to a bar and the bartender wonders, "What are the chances of that?"

- **A *deja vu* walks in to a bar**
  A *deja vu* walks in to a bar and the guy next to her says, "Haven't I seen you somewhere?" And, she says, "I don't know but I've heard that before."

- **Invisible Man walks in to a bar**
  Invisible Man walks in to a bar and orders some wine. Then, he tells the bartender, "If my wife rings and asks for me, tell her that I am not here.

- **Invisible Woman walks in to a bar**
  Invisible Woman walks in to a bar and sees Invisible Man drinking. She takes the stool next to him. Just then, Invisible Man tells the bartender, "If my wife rings and asks for me, tell her that I am not here.

- **A proverb walks in to a bar**
  A proverb walks in to a bar and leaves almost immediately. The bartender murmurs sadly, "It goes without saying."

- **Hindsight walks in to a bar**
  Hindsight walks in to a bar and looks at the New Year's decorations. The bartender smiles and says, "Hindsight, it is 2020."

This joke was written before 9 June, 2019, when it was posted on Twitter, long before anyone thought about it.

- **A cyclone walks in to a bar**
  A cyclone walks in to a bar and the bartender asks, "What happened? You seem to be in a depression."

- **A lightning walks in to a bar**
  A lightning walks in to a bar and the bartender says, "Hi! They said you would be arrested!"

- **A thunderstrike walks in to a bar**
  A thunderstrike walks in to a bar and the bartender says, "I knew I was going to hear from you."

- **An alien walks in to a bar**
  An alien walks in to a bar and orders a drink. The bartender says, "Sure, but you want that in a glass or a saucer?"

- **A blonde walks in to a bar**
  A blonde walks in to a bar and climbs onto the roof because somebody said the drinks were on the house.

- **Count Dracula walks in to a bar**
  It is very late in the night. The streets are empty. The bar is empty. Count Dracula walks in. The bartender is closing the shutters on the windows. The

bartender notices the Count and immediately several bulbs pop out. The bar becomes dark and the bartender can see the Count's orange-red eyes beckoning him from the far end of the bar. The bartender is scared. He moves slowly behind the bar and asks, "Would you like a dee-dee-drink?" Dracula extends a monstrous-looking hand, grabs the bartender by the neck and lifts him off the ground. "Yes. What is your blood group?" The bartender mutters, "Oh puh-puh.... positive." Dracula smiles, "Good. That is exactly the blood group I want." and bares his fangs. The bartender is about to faint when he notices a sign on the wall saying "Be Positive." Summoning his wits, he shouts, "No, it is B positive. I am B positive." Just then, Nosferatu walks in and says, "Give him to me. I am B plus." Count Dracula turns and screams. The windows shatter and explode. So do the lights. They burst. Power goes off in the entire block. The street lights are also out. Even the moon hides behind a thick cloud. Darkness everywhere. Inside the bar, Dracula's eyes are burning brighter than ever before. He drops the bartender, grabs Nosferatu, shakes him violently, shoves him towards the door and shouts, "Hit the road! Get off this block!! This is my racket!!!"

- **A bookie walks in to a bar**
  A bookie walks in to a bar. The bartender winks at him and says, "Sorry, no bets allowed."

- **A skeleton walks in to a bar**
  A skeleton walks in to a bar and orders a drink. Others at the bar are shocked. The skeleton decides to calm them. It says, "You came in here for high spirits, didn't ya? Very well, then." He raises his glass, "Cheers!"

- **A dog walks in to a bar**
  A dog walks in to a bar and the bartender says, "Sorry, no pets allowed." The dog says, "That's okay. I am here for the skeleton."

- **A cat walks in to a bar**
  A cat walks in to a bar and the bartender says, "And, what are YOU here for?" The cat says, "I am a medium. We were contacting a dead spirit and he ran away mid-séance. I think something was dogging him."

- **A taxman walks in to a bar**
  A taxman walks in to a bar. The bartender points to the skeleton and says, "The assessee you are looking for is over there."

- **An alien walks in to a bar**
  An alien walks in to a bar and says, "I come from a galaxy far far away." The bartender shushes him, beckons him closer and says in a hush voice, "You better return. A government guy is already here." The alien looks discreetly sideways and asks, "Will he capture me and perform experiments on my body?" The barman says, "I don't know about. However, if he sees you, he will definitely impound your spaceship. You will not be able to return. Previous visitors from space owe a lot in back taxes." The alien gets up and prepares to leave. The barman accompanies him to the door, "If you pretend to be humans and try to live among humans, you end up suffering like humans."

- **A tactical nuke walks in to a bar**
  A tactical nuke walks in to a bar and orders a drink. The bartender points to the taxman and asks, "Do you think you can kill him?" The nuke says, "Nope! They are like roaches."

- **Death and taxes walk in to a bar**
  Death and taxes walk in to a bar but they don't order anything. After a while, the bartender asks, "You guys ready to order?" Death and taxes reply in unison, "Certainly."

- **A sub-prime loan walks in to a bar**
  A sub-prime loan walks in to a bar. The bartender ties a black cloth across his eyes and pours the loan a drink.

- **An investment bank and a pension fund walk into bar**
  An investment bank and a pension fund walk into bar. The investment bank orders free drinks for everyone and tequila for the pension fund. After multiple shots of tequila, the pension fund passes out on the floor. The bank then searches pockets of the fund and finds a wallet. It takes all the money from the wallet, pays the tab, pockets the rest and leaves the bar.

- **Napoleon walks in to a bar**
  Napoleon walks in to a bar and says, "Give me something to drink." The barman asks, "How about a short beer?"

- **An acupuncturist walks in to a bar**
  An acupuncturist walks in to a bar and orders some champagne.

- **An advocate walks in to a bar**
  An advocate walks in to a bar and summons the bartender. The bartender is his client so he advocates a free drink. The bartender asks, "Is this a COURTesy visit?" The advocate says, "That's the case. I will be brief. How about some decorum?" The bartender says, "No issue."

- **A Communist walks in to a bar**
  An Communist walks in to a bar and the advocate asks if it is okay for Communists to drink. The Communist says, "We are for a class-less society but not a glass-less one. What about you? Is it okay for advocates to be seen in a bar?" The advocate says, "No, there is no bar. In fact, we are the bar."

- **A builder walks in to a bar**
  A builder walks in to a bar and collapses on to a stool.

- **An alligator walks in to a bar**
  A alligator walks in to a bar and asks for a drink 'to drown' his sorrows. The bartender says he is sorry to hear that but believes that it is only crocodile tears.

- **An ant walks in to a bar**
  An ant walks in to a bar and starts drinking. A few hours later, his wife walks in. She says, "I've been searching for you everywhere while you are sitting here and drowning in alcohol. The ant looks up surprised and says, "You and your imagination! It was only a drop."

- **An antelope walks in to a bar**
  An antelope walks in to a bar because there is no use running away from a problem.

- **A bat walks in to a bar**
  A bat walks in to a bar because he can clear obstacles only in the air.

- **A bee walks in to a bar**
  A bee walks in to a bar because he wants a buzz.

- **A bear walks in to a bar**
  A bear walks in to a bar and CLIMBS onto a stool.

- **A beaver walks in to a bar**
  A beaver walks in to a bar, has a drink and smiles at everyone... because he believes in building bridges.

- **A buffalo walks in to a bar**
  A buffalo walks in to a bar because it is his favourite watering hole.

- **A Bactrian camel, a dromedary camel and a llama walks in to a bar**
  A Bactrian camel, a dromedary camel and a llama walks in to a bar and the bartender reaction was... 'harrumph'.

- **If a bartender was born as a fish, what kind would it be?**
  A Barreleye.

This kind of fish has a transparent head.

- **A camel walks in to a bar**
  A camel walks in to a bar and orders a drink. The barman refuses. The camel says, "I may be a camel. Even I need to drink sometime!" The barman says, "Not when you walk in on all fours."

- **A horse walks in to a bar**
  A horse walks in to a bar with its front legs up in the air and orders a drink. (The camel told the horse what happened.) The barman pours the horse a drink. As the horse settles to drink, it hears a remark and leaves without drinking or paying.

- **An lion walks in to a bar**
  An lion walks in to a bar and orders a drink. The barman is amazed, "A lion who drinks!" The lion says, "I am hungry too. I could eat a horse."

- **A cow walks in to a bar**
  A cow walks in to a bar and causes a cow-mootion.

- **A cow and a bear walk in to a bar**
  A cow and a bear walk in to a bar. The bartender asks how their packaged

drinks business is. The bear says it is not all milk and honey.

- **A crow walks in to a bar**
  A crow walks in to a bar and bartender enquires about his mate. The crow answers, "It's on the house."

- **A digital camera walks in to a bar**
  A digital camera walks in to a bar and snaps at the barman, "Give me a drink!" The barman says, "In a flash!"

- **A film camera walks in to a bar**
  A film camera walks in to a bar but the barman refused it a drink. Because? Because it was a roll camera.

- **A tripod walks in to a bar**
  A tripod walks in to a bar but the barman refused it a drink. Because? Because it did not have a steady hand.

- **A deer walks in to a bar**
  A deer walks in to a bar. The bartender points to a sign and says, "Look, dear! No horns".

- **A dog walks in to a bar**
  A dog walks in to a bar, buys a drink and buries himself in a newspaper.

- **A donkey walks in to a bar**
  A donkey walks in to a bar. As he pours the drink, the barman thinks, "I am going to get a big kick out of this."

- **A dolphin walks in to a bar** A dolphin walks in to a bar and orders a drink. The bartender asks, "What's the porpoise?".

- **A duck walks in to a bar**
  A duck walks in to a bar, orders drinks for everyone, and says, "Put it on my bill."

- **A cheetah walks in to a bar**
  A cheetah walks in to a bar and orders a whisky. The bartender asks, "What do you want for a CHASER?"

- **An eel walks in to a bar**
  An eel walks in to a bar. Does that come to you as a shocker?

- **Elephant and Ant walk in to a bar**
  Elephant and Ant walk in to a bar. The bartender smiles at the Ant and pours it a drink. To Elephant, he says, "Do you have an ID?".

Refer to the duo from the 'Elephant And Ant Jokes' section.

- **Elephant and Ant walk in to a bar**
  Elephant and Ant walk in to a bar. Ant orders tequila shots for both. Elephant is suspicious. He switches the shots and drinks Ant's. A few seconds later, Elephant falls backwards from the stool knocked out.

- **Elephant and Ant walk in to a bar**
  Elephant walks into a bar, scares the customers, and destroys a lot of furniture and fixtures. He then sits at the bar, trumpets loudly and pours himself a drink with his trunk. Ant, who was working there as a bouncer, walks over and says, "Hey, buddy, you want me to throw you out?" Elephant puts down his drink, pays his tab and leaves quietly.

- **A fish walks in to a bar**
  An fish walks in to a bar and says, "I desperately need a drink. I feel like a fish out of water."

- **A frog walks in to a bar**
  A frog walks in to a bar because the doctor advised him to lose weight.

- **A giraffe walks in to a bar**
  A giraffe walks in to a bar and orders 20 beers and the bartender says, "That's a tall order!"

- **An lion walks in to a bar**
  An lion walks in to a bar and it causes an uproar.

- **An mosquito walks in to a bar**
  A mosquito walks in to a bar and says, "Give me your strongest liquor." The barman pours a drink and asks, "Don't you mosquitoes drink blood?" The mosquito says, "Oh, this is purely for disinfection purposes. Coronavirus is taking a toll on our community too and the price of handwash liquid has gone through the roof."

- **A shark walks in to a bar**
  A shark walks in to a bar and says to the bartender, "I need a drink and something to bite."

- **A snake walks in to a bar**
  A snake walks in to a bar and says, "Is this a drinking hole or what?"

- **A squirrel walks in to a bar**
  A squirrel walks in to a bar and says, "Give me a drink and spare the nuts."

- **A tortoise walks in to a bar**
  A tortoise walks in to a bar and drinks heavily. The bartender says, "Have you tried to quit?" The tortoise says, "I did but it has been slow progress."

- **A turtle and lobster walk in to a bar**
  A tortoise and lobster walk in to a bar and order drinks. After the drinks arrive, the lobster finishes his drink and then finishes the turtle's drink as well with a "Sorry, bud". The turtle bites the lobster hand and says, "Order again and this time don't be so shellfish."

- **A turkey walks in to a bar**
  A turkey walks in to a bar, buys a drink, meets his friends, sits down and talks turkey.

- **A zebra walks in to a bar**
  A zebra walks in to a bar, and it makes everyone stop and think.

In some countries, a 'road crossing' or 'crosswalk' is known as a *zebra crossing*.

Blonde Jokes

Sorry, sister, blonde jokes are not politically correct... and, this goes right over MY head!

After I finished high school, I read a lot of James Hadley Chase. He was a famous British novelist who wrote crime thrillers. Some of his novels were set in the USA, even though he had not visited the country. He wrote those novels based on what he had read or heard about that country. I had been writing this jokebook based on an American jokebook I read in the 80s. (I do not remember its name or know when it was published.) It had blonde jokes so I wrote a good many for mine. After I wrote this section, I learned that blonde jokes are no longer considered politically correct! Too

late. I will not kill my blonde. She is a real person now.

Many jokes in this book have been inspired by 'Archie' of Duffy's Tavern. (For more information about this show from the Golden Era Of Radio, read section Annexure 1: Vintage Radio Shows.) Apart from routinely killing the English language, Archie gave birth to new words like 'weirdidity' and expressions like 'Perish Forbid'. When Archie hears something, he understands it as something else and when he talks about there is only a little resemblance to what he had heard in the first place. The blonde writer in this section is the female version of Archie. The ads are for India but a blonde has been contrived to write them.

In any case, everyone knows that blonde jokes are dumb because Ms. Alexandria Ocasio Cortes has single-handedly made them obsolete after winning the election in 2018.

- **Blonde Strategy**

  Teacher: This room is stuffy. There is no fan or AC. Anyone has any bright ideas on how to solve it?
  Blonde: Let's bring in the air force.
  Teacher: What do you mean?
  Blonde: Let's open the windows.

  I heard this joke from someone I knew. The blonde owns several educational institutions in Chennai. He probably was also amused after hearing it.

- **Blonde Stalemate**

  Waiter: May I take your order?
  Blonde: You may.
  [Awkward silence]

  When someone mass-emails a question starting with "May I know...", I always reply, "You may."

- **Blonde Reflection**

  Brunette: Have you met my sister? She is my identical twin.
  Blonde: No. What does she look like?

  I am not sure if I am the first one who came up with this joke.

- **Blonde Examination**

  Teacher: Did you study hard for your exams?
  Blonde: Yes, ma'am, I studied hardly.

  One day in my school years, when we were writing an exam, a teacher came in and said, "If some visitor asks you if you studied hard for the exam, don't tell him that you studied 'hardly'." This advice was given to all classes. We followed her advice but if any of our own teachers came in and asked the question, someone would always say,

- **Blonde Mobster**

  Teacher: As the saying goes, is it possible to kill two birds with one stone?
  Class: No, ma'am.
  Blonde: Yes, ma'am.
  Teacher: Really? How?
  Blonde: You tie the birds to a stone and drown them.

This was originally a Chuck Norris Fact but it had no explanation.

- **Blonde Milkmaid**

  Teacher: What does 'put out to pasture' mean?
  Blonde: When a cow starts producing pasteurized milk.

- **Blonde Ultimatum**

  Teacher: Name four animals.
  Blonde: Tom, Jerry, Sylvester and Tweety.

This is based on an old joke by S Ve Shekhar.

- **Blonde Perspective**

  Teacher: What is the difference between a serial killer and a psychopath?
  Blonde: A psychopath kills indiscriminately while a serial killer follows an alphabetical order.

- **Blonde Dictionary**

  Teacher: What do you call a professional who draws for a living?
  Blonde: A drawer.

- **What magazine does a blonde read?**
  Reader's Digest but only when she has indigestion.

- **Blonde Bite Force**

  Teacher: What is an alligator?
  Blonde: The person who makes allegations.

- **Blonde Awareness**

  Teacher: Give an example of man-made Climate Change.
  Blonde: An air-conditioner.

- **Blonde Solution**

  Teacher: One handkerchief takes 12 minutes to dry in the sun. How many minutes will four hankies take?
  Blonde: Eleven minutes.
  Teacher: The correct answer is 12 minutes. How can it be 11 minutes for you?
  Blonde: In our home, we use our washing machine's dryer.

Believe it or not, a good number of people will multiply the number of minutes with the number of hankies.

- **The Blonde Way**

> **British Brunette**: I am a pilot.
> **American Blonde**: Really? Do you drive planes on the left side too?

- **What kind of music do blondes like?**
  Easy listening.

- **Blonde Awareness Day**

  > **British Brunette**: Happy Independence Day.
  > **American Blonde**: Thanks. When do you celebrate *July the 4th* in the UK?

- **Blonde Fortune**

  > **Brunette**: "I am a fortune teller." [Shows her a crystal ball.]
  > **Blonde**: "I am a fortune reader." [Shows her a fortune cookie message.]

- **Why was the blonde shouting at the bartender?**
  She passed the bar several times but no one offered her a law degree.

- **Why did the blonde refuse the manila envelope?**
  She was afraid it would be sent to Philippines.

- **The blonde writes a letter to the editor of a newspaper**
  "I wish to bring to your readers' notice of a harrowing experience I had with
  the *No Passenger Left Behind Railway Company*. Last weekend, I and many other
  passengers in the last compartment of our train were left stranded at a station.
  The railway workers there forgot to shunt the compartment and the rest of the
  train proceeded without us. It was 20 minutes before the train came back for
  us. To avoid such blunders in future, I urge railway companies not to include a
  last compartment in their trains."

- **The blonde drives a train**
  The blonde went to a train driving school. During a test run, a man crossed the
  tracks. The blonde braked suddenly and the train derailed. The instructors told
  her that a train had the right of way and if the motorman saw a person he/she
  can hit the person without any liability. During the next test run, the blonde
  caused another derailment. After the accident, the instructors learned that the
  blonde saw a man standing next to the tracks and she went off the rails to hit
  him.

- **Why was the blonde amazed by the US Marine Corps?**
  She was expecting an aquatic zombie.

- **Why did the blonde buy a *Teach Yourself Latin* book along with the spirit-
  talking (*Ouiji*) board?**
  She wanted to speak to the dead in their language.

- **Why did the blonde cross the road?**
  Her friend had advised her to look at problems from the other side too.

- **What was the blonde doing in the meat section?**

She was looking for organic food.

- **Blonde Botanist**

   Teacher: From what is ketchup made?
   Blonde: From the fruits of the ketchup tree.

- **Why did the blonde break her computer into two after she forgot the password?**
  Someone told her she will have to HACK it.

- **Why did the blonde move her computer near the fireplace?**
  Someone told her she needed to protect her network with a firewall.

- **Why did the blonde send $1000 (USD) to Nigeria?**
  The Bank of Internet announced that she had won a million dollars and the $1000 was just postage fee.

- **Why did the blonde send $100 (USD) to India?**
  A caller from India told her that her IP address was sending Y2K virus to computers all over the world. The only way to stop it was to buy the Y2K Antivirus.

- **Why did the blonde send $10 (USD) to Pakistan?**
  A Pakistani child with terminal cancer wants to buy get-well cards before he dies.

- **Why did the blonde send $1 (USD) to Florida?**
  To get her contact details published in the Internet directory book.

- **Blonde Observation**

   Teacher: Who wrote the book 'How to become an instant millionaire'?
   Blonde: Probably a spammer.

- **Blonde Intuition**

   Brunette: Why does Windows OS get so many viruses?
   Blonde: Maybe **Microsoft** stands for '**Micro**bial **Soft**ware'.

- **Why don't blondes get cold?**
  They run **amuck**.

- **Blonde Judgement**

   Brunette: Why does Windows 10 look so dead-white and lifeless?
   Blonde: Maybe because it is the final version of Windows.

- **Blonde Compassion**

   Blonde: Hi, I would like 3 pounds of that.
   Store Worker: Sorry, ma'am. That's expired meat. That's why it's locked up.
   Blonde: So what? I can't eat a live animal.

- **Why did the psychiatrist die of shock?**
  The blonde had second thoughts.

- **Why did the blonde go to Indonesia?**
  She wanted to learn the Java language.

This is a computer programming joke.

- **Why did the blonde go to an optician?**
  She wanted to learn C language.

- **Why did the blonde go to an optometrist?**
  She wanted to learn C#.

- **Blonde Astrophysicist**

  Teacher: Who wrote the book 'Men are from Mars and Women are from Venus'?
  Blonde: Obviously, a charlatan.

- **The blonde answers a physics question with a geography answer**

  Teacher: What is the unit of charge?
  Blonde: Columbia.

- **Blonde Physicist**

  Teacher: What do you call a unit of force?
  Blonde: For.

- **The blonde answers a chemistry question with a biology answer**

  Teacher: What is 6.023×10^{23} atoms or molecules of any substance known as?
  Blonde: One rat.

- **Blonde Success**

  Brunette: Did you find traces of fluorine in the tests?
  Blonde: No. The tests always come back with an F.

- **Blonde Zoologist**

  Teacher: Nearly 7% of Americans think chocolate milk comes from brown cows. Does anyone from where chocolate milk really comes from?
  Blonde: Yes, Ma'am. Cows produce chocolate milk only when you feed them chocolate.

- **Blonde Killjoy**

  Teacher: Aren't women equal to men?
  Class: Yes, Ma'am.
  Blonde: Ma'am, I think women are more than equal to men.
  Teacher: Ah, I think we have a feminist here. Good. Tell the class why women are more than equal to men.
  Blonde: 'Men' is written as M-E-N while 'women' is written as W-O-M-E-N.

- **Blonde Lemonade**

  Teacher: Can you make lemonade out of an apple?
  Class: No, Ma'am. **Blonde**: Yes, Ma'am.
  Teacher: How?
  Blonde: When I make lemonade, I always leave the apple out.

- **Blonde Supremacy**

  Teacher: How many lines do you need to draw a square?
  Class: Four.
  Teacher: Can you draw a square with three lines?
  Class: No.
  Blonde: Ma'am, I can draw a square with less than three lines.
  Teacher: How's that possible?
  Blonde: Let me show you.

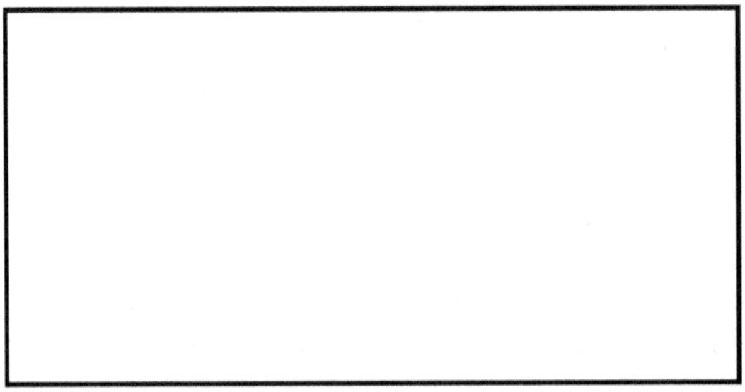

  Teacher: That's not a square. It is a rectangle and already has four lines.
  Blonde: I am not finished yet.

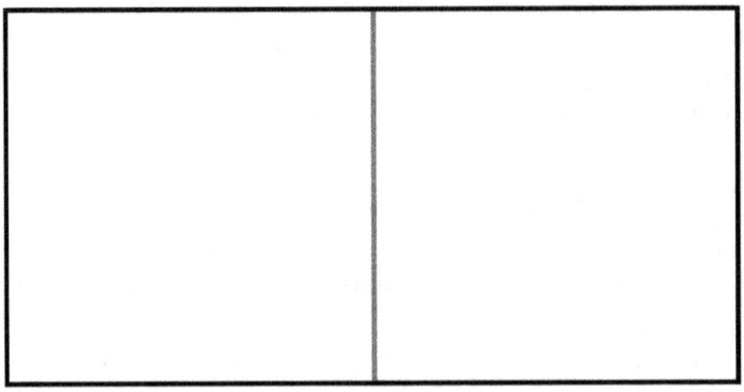

- **How did the blonde get amnesia?**
  She had no idea.

- **Blondes have an answer to everything**

  Brunette: How do you put an elephant in a fridge?
  Blonde: You open the door, find a place for the elephant and put it there.
  Brunette: How can an entire elephant inside a fridge?!
  Blonde: Okay. You remove some of the racks and make space for it.
  Brunette: Even if you remove everything in the fridge, you will still not be able to fit an elephant inside a fridge.
  Blonde: All right. What's an elephant?
  Brunette: Here, read this animal encyclopedia. Then, tell me how can you do it?

> **Blonde**: Still not a problem. It can be done. You just need to go to Asia.
> **Brunette**: What?
> **Blonde**: It says in the book that Asian elephants are much smaller than African elephants.

- **Blondes have an answer to everything – Part 2**

> **Brunette**: How do you put a whale inside a fridge?
> **Blonde**: You cannot.
> **Brunette**: Mm-mm?
> **Blonde**: There is already an elephant in it.
> **Brunette**: Okay. The elephant has been taken out. The fridge is empty now. Then, how do you put the whale in it?
> **Blonde**: I think you should can the whole whale idea and put it in the freezer!

- **Blonde Wonder**

> **Blonde**: I want to return this phone.
> **Salesman**: What seems to be the problem?
> **Blonde**: I getting the same unwanted message from different numbers and I am unable to block them.
> **Salesman**: What's the message you are getting?
> **Blonde**: 'Low Battery'

- **The blonde takes a stand**

> **Teacher**: Why does the stork stand one leg?
> **Blonde**: If it lifts the other leg, it would be in the water.

- **The blonde writer**

A hospital wanted a new radiologist. The recruitment firm asked a blonde to write the ad copy. She wrote: "WANTED RADIATOR: Radical students invited to apply. Will need to see through people's body parts, such as the head, and ensure that there is nothing serious there."

- **The blonde writer**

An airline needed a new pilot. The recruitment firm asked a blonde to write the ad copy. She wrote: "WANTED DRIVER: Valid 18-wheeler license a must. Outstanding candidates need not apply."

- **The blonde writer**

A TV channel wanted a news anchor. The recruitment firm asked a blonde to write the ad copy. She wrote: "WANTED NEWS READER: Must be able to shout above Arnab Goswami levels. Ability/willingness to throw/receive a punch will be a plus."

- **The blonde writer**

A government spy agency wanted a new agent. The recruitment firm asked a blonde to write the ad copy. She wrote: "WANTED CIGARETTE AGENT: Police dogs invited to apply with/without intelligent experience. Should be able to sniff out fire where there is no smoke. Experience in sifting through garbage and analysing the contents is a must."

- **The blonde writer**

An oil company needed a new geologist. The recruitment firm asked a blonde to write the ad copy. She wrote: "WANTED ROCKET SCIENTIST: Should go into the ground and come out with valuable mines. Environmentals need not apply."

- **The blonde writer**
  A space research organization wanted a new astronomer. The recruitment firm asked a blonde to write the ad copy. She wrote: "WANTED ASTRONAUT: Astrology graduates invited to apply. Should be willing to relocate in view of the planets."

- **The blonde writer**
  A pharma company wanted a new chemical engineer. The recruitment firm asked a blonde to write the ad copy. She wrote: "WANTED PHARMACIST: Farming and ecology graduates invited to apply. Past experience in reacting to chemicals will be a plus."

- **The blonde writer**
  A cosmetics company wanted a new herbalist. The recruitment firm asked a blonde to write the ad copy. She wrote: "WANTED BOTANIST: Botanical graduates invited to apply. Experience in extracting plants a must."

- **The blonde writer**
  A suicide hotline wanted a new counsellor. The recruitment firm asked a blonde to write the ad copy. She wrote: "WANTED SUICIDE COUNSELLOR: Psychopaths invited to apply. Past suicide experience will be a plus."

- **The blonde writer**
  A hospital wanted a new psychiatrist. The recruitment firm asked a blonde to write the ad copy. She wrote: "WANTED PSYCHOPATH: Physiotherapy graduates invited to apply. Should be able to closely study patients and put an end to their problems."

- **The blonde writer**
  A software company needed a new programmer. The recruitment firm asked a blonde to write the ad copy. She wrote: "WANTED PROGRAMMER: Should be able to program in HTML and CSS. Photo shop experience would be a positive."

- **The blonde writer**
  A computer training institute needed a new lab assistant. The recruitment firm asked a blonde to write the ad copy. She wrote: "WANTED COMPUTER LAB ASSISANT: Should be able to press the restart button when computers stop responding. Any other kind of computer expertise is not required."

- **The blonde writer**
  A veterinary clinic needed a new doctor. The recruitment firm asked a blonde to write the ad copy. She wrote: "WANTED VETERAN: Should be a domesticated vet. Will need to give birth to new animals as well."

- **The blonde writer**
  A restaurant needed a new chef. The recruitment firm asked a blonde to write the ad copy. She wrote: "WANTED CHIEF: Cratering graduates invited to apply. Chafing experience is a must. Previous experience in leading a team of cookers will be a plus."

- **The blonde writer**
  A book publisher needed a new illustrator. The recruitment firm asked a

blonde to write the ad copy. She wrote: "WANTED DRAWER: Must be good with paints and brushes. Teleportation option available."

- **The blonde writer**
  A law firm required a divorce attorney. The recruitment firm asked a blonde to write the ad copy. She wrote: "WANTED MARTIAL RULE EXPERT: Martial law graduates invited to apply. Should be an expert in settling fights and taking away their money."

- **The blonde writer**
  The history department at a university needed a new archeologist. The recruitment firm asked a blonde to write the ad copy. She wrote: "WANTED EXORCIST: Archery graduates invited to apply. Should have prior experience in bringing back the dead and dating them."

- **The blonde writer**
  A symphony orchestra needed a new conductor. The recruitment firm asked a blonde to write the ad copy. She wrote: "WANTED BAND LEADER: Should lead a team of bandits to siphon public money. The best candidate will get the stick and face the music."

- **A brunette, a blonde, a redhead and a platinum blonde**
  The following conversation appears in my first fiction novel *Unlikely Stories*, which was published in 2022. The conversation is between the lead pair.

  "Shoot! Well, in the US, blonde jokes have become 'politically incorrect'."

  "Because?"

  "Ideally, blondes should not be offended because hair colour has no correlation to intelligence. Blondes look prettier than others. And, pretty people are often assumed to be intelligent as well. When the expectations do not match with reality, it gives rise to the opposite assumption that blondes must be stupid. It seems everyone's stupid."

  "When jokes create the wrong impression about people, they should be banned."

  "You cannot go around and start banning stuff left and right."

  "If something is misused, then it should be banned. Like guns in America."

  "Guns in the US? … If gangsters are found to be making threat calls, should phones be banned?"

  "I don't know. Why do they need so many guns?"

  "They have a gun culture. We don't. It is not for us to judge. We have a small but thriving stabbing and beheading culture. What would happen if knives were banned?"

  She shook her head. "Maybe my example was bad but jokes that ridicule women should not be given respectability."

  "What if men banned jokes that women make to make men look stupid?"

  "No, those jokes are just funny."

  "See? What is funny to you can be offensive to others. If we start banning things that someone considers offensive, then eventually everything will be banned. Only a tyrannical society will ban humour.”

“When did blonde jokes stop being funny?”

“When they degenerated from being about intelligence to being just crass or double-meaning.”

“Then, they are right to ban them.”

“And destroy an entire class of great jokes created over decades? Anyway, my blonde jokes are clean, like all my jokes. The blondes are just a prop to say something funny or clever. In fact, in some of my blonde jokes, they are smarter than others.”

“How?”

“In one blonde joke, a teacher asks a class if they can draw a square with three lines.”

“And, the blonde drew a square with three lines?”

“She drew a square with less than three lines.”

“Less than three lines? How?”

I took a paper towel, placed it flat on the table and drew a rectangle on it.

“That is a rectangle. Not a square. It has four lines.”

I drew a line in the middle of the rectangle connecting the two broader sides.

“Now, you have two squares made from 5 lines. That is 2.5 lines per square.”

“I can draw a square with two lines.”

“How?”

She took the pen and the paper towel, and drew two lines like an L in the top-right corner. The two sides of the corner made the space enclosed by the two lines into a *de facto* square. I took the paper towel back and looked at her with admiration. “Man, you are smarter than I am! I am going to to add this to my jokebook.”

“No, it is my copyright.”

“I will give your idea to a redhead. A brunette, a blonde and a red-head walk into a bar. They do not have money to pay for their drinks so the barman makes them a challenge.”

“What are redheads? People with red hair? Does it even exist?”

“There are people with dark reddish-brown hair. They are called redheads. I do not think the bright red variety exists. I've not seen any. Female redheads are supposed to be hotter than the blondes and even more stupid.”

“This is getting even more stupid than I thought it would be.”

“There is another category of stupid.”

“What?”

“Platinum blondes. Platinum blondes are even more stupid than... I don't know if they are more stupid than redheads but they are definitely stupider than blondes. Platinum does not have much yellow and is a lot more pale."

Vampira slowly shook her head and took the paper towel from me again. She said, "I shouldn't be doing this to my own kind." She then folded the corner square diagonally on to itself. She then folded the whole paper diagonally. It now looked like a half-made paper arrow. She then drew a line on one side of the folded corner and then continued it on the other side of the arrow tip. "There! One line. Give it to the platinum blonde."

Financial Jokes

There are several poems in this section. Feel free to create derivative works. For example, in the FANG stocks poem, you can replace FANG with any other stock code or acronym. You can also set them to tune. You can also set them to the tune of the nursery rhymes mentioned in brackets.

- **What is an artichoke?**
  Something that happens when you become the owner of a million-dollar painting at an auction by waving 'Hi' to a friend.

- **Truth in numbers**
  Numbers: Numbers don't lie.
  Statistics: But, we do.

- **Should you trust statistics provided by a Republican?**
  No. They tend to be conservative.

- **Why would no bank give a loan to Superman?**
  Because he has no immovable assets.

- **Why would you never get a loan from Superman?**
  Because he will see through you.

- **Why was the vampire arrested for insider trading?**
  He had inappropriate dealings with some blood bank employees.

- **Why was Count Dracula asked to take a course on moral hazard?**
  Because he wanted to invest in a blood bank.

- **How can you tell if the economy is in an inflationary spiral?**
  When the vampires start drinking each other's blood.

- **What does it mean when Count Dracula buys life insurance?**
  The tax department has picked him for a 'routine audit'.

- **When is a taxman a good taxman?**
  When he is taxing the filthy filthy-rich, particularly their identity-hiding tax-evading maze of multi-level shell companies, charities, foundations, trust funds, tax-haven-based offshore subsidiaries and bank accounts, etc.

- **Should you count your chickens before they hatch?**
  Consult your tax attorney.

- **When is a taxman not a good taxman?**
  All the time.

- **Why did the cloud get a tax claim?**
  A rumour was floating that it had a silver lining.

- **What did one FTSE stock say to another?**
  "Seems like you have lost a pound or two."

- **What did one startup investor say to another?**
  "What's with the pinched expression?"

- **Why did the barrel of petroleum complain to the commodity exchange board?**
  The financial papers were referring to it in crude terms.

- **What does insider-trading hedge fund manager's school yearbook say about him?**
  "Most likely to learn the abacus...in jail"

- **What does Wall Street investment banker's school yearbook say about him?**
  "Most likely to empty the coffers of the state, city and town too."

- **What does the startup founder's yearbook say about him?**
  "Most likely to take your money and run."

- **What does the derivatives trader's school yearbook say about him?**

"Most likely to lose his shirt on some bet."

- **What does the options trader's school yearbook say about him?**
  "Most likely to be a falling debris hazard near tall buildings."

- **Psychos On Wall Street**
  A high-security prison in New York hired a recruitment firm for filling the post of psychopathologist. The recruitment firm carried ads on several newspapers. One of them printed the ad with a mistake. They titled it with 'Wanted Psychopath'. A total of six candidates were waiting in the lounge when a down-on-his-luck psychopath appeared at the recruitment firm. When the receptionist went to the pantry, the psycho followed her, knocked her unconscious and hid her inside a cupboard. Then, he announced to the other waiting candidates that the position was filled and asked them to leave. He then appeared for the interview as the only interested candidate. The recruiter looked at his résumé and said "This says you are strong, motivated, willing to take risks, can study customer behaviour for deciding future course of action, succeed against all odds, etcetera, etcetera, but there is nothing to suggest that you have a medical or science qualification, which is essential for this position. All you have is some degree in finance." The psycho got enraged by this. He grabbed the recruiter by the collar and placed a knife on his throat. "Would you like to reconsider?" the psycho demanded. The recruiter begged the psycho not to harm him. The psycho freed the recruiter. The recruiter hurriedly took a file out of a drawer and says, "Forget that job. I have a better one for you. I think you are the right candidate for a different but more well-paying job. Would you like to work on Wall Street? There is this investment bank. They need a derivatives trader."

Pyscopaths on Wall Street
https://hbr.org/2012/03/psychopaths-on-wall-street

- **How are credit ratings and junk bonds the same?**
  They are both worthless and intended to deceive in the long term.

- **A credit rating walks in to a bar**
  A credit rating walks in to a bar, orders a drink and pays with an IOU. The IOU has a footnote disclaimer saying that the instrument was subject to market risks and the credit rating is not an indicator for future performance.

- **What is a serial killer's favourite self-help book?**
  The road less travelled.

- **How did the male banker show his love for the female banker?**
  He gave her a token of friendship.

- **Credit Default Swaps**

  > C-D-S!
  > C-D-S!
  > Toxic 'n' infectious!
  > Toxic 'n' infectious!
  > Makes the banks look unsteady!
  > Makes the banks look unsteady!
  > Bail them out!
  > Bail them out!

Set to the tune of 'Bits Of Paper'

- **What kind of cut does a too-big-to-fail Wall Street investment bank not get when it asks for a bailout?**
  Pay cut.

- **FANG stocks are going down**

  > FANG stocks are going down!
  > Going down! Going down!
  > FANG stocks are going down, taking the rest of the market!
  >
  > And, every bottom that FANG stocks hit!
  > FANG stocks hit! FANG stocks hit!
  > And, every bottom that FANG stocks hit, the rest of the market would reel around.

Set to the tune of 'Mary had a little lamb'.

- **Gold Investor Anthem**

  > Markets boom and markets crash
  > Always have some barbarous relic in your hands
  > Even when your government files for bankruptcy
  > Gold is nobody's liability

Set to the tune of 'Eeny, meeny, miny, moe'.

- **Investment Bank**

  > An options trader
  > Sat in a corner
  > Looking at his puts and call
  > He was ready to jump out of the window
  > When he heard a knock on his door
  > It was a pension fund that will take the fall

Set to the tune of 'Little Jack Horner'.

- **Negative Interest Rates**

  > Negative interest rates! Negative interest rates
  > Do you take me for a fool?
  > With negative interest rates!
  >
  > If I lend one dollar, then I lose some cents!
  > Do you take me for a fool?
  > With negative interest rates!

Set to the tune of 'Hot Cross Buns'

- **Startup sequence**

  > One! Two! The money won't do!
  > Three! Four! The angels hit the road!
  > Five! Six! The IPO fails!
  > Seven! Eight! The promoters get out!
  > Nine! Ten! No one's laughin'

Set to the tune of 'One Two Buckle My Shoe'.

- **Stock Investor Anthem**

  Early to invest
  Early to sell
  Ensures an investor retires in style

- **The stockmarket is falling down**

  The stockmarket is falling down!
  Falling down! Falling down!
  The stockmarket is falling down!
  Dear Plunge-Protection Team, are you listening!

  Stop inflating financial bubbles!
  Financial bubbles! Financial bubbles!
  Stop inflating financial bubbles!
  Dear Federal Reserve, isn't it a moral hazard!

  Gold and silver are also manipulated!
  Manipulated! Manipulated!
  Gold and silver are also manipulated!
  Dear Austrian economists, there is just not enough to go around!

  • Set to the tune of 'London Bridge Is Falling Down'
  • "Former JP Morgan trader pleads guilty to manipulating US metals markets for years"; CNBC
  • "Global Banks to Pay $1.2B in Settlement for FX Manipulation"; NASDAQ

- **Tax Jurisdiction Hunting**

  1, 2, 3, 4
  Tech titans escape tax using foreign jurisdictions
  5, 6, 7, 8
  While the IRS is garnishing wages of ordinary minions

  Set to the tune of '1234 Mary's At The Cottage Door'.

- **Vampire squid alert**

  Blood is red
  Veins are punctured
  Beware of vampire squids
  They suck your pension funds

  • Set to the tune of 'Roses are red'
  • "The Great American Bubble Machine: How Goldman-Sachs Blew Up The Economy"; Rolling Stone

- **Universal Basic Income**

  It is raining.
  It is pouring.
  Helicopter money is falling.
  The mayor says the books are red.
  Investment banks will be the only ones smiling.

- **Why do tortoises never become entrepreneurs?**
  They get accused of having a shell company.

- **What magazine do Income Tax officials likes to read?**
  Raider's Digest

Horoscope Jokes

By V. Subhash, a certified astrologer and alumnus of People's *School of Self-Criticism, Pessimism and Astrology,* People's *Republic of China.*

- ♈ **ARIES (March 21 to April 19)**
  Finally, you meet the girl of your dreams. But she wants nothing more than a ticket from the bus conductor.

- ♉ **TAURUS (April 20 to May 20)**
  You will start going out with a North-Indian girl. You will come to realize that, apart from the accent, they are just as problematic as local South Indian ones.

- ♊ **GEMINI (May 21 to June 21)**
  You will be relieved that the guy who has a habit of "looking" at you in the bus stand is no longer doing that. Your relief turns in to a strange feeling of loss when the guy begins to devote his attentions on a more good-looking girl.

- ♋ **CANCER (June 22 to July 22)**

You take great pride in the fact that your girls college attracts a lion's share of Roadside Romeos. Yet, you take part in protest marches against eve-teasing.

- ♌ **LEO (July 23 to August 22)**
  You make great strides in speaking fluent English but this only makes the girls characterize you as boorish and noisy.

- ♍ **VIRGO (August 23 to September 22)**
  You wish you could turn your boyfriend into a cat and keep him as a pet at home. Well, don't.

- ♎ **LIBRA (September 23 to October 23)**
  Your dream of getting a rich girlfriend comes true. Your dream of significant financial savings doesn't.

- ♏ **SCORPIO (October 24 to November 21)**
  Bad news and good news. The bad news is that you will be caught using bits for the physics test. The good news is that you will let off because the bits were for the chemistry test.

- ♐ **SAGITARRIUS (November 22 to December 21)**
  You are outraged that a girl in your college has been teased by a student of a rival college. Though it turns out that the culprit was actually a student of your own college, it is too late because you are arrested for throwing a brick at a bus windshield.

- ♑ **CAPRICON (December 22 to January 19)**
  Your balloon of happiness in joining a co-ed college is pricked by seniors who insist on ragging you in front of female members of your class.

- ♒ **AQUARIUS (January 20 to February 18)**
  Your interest in impressing the ladies with dangerous footboard travel comes to an end after you are run over by a truck after you fall from a bus after you hit a lamp post.

- ♓ **PISCES (February 19 to March 20)**
  You are looking for a guy who listens to you, laughs at your jokes, cares about you, ignores your faults, loves you no matter what, ... Stop it, honey! This man is your father. Take an MRI of your brain and see a psychiatrist.

I wrote this horoscope many many years ago for a magazine for college students.

Jokes In Advertising

These funeral parlour ads were inspired by the 1963 movie *Comedy of Terrors* and the 1940s radio show *Duffy's Tavern* ("If you must drink on Christmas eve, be sure to drive your car. Signed, Cavendish, the undertaker."). Undertakers provide an under-appreciated service to their community. If any undertaker business wants lines for ads, they can use one of these free-of-cost on a non-exclusive non-transferable basis.

- **Funeral Parlour Ad**
  END-TIMES UNDERTAKERS: When your loved ones make their departure, we make our arrival.

- **Funeral Parlour Ad**
  CHECKER & SONS UNDERTAKERS: When loved ones check out, we check in.

- **Funeral Parlour Ad**
  ESPIRIT UNDERTAKERS: We undertake the body when they give up the ghost.

- **Funeral Parlour Ad**
  SLICK & MOB FUNERAL PARLOUR: We finish your unfinished business like nobody's business.

- **Funeral Parlour Ad**
  SPRUCE & BALM UNDERTAKERS: Some of our customers never looked better.

- **Funeral Parlour Ad**
  STORIED UNDERTAKERS: We have been in the funeral business so long that we kill the competition with our impeccable service.

- **Funeral Parlour Ad**
  HOTEL CALIFORNIA INTERNMENTS: You can check-in any time you want but you can never live.

Cremation is an accepted way of disposing a dead body for Christians but interring in a crypt is not.

- **Funeral Home Ad**
  PEARLY GATES PARLOUR: We will deck you up so good that your dead mother will be proud to see you arrive at the pearly gates.

- **Funeral Home Ad**
  EASY-GO UNDERTAKERS: Come hell or high water, go down there in style. Check out our luxury coffin collection.

- **Funeral Home Ad**
  KEVORKIAN UNDERTAKERS: Toughest part is taking the plunge. Come to us. Rest is easy. We will give you a harp and you will float towards heaven like an angel in no time.

- **Funeral Home Ad**
  FRANK & STEIN UNDERTAKERS: You are not taking anything to heaven with you so why bother? Hint: Organ and cadaver donation requests accepted.

- **Funeral Home Ad**
  DEADWEIGHT UNDERTAKERS: You die only once. Don't die cheaply. Check out our elite coffin collection.

- **Funeral Home Ad**
  MAIN STREET UNDERTAKERS: No money? No problem! Check out our affordable luxury coffin collection. Meet your maker in easy instalments.

- **Funeral Home Ad**
  FUNNY & DIE UNDERTAKERS: Worried your death could put a hole in your family's pocket? Perish the thought. Fun fact: Funeral coffins are not that expensive. Check out our value-for-money collection.

- **Funeral Home Ad**
  EARTHLY-WARMTH UNDERTAKERS: Choose us for the warmth of the earth.

Or, burn in hell. Hint: Cremation option available.

- **Funeral Home Ad**
  EARTHLY-WARMTH UNDERTAKERS: Go six feet under. Or, sleep with fishes. Hint: Burial-at-sea option available.

- **Funeral Home Ad**
  TREMBLE-GLEE UNDERTAKERS: You say good-bye first and then do business with us.

- **Funeral Parlour Ad**
  DOOMSDAY UNDERTAKERS: Worried about graverobbers, vandals and the zombie apocalypse? Check out our welded-shut hermetically sealed iron casket options. Even the IRS won't be able to get in... Maybe they will but you get the idea.

- **Funeral Home Ad**
  DRAKE & HULA FUNERAL PARLOUR: You are a vampire? No problem. Our Undead Coffin line models are equipped with battery-powered roller wheels (and hydraulic brakes), an oxygen tank, a digital clock (with *Tocatta and Fugue* alarm tone) and a button-operated sliding door.

- **Funeral Home Ad**
  FINAL-SHOT FUNERAL HOME: Choose us. All the coolest seniors are doing it.

- **Funeral Home Ad**
  BREATHE EASY UNDERTAKERS: You came to this world unprepared and crying. Leave it on your terms, with a smile.

- **Funeral Home Ad**
  O'BAMUH UNDERTAKERS: Burial? We can. Cremation? Yes, we can. Turn you into ashes and shoot you into the sky or disperse over the sea?... Yes, yes, yes, we can!

- **Funeral Home Ad**
  COOL-N-COZY FUNERAL HOME: Don't spend an afterlife shifting and rolling in your grave. Select a comfortable coffin today.

- **Personal Ad**
  Lonely ghoul looking for a gal who is out of this world.

- **Personal Ad**
  Son of the soil moleman wants to meet molewoman with down-the-earth altitude.

- **Personal Ad**
  Lonely male vampire wishes to meet lonely female vampire with knockout looks, impressive teeth and shared personal taste. Call after-hours.

- **Personal Ad**
  Lonely male werewolf wishes to meet lonely female werewolf. Appreciates late-night walks and moonlit dinner. Great if you can bring along a man/woman but will settle for a can of dog food.

- **Personal Ad**
  Lonely male burglar wishes to meet lonely female burglar without stolen heart. Call during daytime.

- **Personal Ad**
  Soft-spoken crime-fighter superhero wishes to go hang out with beautiful

superheroine with no hangups for fast cars or cool gadgets. Batgirl and cave-dwellers need not apply.

- **Personal Ad**
Superhero more powerful than a locomotive wishes to meet beautiful superheroine with better taste in fashion. Supergirl and news reporters need not apply.

- **Personal Ad**
Masked crusader. Lives in the jungle. Moves like a phantom. Appreciates peace and quiet. Old flames and environmentalists need need not apply.

- **Personal Ad**
Lonely male alien seeks lonely female alien from a galaxy far far away. Should have own transport and adequate fuel supply for return trip. Age/looks no bar.

-

- **Advertising Business**
Gotcha! We will waste valuable space like this just to prove that advertisements will attract your attention!

- **Personal Ad**
Lonely male cat would like to meet on-the-fence female cat. Object: Unearthly late-night meowing sessions.

- **Personal Ad**
Slightly overweight male turkey interested in taking extremely overweight female turkey to dinner. Call before Thanksgiving.

- **Personal Ad**
Depressed feed-fed female cow would like to see pasture-raised male cow. Object: Just send your photograph in your natural surroundings. I will never leave this place alive.

- **Personal Ad**
Lonely male dog who chewed the remote would like to meet lonely female dog in the neighbourhood. Object: Watch TV at your place.

- **Personal Ad**
Depressed male hyena would like to meet lonely female hyena with a sense of humour. Object: Could use a few laughs.

- **Personal Ad**
Just-released free bird wishes to meet aspiring mobster chick with clean record. Object: Escape from the man of course but no tricks.

- **Personal Ad**
Lonely male dove would like to meet lonely female dove. I know a place on the father of the nation.

- **Personal Ad**
Me: Romantic female owl. You: Rooting-tooting male hooter. Object: Moonlit dinner. On the menu: One sumptuous snake. Two if the next ad gets a response.

- **Personal Ad**
Overweight male snake wishes to meet curvy female snake who will not recoil in horror at first meeting.

Journalism Jokes

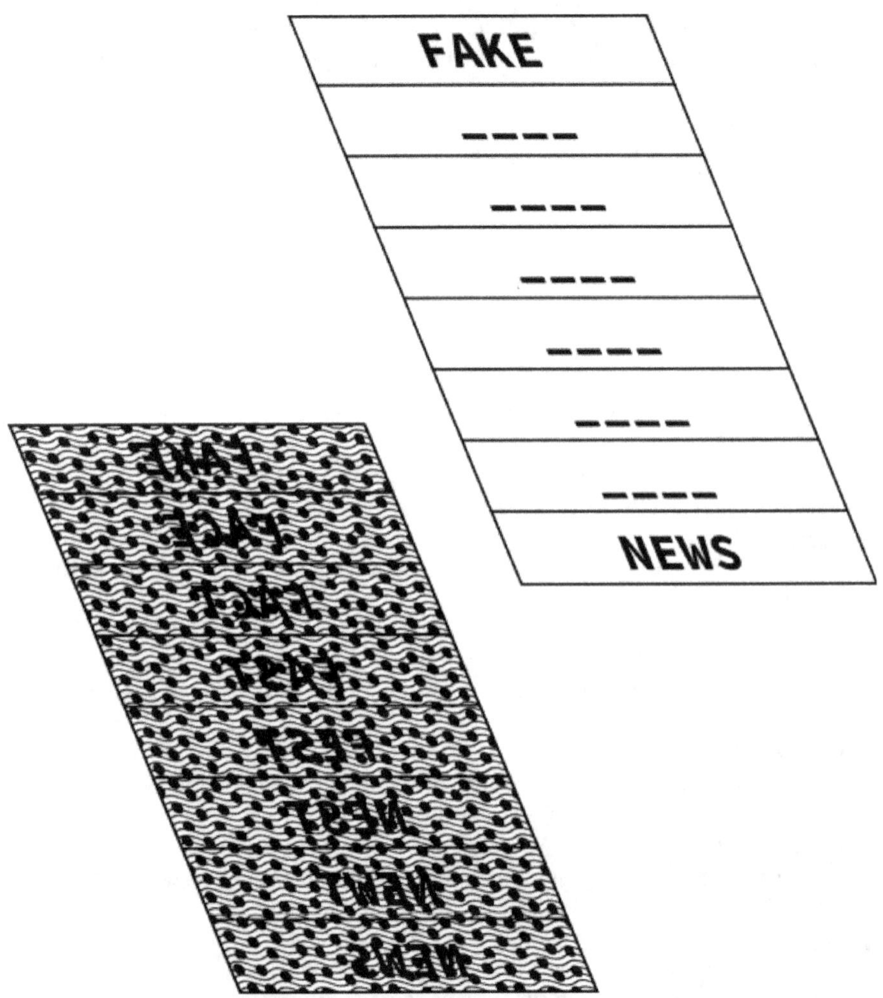

Many newspaper editors habitually deploy turn of phrase and puns when they rewrite the headlines. This can be annoying because not many can conceal the effort. Sometimes, however, the news is so strange, it reads like a pun without any editorial handiwork. As Mark Twain said, fact is stranger than fiction because fiction needs to stick to possibilities. Some of these jokes are headlines that I would have gone with.

- **Personal Ad**
  Me: Emotional therapy male donkey working at a New York state university.
  You: Female donkey with a sense of humour. Conversation piece: "Mentally
  stressed" students. Object: Make you laugh from ear to ear.

- *Donkeys deployed to deter university dolts from acting like jackasses*

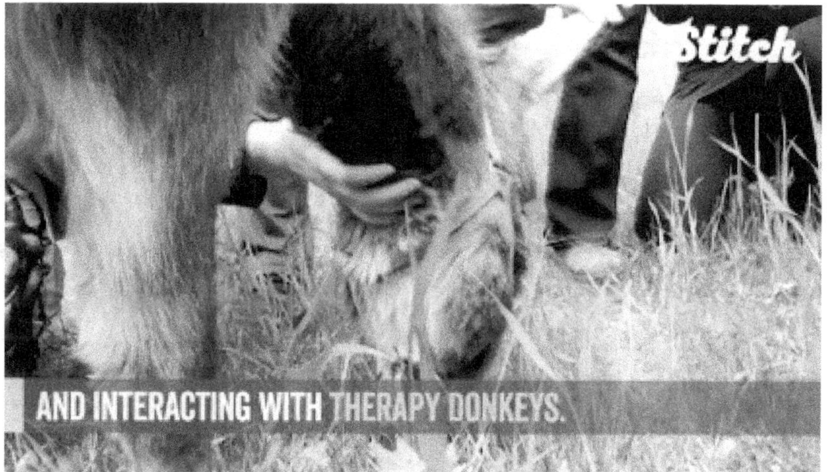

News source: The College Fix/WISN

- *Police suspect crocodile had a hand in lady's death*

News source: Drudge Report

- **Echelon Salt®™**
  During the Iraq war, there were reports about a global surveillance network
  run by the usual suspects US and UK in association with countries like Canada,

Australia and New Zealand. It snooped on emails and other communications of ordinary people and stored the data indefinitely. This surveillance infrastructure was known as the Echelon network. At that time, I had an e-mail signature generator on my website (**http://www.vsubhash.in/html-email-signature-template-generator.html**) I enhanced it with an optional feature that I called Echelon Salt®™. It added several terrorism-associated keywords to the signature in the form of a HTML comment. Ordinary users would not be able to see the keywords but an email surveillance software program that parses emails for keywords might flag it. Echelon Salt immediately won praise from the intelligence 'community'.

Mr. Hayden's statement is of particular significance. At that time, there was a lot of consternation in this alleged community because a cabal of Bush (W) administration officials deliberately avoided official intelligence reports. Instead, they substituted it with their own cherry-picked mishmash of hopscotch intelligence. This was done so they could claim that Saddam Hussein's Iraq had WMDs. The US media blindly accepted these claims and parroted them to the US public. After countless number of people killed/injured/maimed, Iraq was turned into rubble (except for the oil infrastructure (they even hit hospitals and power plants)) and trillions of dollars US taxpayers' money wasted (in military services and civil reconstruction contracts), it was all proved as 'fake news'. Today, Iraq continues to be unstable and is infested with terrorists from around the world. When politicians on all sides and the media agree on something, then something is wrong. Take it with a bit of salt.

"Thanks to Echelon Salt®™, at least someone in the government reads our reports now."

— Michael Hayden (Director, CIA) in *Central Intelligence Agency Magazine.*

- *Bearded men join the fight against phones, computer keyboards and the humble toilet seat for germ-borne crown*
  Alternate title: Bearded men continue to thwart facial recognition tech

> ## Men with beards carry more germs than DOGS with deadly bacteria ...
>
> Daily Mail - 2 days ago
>
> It's bad news for hipsters but **men** with **beards** harbour more **germs** in their whiskers than **dogs** carry in their fur, scientists say. The alarming ...

News source: Daily Mail

- **Superman and Modi**
  Modi was pictured like this at the Hornbill Festival in Nagaland.

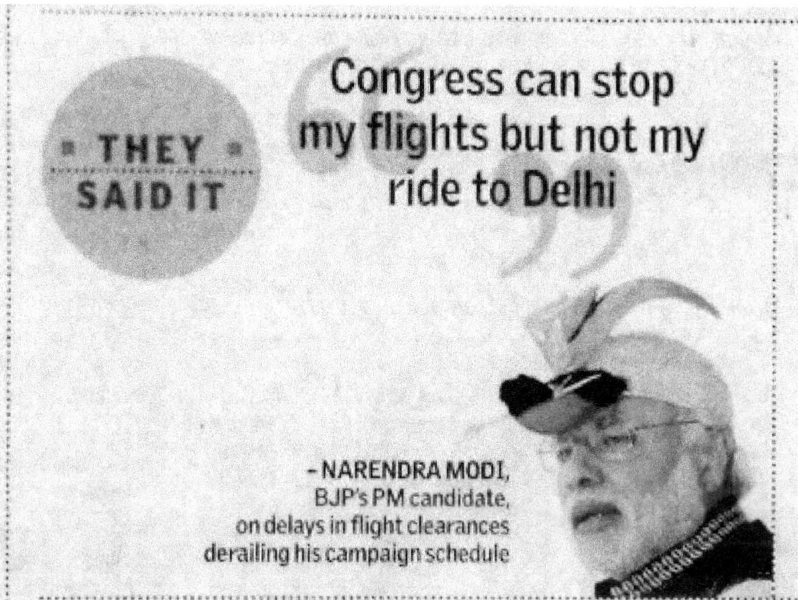

When I saw this news item, I was instantly reminded of this joke (paraphrased from memory) that I found in *Reader's Digest*.

> The famed boxing champion Mohammed Ali was travelling in a plane. When the plane was about to take off, there was an announcement instructing all passengers to wear their seatbelts. An air-hostess noticed that Ali's seatbelt was unbuckled. When reminded by the air-hostess, Ali said, "Superman does not need seatbelts." (This happened when Ali was notorious for claiming that he was the greatest and only Allah was greater than him.) The air-hostess replied, "Superman does not need an airplane either." Ali obeyed.

- *USA accuses China of developing tinfoil-hat technology*

U.S. blacklists 34 Chinese entities over human rights abu...

www.cnbc.com/2021/12/16/us-blacklists-34-chinese-entities-over-human-r

U.S. blacklists 34 Chinese entities, citing human rights abuses and
'brain-control weaponry' Published Thu, Dec 16 2021

- *Personal data predator thinks it should be legal*

Facebook's Mark Zuckerberg proposes four ways to regulate the internet
In related news, the fox has some great ideas for securing your hen house
Source: Engadget

Facebook stored hundreds of millions of user passwords in plain text for years
MarkZ skipped that course on encryption
Source: Krebs on Security

- *Saudi Arabian woman not liking government-ordered social-media detox program*

Saudi Women's Rights Activist Sentenced to 34 Years in Jail Over Twitter Usage

19 hours ago

- *Scientists take the bite out of shark attacks*

Report: Scientists Want Shark Encounters Called 'Bites' Not 'Attacks'

- *Woman gets an earful from restaurant owner*

Woman bites off part of man's ear at Macomb County Chinese restaurant

POSTED: 2:47 PM, Jun 29, 2018
UPDATED: 2 hours ago

- *Name more parasitic worms after women? Because women deserve it?*
  Alternative title: Scientist disguises sneak attack on women as anti-sexist plea

- *Peddler of artificial meat makes off with the real stuff!*

  8:06p   Beyond Meat COO accused of biting man's nose outside football game

- *Store owner caught with expired honey*

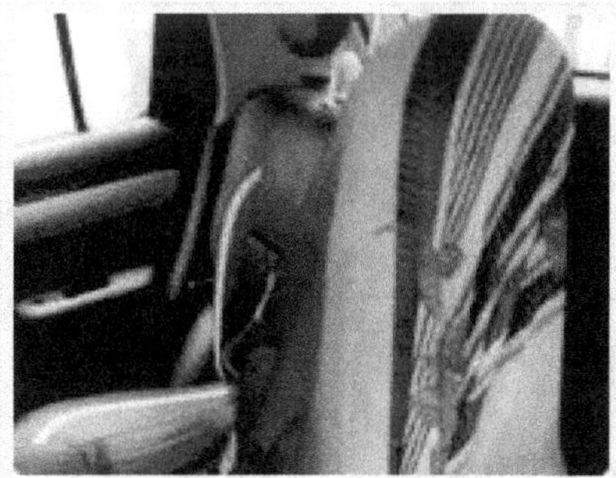

Mumbai Woman Hangs
Herself, Husband Drives
Around With Body For 8
Hours

- **What magazine do jailed convicts like to read?**
  Time

- **What magazine do death-row convicts like to read?**
  Nooseweek

- *Thousands of Americans will scream helplessly at the sky on Trump's election anniversary*

  This really happened. On the appointed day, hundreds of Trump haters assembled in several cities and vented their anger by screaming at the sky. *Trump Derangement Syndrome (TRS)* is real.

Newsweek

THOUSANDS OF AMERICANS WILL SCREAM HELPLESSLY AT THE SKY ON TRUMP'S ELECTION ANNIVERSARY

BY CHRIS RIOTTA ON 10/23/17

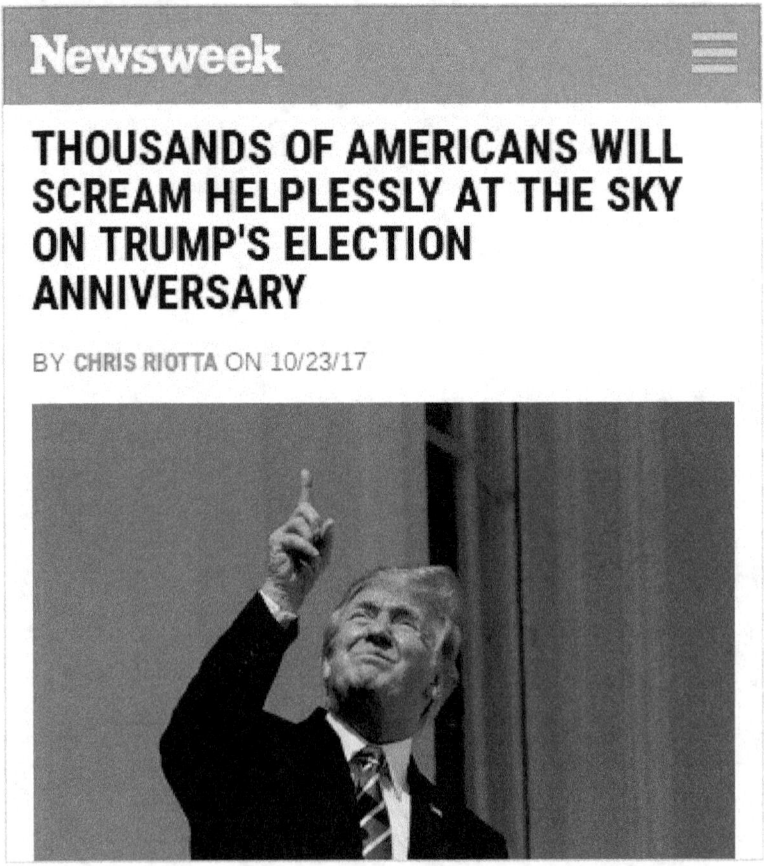

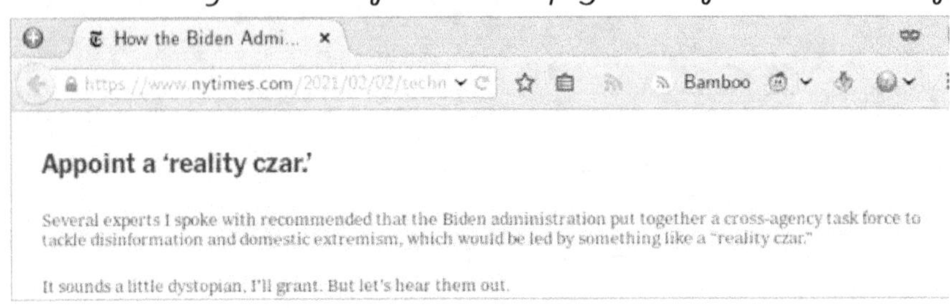

- *New York Times journo seeks government help after losing touch with reality*

How the Biden Admi...

https://www.nytimes.com/2021/02/02/techn

Bamboo

Appoint a 'reality czar.'

Several experts I spoke with recommended that the Biden administration put together a cross-agency task force to tackle disinformation and domestic extremism, which would be led by something like a "reality czar."

It sounds a little dystopian, I'll grant. But let's hear them out.

Some months after this trial-balloon article was published, the US Department of

- *US media plants a fake news story at the White House*

The US media hates US president Trump and the feeling is mutual. In the media's reality distortion field, everything that Trump did was wrong and anything that went wrong was Trump's fault. Trump is nobody's fool and he gives as good as he gets. In 2018, when Macron visited the White House, the two presidents planted a tree sapling in the White House lawn. When the sapling went missing a week later, the heartbroken US media fell on its remains like a starving gopher.

≡ **abcNEWS**

White House tree planted by Presidents Trump, Macron mysteriously vanishes

By JESSE CONVERTINO

Apr 30, 2018, 6:28 AM ET

President Donald Trump and French President Emma...more +

The sapling was a gift from the French president during last week's ballyhooed state visit.

Subsequently, the White House released CCTV footage of Ms. Hillary Clinton and an unknown accomplice, armed with shovels, at the scene of crime.

- *#BlueForSudan hashtag offends Na'vi people because it appropriates their blue identity*

- *Deplatformer-in-chief tricks blind woman into giving her a 'freedom of expression' award, sponsored by her own outfit TheyTube!*

- **What magazine do cannibals like to read?**
  Reader's Digest.

- **What magazine do vampires like to read?**
  Life and *People.*

- **What magazine do terrorists like to read?**
  Wired, Life and *People.*

- **What newspaper do ordinary Americans like to read?**
  USA Today.

- **What magazine do Native Americans like to read?**

India Today.

- **Why are blonde jokes not funny anymore?**
  AOC made them obsolete.

- **What does AOC's school yearbook say about her?**
  "Most likely to have an impact in a decade or so."

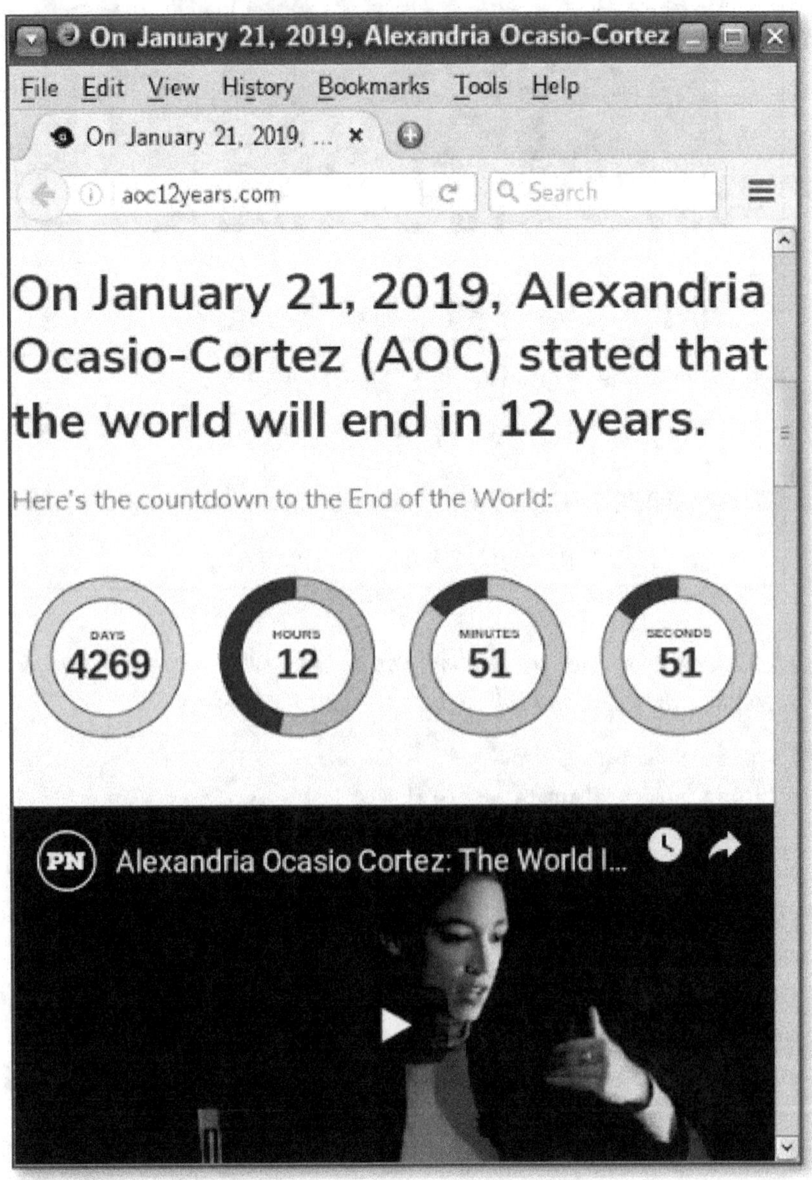

This also really happened. Ms. Alexandria Ocasio Cortes made her doomsday

- *Deer in Spain die in vain to make the Sun shine for green swine*

Inconvenient Truths: Spanish Solar Firm
Slaughters 500 Native Deer to Make Way
for Panels

News source: **StopTheseThings.com**

- *Global warming makes the oceans safe for everyone*

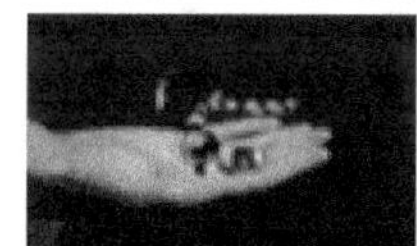

Warming oceans may cause
sharks to be born smaller,
exhausted and
undernourished

News source: The Hindu

- *British Queen sued for crimes against Obamanation*

T   The Times

Kenyan tribes take UK to European Court of Human Rights...
'colonial land grab'

Kenyan tribes have taken
the UK government to the
European Court of Human Rights over allegations of land theft, eviction and torture ...

- *Internet gets its water back after actress deletes pool pic*

Soundarya Deletes Pool Pic After
Internet Reminds Her Of Water
Crisis

- *No more world peace as FARC rebels call the bluff on beauty pageants!*

- *Poacher poached from pachyderm by big pussy*

Suspected rhino poacher is killed by an elephant and eaten by lions

- *Is this a thing now? Take your wife on a long road trip... after she has departed... for heaven?*
  Related: Store owner caught with expired honey

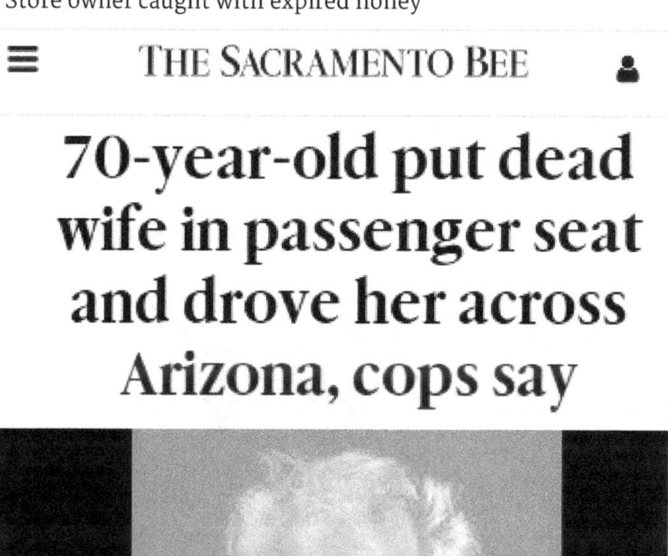

- *Man Proposes; God Disposes*
  Alternative title: Woman falls for man's proposal
  Alternative title: Woman prefers death over living with man

- *There is a God!*

Debt-Ridden Kerala Man Wins ₹1 Crore Lottery Hours Before Selling House

---

News soure: NDTV

- *Body found in sack in drain... NDTV suspects it could be MURDER!!!*

Woman's Body Found Inside Sack In Drain In Mumbai, Murder Suspected

---

The policeman in this stock photo has been involved in all the murder cases reported by NDTV. I find it SUSPICIOUS!!!

Rajinikanth Facts

Meteorite Incidence From 1988 to 2019

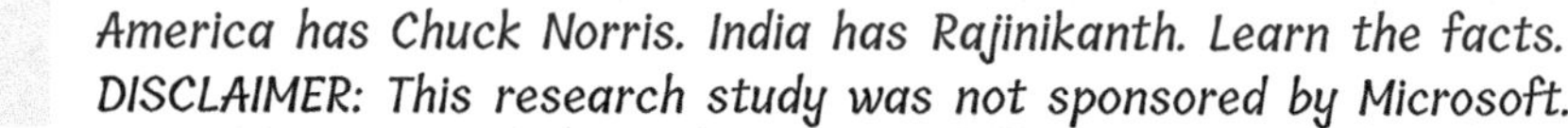

Rajinikanth lives in southern India.
Data source: NASA

America has Chuck Norris. India has Rajinikanth. Learn the facts. DISCLAIMER: This research study was not sponsored by Microsoft.

- **What would happen if you subtract infinity from infinity?**
  Indeterminate.

- **What would happen if Rajinikanth subtracts infinity from infinity?**
  Zero.

- **What would happen if a lightning struck Rajinikanth?**
  Nothing. That's how he lights his smoke.

- **Is not smoking injurious to health?**
  To your health? Of course. It is different with Rajinikanth. Rajinikanth is injurious to smoking.

- **What would happen if a meteorite tried to strike Rajinikanth?**
  It gets classified as a meteor.

- **What would happen if a cyclone tried to strike Rajinikanth?**
  It goes into a major depression.

- **What would happen if a stray asteroid struck Rajinikanth?**
  Who knows? He might let it strike a friendship with him.

- **What would happen if a stray asteroid really struck Rajinikanth with force?**
  It would get bounced back to its belt and become known in its circle as "the one that almost got away".

- **What would happen if a tsunami struck Rajinikanth?**

It will be struck with awe and freeze.

- **Has someone written Rajinikanth's biography?**
  The Limca Book of Records was mostly about him so you could consider it as one.

- **Was Rajinikanth ever reprimanded in school?**
  Yes, many times, such as when for the question, "what do you get when you divide zero by zero", he wrote the actual answer instead of 'indeterminate'.

- **How did Rajinikanth get his driving license?**
  He made the RTO chief do an 8.

- **How did Rajinikanth become the world champion in a staring contest?**
  The statue blinked.

Chuck Norris won against the Sun.

- **What would happen if Rajinikanth loses the election?**
  Rajinikanth will not be losing the election. He would be letting others win.

- **Chuck Norris knows *Victoria's Secret*. What is it?**
  Rajinikanth.

Religious Jokes

- **Divine Commandment**
  One of Mark Twain's friends visited him one day and suggested they go for a walk. When Mark Twain hesitated, the friend said, "But there is a scriptural command for you to go." Twain wondered what it was. His friend opened the Bible and pointed to a line in one of the gospels where it said:

  > And whosoever shall compel thee to go a mile, go with him twain.

  Twain obeyed.

- **Protestant Church vs Catholic Church**
  The priests in the former have other halves but those in the latter have better quarters.

I have forgotten where I read this.

- **Cosmic Audit**
  The following is from a review by Ram Swarup in *The Statesman* of *Seven Hundred Plans To Evangelize The World: The Rise of a Global Evangelization Movement* by David Barrett and James W. Reapsome.

  > The authors give us some very interesting figures. They have no use for the traditional biblical chronology, which allows man a bare 4000 years of sojourn on earth. (According to a 17th century computation, Man appeared on the earth on October 23 of BC 4004 and the apostles were already getting ready for the end of the world in their times). Our authors however take a long stride, back and forth, go back to 5.5 million years when *Homo* appeared on the scene and they traverse 4 billion years in future. Undeterred by the fact that the new perspective involves grave theological problems, they boldly audit for us the missionary activity for all this era. By the time Jesus came, 5.5 million years had already elapsed and 118 billion men and women had already lived and died, all *ipso facto* destined for hell as they did not know Christ. But new prospects opened for mankind after AD 33 when the Kingdom of Heaven was announced and inaugurated. Heaven, empty until then, began to be populated though rather unexpectedly slowly in the beginning. But by 1990, there are already 8 billion dead believers (Church Triumphant), all qualifying for habitation in the new region. They are however still only 5.68% of unbelievers destined for hell, quarters across the street. But the demographic composition continues to improve in their favour. By AD 2100, they are 8.57%, and at the end of 4 billion years, they are fully 99.90%, the Christian heaven holding 9 decillion (one decillion is ten followed by 33 zeros) believers. In AD 1,00,000, believers are still only 85% of the total living population. But by AD 4 billion, the gap practically closes and almost all are believers. The Great commission is fulfilled and missionaries are freed from their obligation to God and His Son. The population figures given here take into account men whose longevity after AD 2500 turns gradually into immortality, and new men and human species artificially created by mass cloning and genetic engineering (Missionaries of the future believing, brave new world will have a different role; they will increasingly be able to raise their own crop of

believers through genetic technology); they take into account humans increasingly living on off-earth space colonies, then across other galaxies and universes. In AD 4 billion, the "ultimate size of the Church of Jesus Christ," the authors estimate, will be "1 decillion believers," not counting 9 decillion dead by then....

- **Year 2000 and the new millennium anomaly**
  If you observe the historical timeline between BC and AD, you will notice that there is no year zero. The years on the negative side progress in descending order until 1 BC. The next year is 1 AD. If you move from 1 AD to 2000 AD, you reach the end of two millennia. In the year 2001, you begin the new millennium.

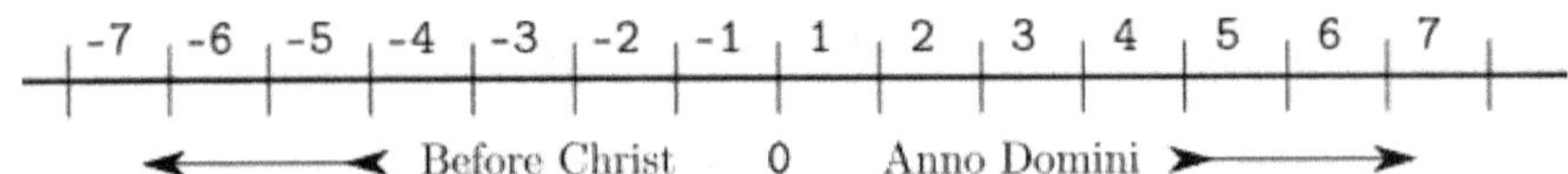

  Wait a minute! Didn't everyone celebrate the new millennium in year 2000? Yes, they did. Did they know? No, they did not. What about scientists and mathematicians of the world? Did they say anything? Most of them did not. Apparently, even in these times with great technologies and powerful computers, something so simple and so important can be missed or got wrong by almost everyone. A few people like the science fiction writer Arthur C. Clarke suggested that both years be celebrated as the end of one millennium and the beginning of another. But, nobody took notice. The new millennium came unheralded, one year late.

- **Year of the Lord**
  A Christian monk named Dionysius Exiguus used the Biblical chronology for the birth of Jesus Christ and divided the timeline with BC and AD. Year 1 was *Anno Domini* or *the year of the Lord*. So, all years before 1 AD became BC or *Befor Christ*. Unfortunately, there was a mistake in his calculations and Christ's birth really falls in 4 AD. Citing this miscalculation and for 'secular' reasons, many historians use BCE (Before Common Era) and CE (Common Era) instead of AD and BC. Calendar problems continued to persist for many centuries. According to the namboothiri.com website:

  > The exact length of the solar year is 365.2422 days. If the length of the year is rounded off as 365 ¼ days, each year the calendar will gain an extra 11 minutes and 14 seconds. This error will grow to a full day every 128 years. By Julius Caesar's time, the difference between the calendric spring solstice and the real solstice had grown to a stupendous three months! Caesar's calendar experts did not know how this error was caused or how to rectify it. Therefore, they proposed an innovation to the emperor: Scrap the old calendar and start a new one beginning with 46 BC. This is how the Julian Calendar came into being.

  According to this article, the problems with the Western calendar were most likely solved using Indian techniques. Learn more at:
  http://www.namboothiri.com/articles/calendar.htm

- **The Jealous Heart**
  A man was extremely jealous of his rival. Unable to beat him, he decided to appeal to God. He went to a forest to sit on *tapas* until God gave him a boon.

God knew the man's intentions so he was prepared when he appeared before him. God added a condition to granting the boon, "Whatever you want, I will give twice the amount to your rival." The man thought for a while and said, "I would like to go blind in one eye."

Romantic Jokes

If this book was named '2000 ways to break up with your spouse', it would not be off the mark. I hate romantic stuff and this book is targeted at kids.

- **What did one fish say to another?**
  "Don't try to get fresh with me"

- **What did one number say to another?**
  "He seems odd."

- **What did the other number reply?**
  "Yes, he seems a bit odd."
  [It was a binary number.]

- **What did one number say to another?**
  "I think she is trying to get even."

- **Why did the two sets break up?**
  They had nothing in common.

- **How did the subset and the superset break up?**
  She took away almost everything he had.

- **What do rabbits like to read?**
  Multiplication tables.

That is arithmetic progression. If only they knew about exponential progression...

- **What did one ultraviolet ray say to another?**
  "I don't think we are on the same wavelength."

- **What did one female lightning say to another?**
  "Oh, he is one down-to-earth fella."

- **What did one male lightning say to another?**
  "I can't get in a word with her because she is always accompanied by that loud

fella."

- **What did the day planner say to the calendar?**
  "Sorry, I already have a date."

- **What did Supergirl do when Superman came home late?**
  She flew into a rage.

- **What did the male kangaroo say to the female kangaroo when he came home late?**
  "Now, honey, don't jump to conclusions."

- **A horse, a donkey, and a mule walk in to a bar**
  A horse, a donkey, and a mule walk in to a bar. The donkey does not drink, saying that he has to work the next day and did not want to wake up with a hangover. The horse also refuses to drink, saying that he has an early-morning church service to attend. The mule orders three bottles of beer, saying, "Oh, very well. I am gonna drink. It's not like I have a family or anything."

- **What did one anteater say to another?**
  "Can you trust him? He always has his tongue hanging out."

- **What did one harp say to another?**
  "Why is he is so strung up?"

- **What did one female tight-rope artist say to another?**
  "You need to cut him some slack."

- **Why did the applied engineering couple break up?**
  Their relationship was good on principle but bad on execution.

- **Why did the civil engineering couple break up?**
  - There was this huge wall between them.
  - The relationship had come to a full circle and they did not want to repeat it.
  - Unresolved issues were piling up and they did not know what to do.
  - Everything came crashing down.

- **Why did the electrical engineering couple break up?**
  The spark had gone of out their relationship.

- **Why did the electronic engineering couple break up?**
  They were always short-circuiting each other.

- **Why did the mechanical engineering couple break up?**
  - They tried but everything came to a complete stop.
  - She threw a spanner in the works.

- **Why did the nanoengineering couple break up?**
  They found mistakes in the smallest of things.

- **Why did the project engineering couple break up?**
  They meant well but there were execution failures at every stage.

- **Why did the software engineering couple break up?**
  They went into an infinite loop of fighting and sulking.

- **Why did the programmer couple break up?**
  No issues.

- **Why did the systems engineering couple break up?**
  It seemed like that they had taken the only way in and if they delayed there

may not be a way out.

- **Why did the structural engineering couple break up?**
  They realized that their relationship was built on a weak foundation.

- **Why did the textile engineering couple break up?**
  They wore each other's patience down to a thread.

- **How did the 3D printing couple break up?**
  He would get all bent out-of-shape over nothing.

- **Why did the absent-minded couple break up?**
  He forgot her birthday.

- **How did she know it was her birthday?**
  Yahoo Mail wished her 'Happy Birthday' when she logged in.

- **Why did the absent-minded couple make up?**
  They forgot everything.

- **Why did the accountant couple break up?**
  Marriage cost his mental peace.

- **Why did the accountant couple make up?**
  Separation cost his bank balance.

- **Why did the actor-actress couple break up?**
  - He was tired of her daily drama and felt upstaged by her.
  - He refused to stick to the script and was always acting up.
  - They were not entertaining any questions now.

- **Why did the actuary couple break up?**
  He was not all he was cracked up to be.

- **Why did alien couple break up?**
  - He was so insincere she felt like she was talking to an alien.
  - Although they were on the same planet, it seemed like they were light years away.
  - The atmosphere was just not right.

- **Will the alien couple make up?**
  It seems like a remote possibility.

- **Why did alien couple make up?**
  There was nobody like her in the big wide universe.

- **Why did the archeologist couple break up?**
  They were again and again fighting over issues from ages past.

- **Why did the art critic couple break up?**
  They criticised each other using utterly unintelligible sentences.

- **Why did the astronaut couple break up?**
  - Their relationship had cratered.
  - Ever since she went to space, she just was not the down-to-earth girl she once was.
  - She would speak to him only through mission control.

- **Why did the astronaut couple make up?**
  - They went over the moon.
  - He promiser her the moon.
  - They went on a second honeymoon.

- o It was written in the stars.
- **Why did the atheist couple break up?**
  - o They did not believe in each other.
  - o He sickened her beyond belief.
- **How did the bartender couple break up?**
  - o What he brought home was peanuts.
  - o He could not stay away from alcohol.
- **How did the biologist couple break up?**
  - o They hated each other with every cell of their being.
  - o He thought she was like a rose when they first met but now he thinks of her more in terms of stinging nettles.
- **Why did the book critic couple break up?**
  - o She said his promises were empty words.
  - o He remained a big mystery to her.
  - o She claimed she had read him from cover to cover and there was nothing of value between them.
- **How did the book critic couple break up?**
  During the court proceedings, she threw the book at him.
- **Why did the book critic couple make up?**
  He promised to be more understanding.
- **How did the bomb-disposal squad couple break up?**
  He was totally blown away by her decision.
- **How did the botanist couple break up?**
  She felt that he was at the root of all her troubles.
- **Why did the builder couple break up?**
  - o He failed to take concrete steps to de-escalate the situation.
  - o Her allegations were without any foundation in truth.
  - o It was not a real breakup. They had a temporary falling out.
  - o He would not take any constructive criticism.
- **Why did the builder couple make up?**
  Flattery will get you places.
- **How did the bungee-jumping couple break up?**
  They were literally crushed. (The rope broke.)
- **What happened to the cannibal who fought with his wife?**
  He got roasted.
- **What did the cannibal say after eating a diabetic?** "He was such a sweet person."
- **Why did the cannibal couple break up?**
  - o Each time he made a small mistake, she chewed his head off.
  - o When food was low, she took an unhealthy liking for him.
  - o They were both consumed by visceral hatred for each other.
  - o He got seriously burned by her.
  - o He asked for her hand and she refused.
  - o She savagely attacked him when he revealed his political affiliation.
- **Why did the cannibal couple make up?**

- o He was prepared to make the sacrifice.
  - o The marriage cost him an arm and a leg but he was ready to go out on a limb for her.
- **Why did the carpenter couple break up?**
  She told him not to darken her doorway again.
- **Why did the carpenter couple make up?**
  Her door was always open for him.
- **Why did the cartoonist couple break up?**
  They had changed into caricatures of what they initially thought of each other.
- **Why did the chef couple break up?**
  - o No matter how how they sliced and diced it, it did not feel right.
  - o He catered to her every wish and whim, but it was never enough.
- **Why did the chef couple make up?**
  - o They warmed up to each other.
  - o They hashed together a compromise.
- **Why did the chauffeur couple break up?**
  - o Their relationship hit a roadblock.
  - o She drove him crazy.
  - o He put the relationship on a permanent overdrive.
  - o She got him right where he wanted.
  - o She drove him to despair.
- **Why did the chiropractor couple break up?**
  - o He cramped her style.
  - o She restricted his freedom of movement.
- **Why did the chiropractor couple make up?**
  He moved her heart with a passionate love letter.
- **How did the clean-freak couple break up?**
  - o She cleaned out everything he had.
  - o Whatever his concerns, she just brushed them off.
  - o She treated him like dirt.
- **How did the clean-freak couple make up?**
  They decided to begin with a clean slate.
- **Why did the clown couple break up?**
  - o Living with him was a big joke.
  - o He refused take her seriously.
  - o She was tired of his silly excuses.
- **Why did the clown couple make up?**
  He mimed his way back into her heart.
- **How did the CNC machine operator couple break up?**
  - o He expected her to work like a machine all day.
  - o He got cranky all the time and she broke down under the stress.
- **Why did the conspiracy theorist couple break up?**
  - o They did not believe in each other.
  - o She was suspicious by nature.
  - o She said he was being 'impossible'. He said that was 'unbelievable'.

- **Why did the conspiracy theorist couple make up?**
  They realized that their misunderstanding was a government plot all along.

- **Why did the contortionist couple break up?**
  - He was willing to bend backwards to accommodate her but she remained stiff that the relationship was permanently broken.
  - His tolerance to her antics was stretched to the limits.

- **Why did the contortionist couple make up?**
  Any reports that said they were breaking up was quite a stretch.

- **How did the coronavirus couple break up?**
  - When it came to spending money, his wallet was in a permanent lockdown.
  - They were social-distancing even before the pandemic hit.

- **How did the coronavirus couple make up?**
  They had been in love before but not with the same ~~fever~~ fervour.

- **How did the costume designer couple break up?**
  Don't worry. It was like a blessing in disguise.

- **How did the courier couple break up?**
  - He made sky-high promises but could not deliver.
  - They had it coming for them for a long time.
  - They got carried away.

- **Why did the coronovirus couple break up?**
  Social distancing.

- **How did the cricket batsman-batswoman couple break up?**
  - They hoped for a long innings but it is over now.
  - He ran out when he could.
  - He was tired of playing defence.

- **How did the cricket batsman-batswoman couple make up?**
  She was a quite catch.

- **How did the cricket bowler couple break up?**
  - She threw him out.
  - Maiden over.

- **How did the cricket bowler couple make up?**
  - He was always her fowl-weather friend.
  - They were ready for a second innings.

- **Why did the crossword hobbyist couple break up?**
  - He remained a puzzle to her.
  - He can take a hint when he was not wanted.
  - They accused each other of being very difficult.
  - He could not get it across to her that her attitude was going down.
  - She left him many hints but he would not catch a clue.
  - He was an annoying stickler for correctness.

- **Why did the crossword hobbyist couple make up?**
  They put their heads together and came up with the solution.

- **How did the crossword hobbyist couple make up?**
  They were lost for words.

- **Why did the curator couple break up?**

The initial euphoria of finding each other grew old quickly after the wedding.

- **Why did the DIY/maker couple break up?**
  They tried to fix the relationship themselves but realized that it was beyond repair.

- **Why did the DIY/maker couple make up?**
  - They could not stay aPART.
  - If you break it, you fix it. That was their policy.
  - They were really made for each other.
  - They had vowed to make it work.

- **Why did the electrician couple break up?**
  He said it was no fault of his that she blew her fuse every day. What exactly happened afterward is not known. Sparks flew all over the place.

- **Why did the electrician couple make up?**
  - It was just another phase in their relationship.
  - Her smile puts the sparkle in his day.

- **Why did the Eskimo (Inuit) couple make up?**
  - She made him take two baths every day. If he said it was freezing weather outside, it did not cut any ice with her.
  - There was no warmth in her soul.

- **Why did the exorcist couple break up?**
  - The stakes were high. She screamed at him day and night. When she smiled, he half-expected her to turn her head a full 360°.
  - He thought she was her soul mate but only later did he realize that she did not even have a soul.
  - She was like a demon-possessed and scared the bejesus out of him.
  - He could stand the cold stares and harsh words but the beatings and the lashings... no he could not... not anymore.

- **How did the fashion designer couple break up?**
  - Don't know but they always behaved in a strange fashion.
  - Wonder who wears the pants in this family?
  - Despite working for so many years, they were still living in an unfashionable part of the town.

- **Why did the fat couple break up?**
  - They were fed up with each other.
  - He has had enough of her. She is an unbearably difficult person.
  - He expected a huge weight to be lifted off his mind.

- **Why did the thin couple break up?**
  - Their love for each other was swept away by their constant quarrels.
  - Their tolerance for each other wore thin.
  - She accused him of belittling her.
  - There was not an ounce of truth in his allegations.

- **Why did the fat-thin couple break up?**
  - On all issues, they were at the opposite ends of the spectrum.
  - They were diametrically opposed to each other.
  - He went overboard and she was having none of it.
  - In all matters, her needs outweighed his.
  - She knew he will eventually come around... to her side of the argument.

- **Why did the fit couple break up?**
  - He was tired of her saying he was unfit for anything else.
  - He said the strain of living with her made it an exercise in futility.
  - They felt they were running round and round in circles and going nowhere.
  - Marrying him was a giant mistake.

- **Why did the fat couple make up?**
  - They could not bear the weight of separation any longer.
  - Fat chance they would split!
  - The breakup left a giant void in their life.
  - Sometimes, it takes a big man to admit he was wrong.
  - He came around and saw her point of the view.

- **Why did the thin couple make up?**
  - This was a serious relationship, one that could not be taken lightly.
  - Being together, they felt, carried more weight.
  - He swept her off her feet… again.

- **Why did the fit couple make up?**
  There was slim chance they could survive without each other.

- **Why did the fat-thin couple make up?**
  - Opposites continued to attract.
  - He meant the world to her.
  - There was nobody like her in the whole wide world.
  - She promised to treat him on par with herself.
  - There was a world of difference between being with her and without her.
  - He literally told her she should not be taking a high-fat diet.

- **Why did the fireman-firewoman couple break up?**
  - The fire in their relationship had died out.
  - The marriage was beyond rescue.
  - He just could not handle the pressure of being married to her.

- **Why did the fireman-firewoman couple make up?**
  When things cooled down, they realized their love for each other was still burning inside them.

- **Why did the flat-earther couple break up?**
  - This time she had gone too far.
  - She drove him to the edge and pushed him over.

- **Why did floral designer couple break up?**
  - It was a thorny relationship all along.
  - It was no bed of roses for them.
  - Whatever fascination they had for each other just withered away.

- **Why did the forensic expert couple break up?**
  They both had overwhelming evidence against each other.

- **Why did the forensic expert couple make up?**
  They both had overwhelming evidence against each other.

- **Why did the Frankenstein monster couple break up?**
  - When he came home late, she just lost her head.
  - "They start off real nice when you marry them. Then, they turn into real monsters." [Thank you, Johnny Bravo.]

- **Why did the Frankenstein monster couple make up?**
  - The sum of all parts were greater than the whole.
  - For him, there was nobody like her - a real one-of-a-kind woman.
- **Why did the gun enthusiast couple break up?**
  They gave it their best shot but missed by a mile.
- **How did the gun enthusiast couple make up?**
  - She does get triggered easily but she is loaded with money.
  - They wanted to give it another shot before going ballistic again.
- **Why did hairstylist couple break up?**
  Some serious differences cropped up.
- **How did the historian couple break up?**
  Marrying her was a monumental blunder.
- **Why did the hypnotist couple break up?**
  - He was out of his mind all the time.
  - She was always under a state of delusion... pretending like she were a queen or something.
  - He was tired of her mind games - always interfering with his thought processes.
- **Why did the hypnotist couple make up?**
  He could not get her off his mind.
- **How did the historian couple break up?**
  - They could not forget the past.
  - They would not let bygones be bygones.
- **How did the historian couple make up?**
  - History repeats itself.
  - They decided to bury the past.
- **How did the hospital clerk couple break up?**
  They both refused to admit anything was wrong with their individual selves.
- **Why did the personnel manager couple break up?**
  - Don't know but both claimed the other was not qualified to lead a normal life with anyone.
  - This is an intensely personal matter and they do not wish to talk about it.
  - She did not know he was the wrong person for her.
  - She considered being married to him as akin to 'indentured labour'.
- **Why did the personnel manager couple make up?**
  She knew what was in his résumé and there was no chance he would survive in this world alone.
- **Why did illusionist couple break up?**
  When the illusion crumbled, they were not happy with the reality that remained.
- **Why did Invisible Man and Invisible Woman break up?**
  - They saw through each other and did not like it.
  - He wouldn't accept her for who she really was.
  - When he looked at her, he looked at her flaws. Not the real HER!
- **Why did the janitor couple break up?**

- o Serious problems piled up. They could not be just brushed away.
  - o She would not touch him with a ten-foot pole.
- **Why did the janitor couple make up?**
  He swept her off her feet.
- **Why did the jailbird couple break up?**
  - o Being married to her makes a death sentence immensely more likeable.
  - o He returned to a life of crime because he knew he would be safe from her in jail.
  - o Living with her all these years was punishment enough.
  - o Being married to her was like a death sentence.
- **How did the jail warden couple break up?**
  - o He tried to escape many times but she always beat him into submission.
- **Why did the jeweller couple break up?**
  The relationship was flawed to begin with.
- **Why did the jester couple break up?**
  They were at their wits' end.
- **Why did the journalist couple break up?**
  - o He was the bearer of bad news.
  - o "No comment!"
  - o Marriage is not a democracy and freedom of speech exists only in denial.
- **Why did the judge couple break up?**
  - o Whenever she wanted to talk, he asked her if the matter was scheduled for a hearing.
  - o Whenever she wanted to talk and said it was important, he asked her to file a review petition.
  - o She held him in utter contempt.
  - o He would not abide by her rules anymore.
- **Why did the judge couple make up?**
  The matter was settled out of court.
- **How did the launderer couple break up?**
  Don't know. They didn't want to wash their dirty linen in public.
- **How did the lawyer couple break up?**
  - o They acquitted themselves with much credit.
  - o He summoned up the courage to say no.
  - o If there is a will, there is a way (out).
- **Why did the lawyer couple make up?**
  He rejected all charges without prejudice and she decided that reconciliation was the best course of action.
- **How did the lazy couple break up?**
  His lackadaisical attitude became his undoing.
- **Why did the lexicographer couple break up?**
  - o His love had lost its meaning to her.
  - o She was not careful in picking her words.
  - o It was a silly misunderstanding.
  - o He gave her a word of advice.
- **How did the lexicographer couple break up?**

They hurled the choicest epithets against each other.

- **How did the lexicographer couple make up?**
  They could not describe it. Words failed them.

- **How did the lift operator couple break up?**
  He said her upper floors were empty.

- **How did the lift operator couple make up?**
  They did not want to escalate the situation.

- **Why did the librarian couple break up?**
  o Their marriage was long past its due date.
  o Don't know. They are a reserved couple.

- **Why did the librarian couple make up?**
  New arrivals.

- **Why did the locksmith couple break up?**
  They were picking on each other like no tomorrow.

- **Why did the locksmith couple make up?**
  They both realized that their key to happiness was with the other.

- **Why did the lyricist couple break up?**
  They were tired of singing the same old song, accusing each other of causing all kind of ills.

- **How did the magician couple break up?**
  o The magic had gone out of the relationship.
  o He had had enough of her cruel tricks.
  o She said living with him was like being skewered by a dozen swords.
  o She said living with him was like being sawed in half and torn apart.
  o All happiness had vanished.
  o Life with him was no bed of roses. In fact, it included a bed of nails!
  o The money he brought home just disappeared into thin air.

- **Why did the makeup artist couple break up?**
  They saw each other's true colours.

- **Why did the makeup artist couple make up?**
  o They decided to accept each other as they were.
  o He promised her he will make it up to her.
  o To save face.

- **Why did the mascot couple break up?**
  o The cheer had run out of their life.
  o He would not accept her for who she really was.
  o Who could have guessed? For all outward appearances, they seemed to be happy.

- **Why did the mascot couple make up?**
  o He promised to pay more attention to the 'real HER'.
  o Behind all that fluffy exterior, there was a real person hiding inside.
  o They could not hide their sadness behind a mask.

- **Why did the mayor couple break up?**
  This town was not big enough for the two of them.

- **Why did the military couple break up?**

There was not a kernel of truth in her allegations.

- **Why did the military couple make up?**
  All is fair in love and war.

- **Why did the mime couple break up?**
  They could not carry on the charade any longer.

- **Why did the mime couple make up?**
  Everything indicated to them that they would be miserable apart.

- **Why did the minimalistic couple break up?**
  - Whatever excuses he gave, she was having none of it.
  - He did not mean much to her anymore.
  - He gave her his 100% but it still was nothing.
  - He was economical with truth.

- **Why did the minimalistic couple make up?**
  - Something is better than nothing.
  - She said he was good for nothing.
  - There is more to a marriage than a man and a woman living together. There was also this other thing called love.
  - She was worked up over nothing.

- **Why did the mine-clearing machine operator couple break up?**
  - She would explode like a shell every time he made a small mistake.
  - He always had to tip-toe around her.

- **Why did the money-laundering couple break up?**
  She does not want his dirty money anymore. She has her own *hawala* channel now.

- **Why did the motorcyclist couple break up?** He was cruising for a bruising.

- **Why did the neurologist couple break up**
  - He gathered the nerve to do it.
  - They were getting on each other's nerves way too often.
  - He was always a bundle of nerves when she was around.
  - The marriage had turned him into a nervous wreck.
  - He had no feelings for her anymore.

- **Why did the neurologist couple make up**
  He did not have the nerve to say 'no' to her.

- **Why did the newscaster couple break up?**
  They had nothing but bad news for each other from the beginning.

- **Why did the nurse couple break up**
  - She left him in stitches.
  - She left him in splits.
  - She lost her patience.
  - There was a limit to his patience.

- **Why did the nurse couple make up**
  He was exactly the medicine she was prescribed.

- **Why did the outdoor explorer couple break up?**
  - They both wanted a way out of their current existence.
  - She told him to get lost.

- **Why did the outdoor explorer couple make up?**
  Nothing in this world could separate them.

- **How did the optician couple break up?**
  - She was sharply focussed on her career and he became just a blur.
  - He had serious flaws. That much was very clear.

- **How did the optician couple make up?**
  He was a sight for sore eyes.

- **How did the optimist couple break up?**
  He said he felt very positive that they were better off apart.

- **Why did the pessimist couple break up?**
  He said he always knew the relationship was doomed from the beginning.

- **Why did the painter couple break up?**
  [Go for it!...] The colour had gone out of their relationship.

- **Why did the panhandler couple break up?**
  - He begged to differ.
  - What he brought home was chump change.
  - With the money he brought in, you could not make a phone call.
  - He was literally begging for it.

- **Why did the parliamentarian couple break up?**
  - She used unparliamentary language.
  - He could never get to be the speaker.
  - If he came late, question hour could drag on for several hours.
  - She had no confidence in him.
  - Every day, she would unload a litany of complaints about him and before he could reply to any of that, she would say, 'End of discussion!' and adjourn.

- **Why did the party planner couple break up?**
  It was not all fun and games that she hoped for.

- **Why did the pest exterminator couple break up?**
  There were just too many problems bugging their marriage.

- **Why did the pharmacist couple break up?**
  They both thought they got the wrong prescription for happiness.

- **Why did the philatelist couple break up?**
  Every day, he would try to stamp his authority while she painfully recollected her enormous contribution to the marriage.

- **Why did the photojournalist couple break up?**
  They just failed to click.

- **Why did the photographer couple break up?**
  They didn't like the sight of each other.

- **Why did the pilot couple break up?**
  - He did not maintain the right attitude.
  - She called him the flying doofus.
  - No matter what accusation she threw at him, he always had an ace up his sleeve.

- **How did the pilot couple break up?**
  - It was like a train wreck.

- o It went down like a dive bomber and had a rough landing.
  - o When they yelled at each other, all you could hear was static.
  - o He praised her sky high. It was not enough for her.
- **How did the pilot couple make up?**
  He took off the moment he had a chance to but she forced him to land.
- **Why did the postal worker couple break up?**
  - o He said she was bad news and she said he was a certified mental case.
  - o She was like an overweight package with insufficient postage.
  - o His brain seems to have been put in a package and returned to sender.
  - o She tried to stamp her authority and refused to address his concerns.
  - o He had a hate-hate relationship with her dogs.
  - o He was nothing to write home about.
- **Why did the postal worker couple make up?**
  - o He sent her a message that melted her heart and she sealed the deal.
  - o The decision was taken in a rush and they got carried away.
- **Why did the police couple break up?**
  - o Living with her was like institutional torture.
  - o She beat him with his *lathi* when he (out of habit) demanded a bribe to do household chores.
  - o When he came home late, she just lost it.
- **Why did the police couple make up?**
  He stole her heart... again.
- **Why did the physicist couple break up?**
  Things had reached a boiling point in their relationship.
- **Why did the physicist couple make up?**
  She melted on seeing drops of condensation in his eyes.
- **Why did the plumber couple break up?**
  - o Suddenly, everything took a turn for worse.
  - o For years, it was leaking but one day it turned into a flood.
  - o Living with her left him emotionally drained.
- **Why did the plumber couple make up?**
  If she was resin, he was like bonding material.
- **Why did the printer couple break up?**
  - o He did not like to stay on the margins while she took up all the space.
  - o She left him in the gutter to bleed.
  - o He did not want to be bound by her rules.
  - o They fell out of line with each other.
- **Why did the printer couple make up?**
  - o There is no need to get wrapped up over nothing.
  - o They did not want to put themselves in a bind over nothing.
- **Why did the professor couple break up?**
  He was tired of listening to her lecture every day.
- **Why did the programmer couple break up?**
  They needed a break from each other. (Maybe Rachel was a programmer at heart.)
- **How did the programmer couple break up?**

They are still processing what happened.

- **Why did the publisher couple break up?**
  - They were not on the same page on many things.
  - That chapter of their life is over.
- **Why did the psychiatrist couple break up?**
  - Attention deficit disorder.
  - Hyperactivity disorder.
  - Foot-in-the-mouth disorder.
  - Oppositional defiant disorder. [This medical term was probably coined by a three-year-old child. It refers to opposition to 'authority figures'.]
  - She gave him a piece of her mind.
- **Why did the psychiatrist couple make up?**
  - They went nuts.
  - They were still crazy for each other.
  - They could not stay mad at each other for too long.
- **Why did the psychopath couple break up?**
  They tore each other to shreds… emotionally.
- **Why did the pyromaniac couple break up?**
  - Their love for each other had stopped burning.
  - She gave him a serious burnout.
- **Why did the quiz couple break up?**
  - When asked why he was late, he never gave the correct answer.
  - Even when food was low, he always asked for a bonus round.
  - Their time was up.
  - He said something was seriously wrong with her and she said he could not be more wrong.
  - She would not give him a second chance.
  - He left her with no choice.
- **Why did the quiz couple make up?**
  - They really liked their consolation prizes and wanted a do-over.
  - They did not want to take any chances.
- **Why did the religious fanatic couple break up?**
  They were fundamentally opposed to each other.
- **Why did the religious fanatic couple make up?**
  They were still fanatically in love with each other.
- **Why did the liberal couple break up?** She felt that there was something fundamentally wrong with him.
- **Why did the rock climber couple break up?**
  - She was condescending towards him.
  - She told him to take a hike.
- **Why did the rocket scientist couple break up?**
  He may be a rocket scientist but he was a stupid ordinary man when it comes to 'understanding' her.
- **Why did the sailor couple break up?**
  The relationship was off to a rocky start and it was not long before it sunk without a trace.

- **Why did the sales executive couple break up?**
    - He felt compelled to tell her the truth.
    - She waged a campaign of attrition against him.
    - He threatened to give a free demonstration and she booted him out of the door.
    - He was not what she had bargained for.
- **Why did the screaming banshee couple break up?**
    - Every day, they screamed at each other at the top of their voices.
    - This marriage had nothing but tears for both of them.
    - He did not expect that this marriage would end in tears.
    - There was no point in crying about it now.
- **Why did the screenwriter couple break up?**
    - They lost the plot of why they liked each other.
    - They would speak to each other only if it was integral to the plot.
- **Why did the film director couple break up?**
  She gave him the silent treatment.
- **Why did the film director couple make up?**
  They decided see the big picture.
- **Why did the set decorator couple break up?**
  Everything was in the wrong place in that marriage.
- **Why did the stand-up comic couple break up?**
    - His jokes were mostly about her and she failed to see the humour in them.
    - He could not take her insults sitting down.
    - They could not stand each other.
- **Why did the stock analyst couple break up?**
    - They did not speak to each other even after trading hours.
    - They said it was a wild rumour and did not want to comment on speculation.
    - He tried to rally support but could not withstand her persistent hammering.
    - The fundamentals did not support them.
- **Why did the stunt coordinator couple break up?**
  They were tired of each other's stunts and were constantly thinking of new ways to fight.
- **Why did the soap writer couple break up?**
  Their feud had reached epic proportions.
- **Why did the sculptor couple break up?**
    - They had been chipping away at each other's patience for too long.
    - She felt objectified.
- **Why did the sculptor couple make up?**
  It is not written in stone that they should split up.
- **Why did the serial killer couple break up?**
    - Their love for each other was seriously out of order.
    - He was not all that he was cracked up to be.
    - She made him think of killing himself.
- **How did the snow-clearing machine operator couple break up?**

Too many problems piled up in their marriage and this was the only way out.

- **Why did the speech therapist couple break up?**
  - She just would not shut up.
  - Whenever he wanted to speak, she shushed him into silence.
  - He was so terrified that whatever he wanted to say just died in his throat when he looked at her.
  - He wanted to end the many years of suffering in silence.

- **Why did the speech therapist couple make up?**
  They decided to talk things over.

- **How did the speech therapist couple make up?**
  They were speechless.

- **Why did the spelling bee couple break up?**
  They both wanted to have the last word on everything.

- **Why did the spokesperson couple break up?**
  - Whenever he raised his hand to say something, she would say, "Don't be rude!", "Wrong!", or "You are fake news!"
  - She told him to speak only when spoken to.

- **Why did the surfer couple break up?**
  He went overboard and she decided he had jumped the shark long ago.

- **Why did the tailor couple break up?**
  She asked him if she looked fat in that dress.

Attention all husbands: This question has only one right answer. It is a time for compliments. It is a test of attitude rather than aptitude. You are not the only one with the critical eye. But, if you are like the battered husband Wallace Wimple of *Fibber & Molly* show (read **Annexure 1**..), shoot one of the following and scoot.

  - "If you turn sideways, you enter another dimension."
  - "The mirror does add 200 pounds."
  - "No, you look thin. It's the dress that looks fat."
  - "Did you borrow it from a sumo wrestler?"
  - "What are you hiding in that dress? An elephant?"
  - "The Air Force called. They want their blimp back."
  - "I read in the paper that somebody stole the clothes off the *Statue of Liberty* in New York. Now, I know what really happened."

- **Why did the tailor couple make up?**
  - They were tailor-made for each other.
  - Modesty was his strongest suit.

- **Why did the terrorist couple break up?**
  - He came home late and she just exploded.
  - Break? He totally blew it out of the sky.
  - She welcomed him with open arms.
  - They had quite a blast.

- **Why did the tight-rope walker couple break up?**
  - He had really gone out of bounds this time.
  - She dumped him because her faith in him was shaken.
  - She could not be swayed by his honeyed words.
  - She thought she was in good hands but he let her down.

- o Famous last words: "You know what your problem is? You need to loosen up a little."
  - o She was nagging him and he said, "Will you cut it out?"
- **Why did the tight-rope walker couple make up?**
  - o The bonds between them just would not break.
  - o He promised to do better managing his life-work balance and she was inclined to believe him.
  - o It was time to take the plunge again.
- **Why did the time-travelling couple break up?**
  - o They were brought back to reality.
  - o They saw no future in their marriage.
- **Why did the time-travelling couple make up?**
  They decided to let bygones be bygones.
- **Why did the ticket seller couple break up?**
  - o They had serious reservations about each other.
  - o Their relationship was going nowhere.
- **Why did the traffic cop couple break up?**
  - o She would stop at nothing.
  - o They drove each other to the extreme.
- **Why did the train driver couple break up?**
  - o She would go off the rails every time he asked for the remote.
  - o He would huff and puff like a steam engine if she asked when food will be ready.
  - o If she started talking, she would go on like an express train.
- **Why did the train driver couple make up?**
  At this junction, they decided to go by each others' wishes for all future decisions.

The correct word is juncture.

- **Why did the trapeze artist couple break up?**
  They had reached the end of the rope in their relationship.
- **Why did the truck driver couple break up?**
  She was always taking him for granted.
- **Why did the truck driver couple make up?**
  They were in it for the long haul.
- **Why did the undertaker couple break up?**
  - o It killed them to be together.
  - o He was always buried in work.
- **Why did the undertaker couple make up?**
  They decided to bury the hatchet.
- **Why did the vampire couple break up?**
  - o He became a real pain in the neck and she began baying for his blood.
  - o He could not put food on the table.
  - o His table manners were atrocious.
  - o When she said he sucked the life blood out of her, he just smiled.
  - o It was beyond the pale of expression.

- He was not much of a talker. (Dead men tell no tales.)
- He did not know when to quit.
- He could not give a satisfactory explanation as to where he was going at midnight or what he was doing at that time.
- After feasting on an anæmic victim, he put the bite on her.
- She threatened to knock his teeth out and use it as a paper-punching machine.
- He left a bad taste in her mouth.
- Living with her was a constant nightmare for him.
- Sometimes, she scared the living daylights out of him.
- She was always in a comBATive mood.
- She gave him high blood pressure and he gave her low blood pressure.
- He was a shadow of his former self.
- It was clear as day to her that he was emotionally a dead man.
- Her batty disposition was a sad reflection on her part.
- Just after she got her hair a nice perm, he frightened her and straightened it all out.
- They were facing an existential crisis but he was more interested in rolling out impressive party tricks.
- He told her she was getting long in the tooth and she said, "Take a look in the mirror!"
- He took an eternity to take decisions.
- He always said he was buried in work.
- This relationship was past its expiry date.
- She would pretend to be catatonic if he asked her to help with housework.
- He did not want to be caught dead with her.
- She punctured his ego.
- He left her emotionally drained.

- **Why did the vampire couple make up?**
  - Love was at stake.
  - He was very good at flying to the ceiling and cleaning those hard-to-reach places. Very useful when you live in a castle.
  - He was low maintenance and always… always appreciated her 'good' looks.
  - She was a hæmophiliac and seeing him always made her blood freeze… clot immediately.
  - He was good at disposing door-to-door salesman and tax collectors.
  - He was very good at removing bottle caps and opening tinned food.
  - He does not hog the remote during the day.
  - He was a good listener. There is something to be said for men who do not talk back.
  - His smile always excited her.
  - He said he will always be there for her.
  - They did not want their past cast a shadow on their future.
  - Before he realized he was neck-deep in trouble, she made a sucker out of him.
  - Their love lasted hundreds of years yet they felt like it had just begun.
  - Dental insurance is cheaper under the family plan.
  - It was too early to write the epitaph on this relationship.
  - He promised to be very much alive to her discomforts.
  - There was not a shadow of doubt that he loved her with all his heart.
  - This time they were dead-serious.

- **Why did the werewolf couple break up?**
  - What he brought home was just dog food!
  - When she got angry, she would turn into an animal!
- **Why did the Sasquatch couple break up?**
  She was getting too close for comfort.
- **Why did the Sasquatch couple make up?**
  Contrary to urban legend, he is not as reclusive as he is believed to be. She caught him when he sneaked in to pick up the morning newspaper.
- **Why did the vandal couple break up?**
  - The writing was on the wall but they did not see it.
  - He broke every promise he made to her.
  - She gave him a piece of her mind.
  - He brought nothing to the marriage that would set the house on fire.
- **Why did the vandal couple make up?**
  - He does not handle breakups very well.
  - Life without her just broke him.
  - They were too broke to live separately.
  - With the economy in shambles, they needed to stick together.
- **Why did the wall-of-death car couple break up?**
  He felt like his life was going around in an endless circle with her tailgating him every time he slowed down.

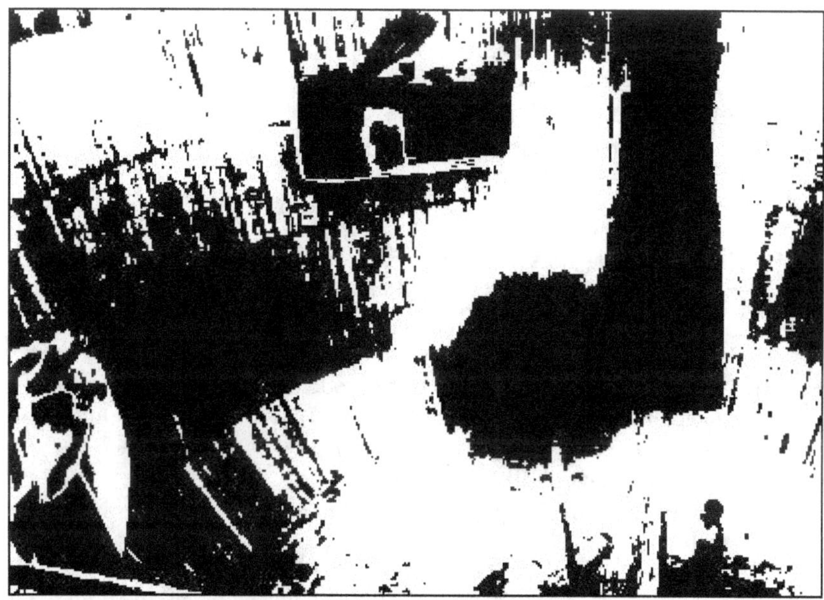

- **Why did the wardrobe supervisor couple break up?**
  She covered up for his mistakes for a long time and finally said, "I am getting out!"
- **Why did the weatherperson couple break up?**
  They cast a shadow on each other and this clouded their relationship.
- **Why did the weatherperson couple break up?**

She claimed he was trying to rain on her parade every time the Sun shined on her.

- **How did the weatherperson couple break up?**
  Don't worry. It was like a blessing in the skies.

- **Why did the weatherperson couple make up?**
  They did not want minor disasters cloud their relationship.

- **Why did the window-cleaner couple break up?**
  Every day, he would hyperventilate over nothing and one day she threw him out of the door.

- **Why did the writer couple break up?**
  There was this unwritten rule she thought he would not cross but he did.

- **Why did the writer couple make up?**
  It is a closed chapter now.

- **How did the Zamboni operator couple break up?**
  They hit a rough patch and wanted a smooth way out.

- **How did the zombie couple break up?**
  - Their marriage literally disintegrated.
  - He could not relax even when her back was turned. One of her eyes out of place... it was hanging behind her head.
  - He said "Your cadaver days are over!" and she said "I will dance on your grave."
  - The marriage was D.O.A. (dead on arrival).
  - He was a dirty rotten scoundrel!
  - He was intellectually challenged.

- **Why did the zombie couple make up?**
  - They decided to put past issues in cold storage.
  - The taxman was after them.
  - ...in sickness and death...
  - She made him turn in his grave.
  - Buried deep in her was an aching heart.
  - Their love for each other got reanimated.

- **Why did the zoologist couple break up?**
  - They were tired of playing cat-and-mouse.
  - He felt like she was not giving him the courtesy due to a laboratory animal.
  - When she questioned why he came home late, he made fun of her 'wild imagination'.

- **Why did the teacher couple break up?**
  - She wanted him to be quiet and raise his hand if he wanted to say something.
  - She made him stand up on the bench if he did anything wrong.
  - She would not let him inside the house when he came late without a note from his father.
  - She blamed her but he felt he was the wronged person.
  - She wanted to teach him a lesson.

- **Why did the English teacher couple break up?**
  - They were not speaking the language of love anymore.
  - When asked to merely pick true or false, she would give a 100-word essay.

- o She would not take 'No' for an answer. She wants an explanation in 100 words or more.

- **Why did the English teacher couple make up?**
  - o He cast a spell on her.
  - o She forgave him after he wrote a 1000-word essay, to her satisfaction, on how much she meant to him.

- **How did the maths teacher couple break up?**
  - o They had irreconcilable differences.
  - o They did not know the answers to many of their problems.
  - o She could not count on him for anything good.

- **Why did the physics teacher couple break up?**
  There was no chemistry between them.

- **Why did the chemistry teacher couple break up?**
  - o It was an overreaction.
  - o Their feud reached a boiling point.

- **Why did the biology teacher couple break up?**
  They magnified each other's faults under a microscope.

- **How did the history teacher couple break up?**
  They wanted to forget the past.

- **How did the geography teacher couple break up?**
  They were poles apart.

- **Why did the kindergarten teacher couple break up?**
  She got angry for no rhyme or reason.

- **Why did the sports teacher couple break up?**
  - o They decided to quit playing games and called it a day.
  - o When it came to playing by the rules, she was a game changer.

- **Control Freak**
  After being trapped by Scotland Yard, Invisible Man was arrested and sentenced. He was then jailed in a mental health facility for 18 years. After completing his term, Invisible Man was released. When he arrived home, his wife opened the door and said, "You've changed. I can barely recognize you."

- **Why did the Stone Age couple break up?**
  When asked to do the dishes, he intentionally broke his mother-in-law's favourite china.

- **Why did the Stone Age couple make up?**
  She said a man like him ought to live in a cave.

- **What do feminists like to read?**
  Obituaries of men.

- **What do battered men like to read?**
  Obituaries of women.

- **What has low life expectancy, poor hygiene, deficient vision, inadequate sense of direction, risk of going bald and high self-esteem?**
  Men.

- **What has high life expectancy, better hygiene, superior vision, adequate sense of direction, zero risk of going bald and low self-esteem?**

Women.

- **What does it mean when Count Dracula sleeps in a cupboard?**
  He has been divorced and his wife got everything (including the famous castle and the luxury coffin).

- **What does it mean when Superman travels in a plane?**
  He has been divorced and his wife got everything (including his super powers).

- **Why does Batman speak in hushed tones?**
  He is deathly afraid of his wife Batwoman, who might echo-locate him.

- **What does it mean when Batman rides the train to work?**
  He has been divorced and his wife got everything (including his Batmobile).

- **Does Invisible Man still have his super power?**
  He has not been divorced or anything and he still has his super power. But, he remains invisible just to avoid meeting his wife.

- **Why does Phantom have no super powers?**
  Even before the series began, Phantom was divorced and his wife got everything. That's why he lives in a jungle and wears a mask just to stay out of her way.

- **Why doesn't Julie, the female Phantom, have no super powers?**
  The divorce lawyer of Phantom's wife met Julie's husband. Now, both Phantoms, brother and sister, live in the jungle without any super powers.

- **Does He-Man still have his super powers?**
  In the absence of serious romantic development of Teela, her lawyers have not

been able to lay claim to He-Man's super powers and other assets. He-Man's sister She-Ra is also safe... for now.

- **How matriarchy exploited men – a likely story!**
In pre-historic times, early man and woman were equals. Or, nobody gave it a thought. Because of superior physical strength, men became hunters. And, women became gatherers. But, they both had to work all day to fend for themselves and their families. One day, a woman discovered that food cooked on fire tasted better. She taught other women how to use fire for cooking food and for heating the dwelling place. The stupid men were afraid of the fire. They liked the food and the warmth of the fire but did not want to deal with fire directly. So, the women decided to take advantage of the situation. They offered to stay at home and mind the fire and do household chores while the menfolk went out and brought the food. Thus, for thousands of years, the matriarchy exploited men. Women would do the cooking, clean the house and mind the children. This left them with a lot of free time to while away. Their lot was better than that of men because the latter had to till the ground, raise the animals, build roads, transport goods, pay taxes, fight wars, etc. With industrialization and urbanization, possession of money (rather than manual labour) mattered more. Many men's jobs had became sedentary. They worked in air-conditioned offices and enjoyed many perks, instead of having to toil on the factory floor or dig dirt in a coal mine. Men were now having a good time while women thought they were slaving over a hot stove all day. Women became jealous and wanted to leave the kitchen. And, many of them did. Of course, they were paid a lot less and had to make more sacrifices than men. They still considered themselves liberated -- from the kitchen, that is.

- **What kind of films do men hate to see?**
Watch-and-cry.

- **What kind of films do women hate to see?**
Watch-and-cry.

- **What computer game do women like to play?**
Crysis.

- **What computer game do men like to play?**
Far Cry.

- **What computer game do SJWs like to play?**
Devil May Cry.

- **What computer game do unmarried Feminist women like to play?**
Need For Speed: Hot Pursuit.

- **What computer game do married Feminist women like to play?**
Unreal Tournament and Mortal Kombat.

- **What computer game do separated Feminist women (filing for divorce) like to play?**
Assassin's Creed.

- **What computer game do divorced Feminist women like to play?**
Doom.

- **Marry Nay Oblige**

I found this in a yearbook.

Billet–Doux

Darling,

Most worthy of your estimation after a long consideration and much meditation, I have a strong inclination to become your relation. As for my education and qualification it is not exaggeration or fabrication that I have passed matriculation with very little preparation. What do you say to the solemnisation of our marriage celebration according to the regulations, to the glorification of the modern civilization. On your approbation of this application I shall make preparation to improve my situation and if such obligation is worthy of commiseration it will be the augmentation of joy and exaltation of our joint dissimulation.

Thanking you in anticipation.

I remain,
A victim of your fascination.

Reply

Dear Mr. Victim,

Congratulations for your lengthy narration, of course, with full affection aimed at an application for a combination, which on examination I find it a fine presentation of your affirmation. But your inclination to become my relation should embrace more so that you may reach a high position. You have passed the matriculation with little preparation. What about my graduation after a long botheration. So, improve your situation in education and make an application by acquisition of post graduation, the minimum qualification for consideration of marriage celebration. After your education attend the convocation and before taking your photo undergo beautification. Further strict observation of the following condition is the regulation for the determination of our relation: consultation with my parents before approaching for any correction, communication of the confirmation that you are not a victim of any other fascination.

In anticipation of solid action instead of continuation of paper conversation.

I remain,
Unaffected by your attraction.

Wit and Wisdom

- **Ambrose Bierce**
  - ALLIANCE, n. In international politics, the union of two thieves who have their hands so deeply inserted in each other's pockets that they cannot separately plunder a third.
  - BRIDE, n. A woman with a fine prospect of happiness behind her.
  - CLAIRVOYANT, n. A person, commonly a woman, who has the power of seeing that which is invisible to her patron, namely, that he is a blockhead.
  - FEMALE, n. One of the opposing, or unfair, sex.
  - GUILLOTINE, n. A machine which makes a Frenchman shrug his shoulders with good reason.
  - HAPPINESS, n. An agreeable sensation arising from contemplating the misery of another.
  - IGNORAMUS, n. A person unacquainted with certain kinds of knowledge familiar to yourself, and having certain other kinds that you know nothing about.

From his *Devil's Dictionary* (available as a free e-book at **www.vsubhash.in**)

- **Charles Summer**
  War crushes, with bloody heel, all justice, all happiness, all that is God-like in Man.

- **Donald Rumsfeld**, Secretary of Defense under George W. Bush.

- o I am shocked ...sort of.
- o It's like, you know, stirring for troubled waters.
- o We do have a saying in America: if you're in a hole, stop digging... I'm not sure I should have said that.
- o We do know of certain knowledge that he [OSAMA BIN LADEN] is either in Afghanistan, or in some other country, or dead.
- o I believe what I said yesterday ... I don't know what I said... but I know what I think, and ... well, I assume it's what I said.
- o The message is that there are known knowns – there are things that we know that we know. There are known unknowns – that is to say, there are things that we now know we don't know. But there are also unknown unknowns – there are things we do not know we don't know. And each year we discover a few more of those unknown unknowns.

- **Donald J Trump**
  Remember, there's no such thing as an unrealistic goal – just unrealistic timeframes.

- **Dwight D. Eisenhower**
  I hate war as only a soldier who has lived it can, only as one who has seen its brutality, its futility and its stupidity.

- **E. M. Forster**
  Two cheers for democracy. One because it admits variety and two because it permits criticism.

- **Gabriel Laub**
  The most beautiful women are the ones who like us.

- **George W. Bush**
  - More and more of our imports come from overseas.
  - Fool me once, shame on... shame on you. If you fool me, you can't get fooled again.
  - Rarely is the question asked: IS our children learning?
  - We ought to make the pie HIGHER.
  - If you're sick and tired of the politics of cynicism and polls and PRINCIPLES, come and join this campaign.
  - The fact that he relies ON FACTS ... says things that are not factual ... are going to undermine his campaign.
  - I know how hard it is for you to put food ON your family.
  - I know the human being and fish can coexist peacefully.
  - The war on terror involves Saddam Hussein because of the nature of Saddam Hussein, the history of Saddam Hussein, and his willingness to TERRORIZE HIMSELF.

- **Henrik Ibsen**
  The strongest man upon earth is he who stands most alone.

- **Hillary Clinton**
  Our ... market economy... knows the price of everything but the value of nothing.

- **Oscar Wilde**
  A cynic is a man who knows the price of everything but the value of nothing.

- **Karl Marx**
  The theory of Communism may be summed up in one sentence: Abolish all private property.

- **Kurt Tucholsky**
  The advantage of being clever is that it is easy to play the fool. The opposite is much more difficult.

- **Margaret Thatcher**
  The problem with Socialism is that you eventually run out of other people's money.

- **Mark Twain**
  - Adam was but human – this explains it all. He did not want the apple for the apple's sake, he wanted it only because it was forbidden. The mistake was in not forbidding the serpent; then he would have eaten the serpent.
  - A friend is someone who supports you when you are in the wrong. Just anyone will support you when you are in the right.
  - If you always tell the truth you don't have to remember anything.
  - All you need in this life is ignorance and confidence, and then success is sure.
    [Makes you jealous of their success, does it not?]

- **Navjot Singh Sidhu**
  Early in his career as a cricket commentator, former cricketer Navjot Sidhu was famous for his *Sidhuisms*. Here are some:
  - Even a dog can take on a crocodile on the land but the real test is to win when the croc is in the water.
  - It is a bad omen if the jackal is licking the lambs.
  - Nobody travels on the road to success without a puncture or two.

- o Its very difficult to kill a man who is hell bent upon committing suicide.
  - o Experience is like a comb that life gives you when you are bald.
  - o The cat with gloves catches no mice.
- **Ram Jethmalani**
  I don't need a microphone; I need a silencer.

- **Rajiv Gandhi**
  Our press is absolutely free. In fact, I feel sometimes that it's even worse than your press.

- **Shakespeare**
  - o Alack, there lies more peril in thine eye than TWENTY of their swords. [Romeo and Juliet]
  - o The devil can cite the scripture for his purpose.
- **V. Subhash**
  To succeed, you need hard work and luck. You can rely on hard work.

- **Tacitus**
  The more corrupt the State, the more laws.
- **Thomas Jefferson**
  - o Liberty is a boisterous sea. Timid men prefer the calm of despotism.
  - o Resistance to tyrants is obedience to God.
- **Wendell Phillips**
  Eternal vigilance is the price of liberty.

Part 3 - Only For Intellectuals

WARNING: This part of the book is NOT meant for people who are easily offended.

Confucius-Say Jokes

Do you believe in political correctness? Do you get easily offended? Then, this section is not for you.

> **TRIGGER WARNING**
>
> Contains facts, fiction and opinions.
>
> Symptomatic treatment is recommended.

*Mel Blanc, the man of 1000 voices, who gave voice to Daffy Duck, Bugs Bunny and many other unforgettable cartoon characters, used to have a radio show called the Mel Blanc Show. (Read more about it in '**Annexure 1: Vintage Radio Shows**'.) In this show, Mel played himself and his assistant Zookie. Zookie speaks like Porky Pig but with more stutter. In the episode 'The Chinese Philosopher', Mel asks Zookie to pick up a Chinese philosopher who was arriving at the railway station. A series of misunderstandings results in the philosopher angrily abandoning his visit and returning back. Mel is then hard-pressed to produce the philosopher and asks Zookie to take his place. I think that was probably how Confucius-say jokes began. Or, at least, Mel Blanc must have had something to do with it. My Confucius-say jokes are all inspired by Zookie. When you read them, out aloud or in your mind, you should read them using Zookie's tone and intonation. Otherwise, it will not be funny.*

- **ART:**
  A PICTURE WORTH THOUSAND WORDS. BUT CONFUCIUS SAY TEACHER DRAW ZERO NEXT TO ESSAY.

- **BEAUTY:**
  BEAUTY ONLY SKIN-DEEP. AND, CONFUCIUS SAY THAT IS WHY SWIMSUIT EVENT NOT CONDUCTED IN SWIMMING POOL.

- **BEAUTY:**
  BEAUTY IS IN EYE OF BEHOLDER. BUT CONFUCIUS SAY DO NOT KISS EYE OF HONOURABLE BEHOLDER.

- **BLACK CAT:**
  CONFUCIUS SAY: IT IS DIFFICULT TO FIND BLACK CAT IN DARK ROOM PARTICULARLY WHEN THERE IS NO CAT.

- **BOYS:**
  IF BOYS WILL BE BOYS THEN CONFUCIUS SAY HONOURABLE BOYS

WILL BE HONOURABLE MIDGETS.

- **CARNIVOROUS FISH:**
CONFUCIUS SAY: BIG FISH EAT LITTLE FISH... AND ACCUMULATE HEAVY METALS.

Carnivorous fish like shark taste great but eat them infrequently.

- **CONFUCIUS:**
DO NOT MISS FOREST FOR THE TREES. CONFUCIUS SAY CONFUCIUS IS THE TREE.

- **CONTRADICTION:**
LEOPARD CANNOT CHANGE SPOTS BUT CONFUCIUS ASK HOW LEOPARD HUNT.

- **CREDIT:**
CONFUCIUS SAY: GIVE CREDIT WHERE CREDIT IS DUE... AND FILE FOR BANKRUPTCY.

- **CREDITORS:**
TOMORROW NEVER COMES BUT CONFUCIUS SAY CREDITORS WILL.

- **CRIME:**
CONFUCIUS SAY: CRIME DO NOT PAY... IF YOU BE LAZY CRIMINAL.

- **DOG VS. FRIEND:**
DOG IS BEST FRIEND FOR MAN BUT CONFUCIUS SAY FRIEND WHO BARKS IS HAVING RABIES.

- **DEAD MEN:**
DEAD MEN TELL NO TALES AND SO CONFUCIUS SAY NOT WAIT FOR SURPRISE ENDING.

- **DUES:**
GIVE DEVIL HIS DUE. AND, CONFUCIUS SAY INFORM TAX MAN.

- **EAST AND WEST:**
CONFUCIUS SAY: EAST IS EAST. WEST IS WEST. TWO NOT MEET. EXCEPT ON INTERNATIONAL DATELINE.

- **FEMALES:**
FEMALE OF SPECIES DEADLY THAN MALE BUT CONFUCIUS SAY THAT IS WHY MEN ARM TO TEETH.

- **FEMININE (C)HARM:**
CONFUCIUS SAY JOKE. A MISS IS AS GOOD AS HER SMILE, MANY MISTERS SAY.

- **FILM CAMERA:**
CONFUCIUS SAY: FIRST IMPRESSION BEST IMPRESSION. SO NOT FORGET TO TURN THE ROLL.

- **GIFT HORSE:**
CONFUCIUS SAY: DO NOT LOOK GIFT HORSE IN MOUTH. HONOURABLE HORSE CHEW YOU OUT.

- **HOUSE VS HOME**
CONFUCIUS SAY: HOUSE MADE OF BRICKS. HOME MADE OF LOVING HEARTS.

- **HONESTY POLICY:**

CONFUCIUS SAY: HONESTY IS BEST POLICY... BUT NO HONOURABLE INSURANCE AGENT HAVE THAT.

- **HISTORY:**
CONFUCIUS SAY: HISTORY REPEAT ITSELF... BECAUSE HONOURABLE GENTLEMAN MAKE SAME MISTAKE.

- **LAUGHTER:**
LAUGHTER IS BEST MEDICINE. CONFUCIUS SAY IT MAKE DOCTORS LAUGH.

- **LOVE & IRONY:**
LOVE IS BLIND. CONFUCIUS ASK IS THAT WHY PLASTIC SURGEONS SO RICH.

- **LOVE AND MEN:**
LOVE IS BLIND BUT CONFUCIUS ASK WHY MARRIED MEN SPEECHLESS.

- **A MAN'S PRICE:**
CONFUCIUS SAY: EVERY MAN HAS HIS PRICE. BUT, WHEN TRAVEL IN TRAIN, EVERY MAN HAS SAME PRICE.

- **HEALTH CHOICE:**
CONFUCIUS SAY: MARRY IN HASTE... REPENT AT LEISURE. DELAY MARRIAGE... GET KID WITH DOWN SYNDROME.

- **MARRIAGES:**
CONFUCIUS SAY: MARRIAGE MADE IN HEAVEN. AWAY FROM GROUND REALITY.

- **MEN AND WOMEN:**
NO MAN IS ISLAND BUT CONFUCIUS SAY ANY WOMAN IS A CONTINENT.

- **MONEY:**
MONEY NOT GROW ON TREES. CONFUCIUS SAY MONEY MADE FROM TREES.

Of course, Confucius would say that because the Chinese invented paper.

- **PRICES:**
CONFUCIUS SAY: WHAT GOES UP MUST COME DOWN... EXCEPT PRICES.

- **QUANTITY MATTERS:**
A PENNY SAVED IS PENNY EARNED BUT CONFUCIUS SAY BETTER SAVE IN POUNDS.

- **QUESTIONS AND ANSWERS:**
CONFUCIUS SAY: TELL SILLY QUESTION, GET SILLY ANSWER. TELL SILLY ANSWER, GET LOTS OF QUESTIONS.

- **SAFETY:**
CONFUCIUS SAY: IT IS BETTER TO BE ON SAFE SIDE... UNLESS SAFE SINK BOAT.

- **SUCCESSFUL MAN:**
CONFUCIUS SAY: BEHIND SUCCESSFUL MAN IS STRONG WOMAN. BEHIND HER IS TAX MAN.

- **RISE EARLY:**
  Confucius say: Early to bed. Early to rise. Makes milkman healthy and wealthy.

- **TAX MAN:**
  Confucius say: Easy come. Easy go. Tax man come. Everything goes.

- **TALK:**
  Talk is cheap but Confucius say some payoffs rich.

- **TIME:**
  Confucius say prepare for worst and hope for best.

Ethnic Jokes

This is the CPU or the main chip

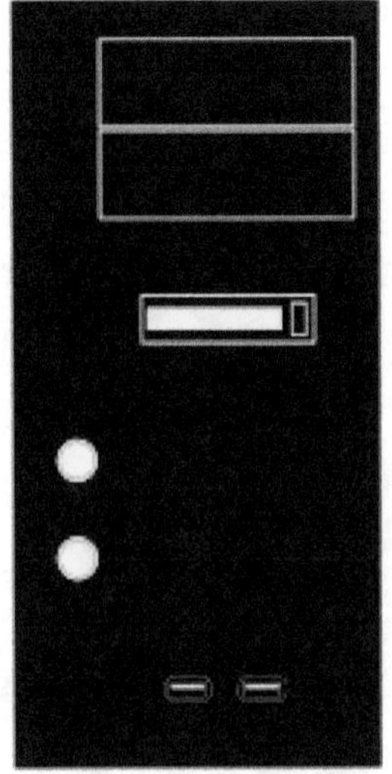

This is the computer dabba or ATX case

Any questions?

Are you a fan of political correctness? Do you get easily offended? Then, this section is not for you.

Several of these jokes are based on ethnic stereotypes. They should be.

- **Intel Inside**

  Indian: Are you the CPU?
  ATX Case: Are you an Indian?

- **Hindi-Pakistani Bye-Bye**
  A Russian, an American, an Indian and a Pakistani are travelling in a plane. Suddenly, the pilot announces that the plane is running out of fuel and all passengers should to ditch their baggage to reduce the load of the plane. The Russian says, "The Soviet Union is the world's largest producer of diamonds and I don't need this big bag of diamonds," and kicks it out of the door. The American says, "The USA is the richest country in the world and I don't need all this gold." He then opens several suitcases full of gold and heaves them out of the door. Now, it's the Indian's turn because the Pakistani is still sleeping. The Indian has nothing valuable or heavy so he throws his Pakistani brother out of the door.

- **"Saare Jahan Se Achcha"**
  A Russian, an American and an Indian are circling around the earth in an international space station that has gone out of control. As the craft is drifting around the earth, the American astronaut puts his hand out of the window to see what was happening. After a while, he yells and yanks his hand inside. "We are flying over New York. I know because one of the tall buildings there just scraped my hand." The Russian cosmonaut puts his hand out of the window and after a while brings it back in with a yell. "We are flying over Russia. One of our Soviet rockets just flew by and singed my hand." This causes a stalemate and they both look at the Indian. The Indian does not have much hope but out of modesty he puts his hand out of the window. After a while, he also lets out an yell and withdraws his hand. The Indian says, "I guess we are flying over India." The Russian and American are puzzled and ask him how he found that out. The Indian replies, "A few minutes after I put my hand out, I realized that my watch had gone missing."

- **Pre-crime without AI or data mining**
  At an international convention of police officers, an informal discussion went like this:

  > **Briton**: The Scotland Yard solves most cases in less than a week.
  > **Russian**: In Soviet Russia, there are very few crimes. And, if there is any, the *militsiya* will solve it in half an hour.
  > **American**: In the USA, the police will reach the spot within 10 minutes of the first emergency phone call.
  > **Indian**: In India, the police knows about any crime before it is committed.

I heard this joke from someone I knew.

- **Grime Fiction**
  This is a real incident that happened to a relative of someone I know. It is a reminder of how fact is stranger than fiction. This man was walking to a bus stop when a stranger bumped into him in an odd way. The suspicious man noted a few minutes later that his expensive watch was missing. As he was friends with the circle inspector, he immediately went to the police station to complain. The inspector dialled a number, inquired about someone, dropped some curse words, asked a few questions and ordered the person to come to the police station immediately. Sometime later, the thief came to the station and and handed the watch over to this guy's relative.

This event occurred in the 80s when landlines were a luxury and even rich people could not get a connection because of the waiting list.

- **A Christian priest, a Hindu godman and a Buddhist monk walk in to a bar**
  A Christian priest, a Hindu godman and a Buddhist monk walk in to a bar. The monk says that alcohol is prohibited in his religion and does not order any drink. The godman says something similar and does not drink. The priest orders a bottle of whisky and starts boozing. His companions ask him if alcohol is not prohibited in his religion. The priest says, "It is prohibited but I am an Irishman!"

- **A Catholic priest, a Anglican priest and an Eastern Orthodox priest**
  A Catholic priest, an Anglican priest and an Eastern Orthodox priest walk in to a bar. The Catholic says alcohol is prohibited in his church and does not order any drink. The Anglican says something similar and does not drink. The Eastern Orthodox priest orders a double vodka and starts boozing. His companions ask him if alcohol is not prohibited in his church. The priest says, "It is prohibited but I am a Russian!"

- **The blonde goes to a Japanese restaurant**

  > **Blonde**: I would like a fried duck.
  > **Waiter**: One duck fly.
  > **Blonde**: In that case, a fried chicken.

I usually order 'One chilli chicken, dry' and the waiter almost always converts it to 'One chicken fry'.

- **How do you transport a whale in a train?**
  With or without luggage?

- **How do you transport a whale in a train without luggage?**
  A whale cannot travel without luggage.

- **How do you transport a whale in a train with luggage?**
  You place the luggage underneath the seat.

- **Where do you place the whale after you take care of the luggage?**
  Does the whale have a ticket? The coach and seat number will be printed on it.

- **How can you fit an entire whale inside a train compartment?**
  You bribe the TTE.

- **How do you transport a dinosaur in a train?**
  You ship it in a box.

- **How can you make a dinosaur fit inside a train compartment?**
  You give it slimming pills.

- **How can a big animal like a dinosaur fit inside a train compartment?**
  If you have travelled in a third-class (unreserved) compartment, then you know it is not a real problem.

- **How do you transport a camel in a train?**
  That's against the regulations. It is not possible.

- **What if the camel is the mother-in-law of the railway minister?**
  Then, anything is possible.

- **How many Indians does it take to a change a lightbulb?**
  One Indian to speak eloquently about the state of the true lightbulbness. Another to declare him to be an enlightened spiritual savant. Three Indians to spread the news. Four Indians to start a cult. Five Indians to build an ashram. Six non-resident Indians (NRIs) to form a trust, register a trademark, and start collecting donations. Several American MBAs and a lawyer to open *True Lightbulbness*® branches in the West. None to screw the lightbulb because *True Lightbulbness*® is now receiving lots of foreign donations. They don't screw light bulbs anymore like neanderthals. They have expensive computer-controlled LED systems now.

- **How many Pakistanis does it take to a change a lightbulb?**
  One Pakistani to start the *Hizb-e-Antibulb* to fight the oppressive influence of the Indian cult of *True Lightbulbness*®. Two Pakistanis to write letters to newspapers asking for donations. Three Pakistanis to register *Hizb-e-Antibulb* as a religious charity. Four Pakistani generals and several visits to Langley to seek American aid. Several American NGOs to route the aid money to *Hizb-e-Antibulb*. One *Hizb-e-Antibulb* terrorist to bomb an American embassy. None to screw the lightbulb because the Americans are now bombing the country and Pakistanis are living in caves.

- ***The Great Mutiny*** **by Christopher Hibbert**
  India's 'first war of independence' or 'the revolt of 1857' was given the name *Sepoy Mutiny* by the East India Company (EIC). After the revolt was quelled, the British Crown formally took over the Indian possessions of the company. (Until then, the British monarch was only a shareholder.) The British colonial government maintained the *Sepoy Mutiny* name for the revolt. According to the British, an Indian soldier named Mangal Pandey, high on local hemp, shot a British officer and started a revolt among the 'sepoys' or British Indian army soldiers. It was a minor disciplinary matter... such and such.

Opinion is divided even among Indian historians. The revolt against the Company government was led by soldiers of Indian kingdoms ('princely states') and the sepoys. The Indian public did not take part in the revolt, some say. However, it is a historical fact many Indian kingdoms including Hindu ones elected the last Mughal Bahadur Zafar Shah as India's emperor and fought under his nominal leadership. (His descendants were exiled to Burma.)

I read the book by Hibbert two decades ago and this is all my recollections from it. However, some incidents mentioned by Hibbert have remained etched in my memory. (Hibbert did not only rely on official archives but also diaries and personal papers of EIC officials and soldiers.)

- History books never mention the Chappathi Movement. This was not a people's movement. It was literally a movement of chappathis. In order to spread the news of the revolt against the Company to the far corners of India, the rebels invented this unique technique. The headman in every village was supposed to send a few chappathis with a courier to all nearby village, town or city and ensure that his counterpart there also did the same. On receipt of the chappathis, somebody ate them but a new set was cooked and sent to nearby villages on foot. Company intelligence sources found that chappathis were travelling at a great speed and within a short period of time the entire subcontinent would be baying for the blood of the British.
- An Islamic cleric issued a fatwa declaring Hindus and Muslims as brothers and the British as invaders. He exhorted Muslim soldiers that it was their religious duty to ally with their Hindu brothers and defeat the invaders. One of the lessons that the British learned from the revolt was to never let Hindus and Muslims act on anything together. Since then, divide-and-rule became the foundation of British colonial policy in India.
- When Company men were on the run, one British soldier found a unique way to escape being killed by his captors. This man was familiar with Arabic/Urdu. The moment he was about to lynched or harmed, the soldier would start reciting verses in praise of Allah. As no Muslim can harm a man praising Allah, the soldier escaped death each time.
- When the Indians were on the run, British soldiers used to prey on Indian road travellers. One Muslim traveller was caught hiding several veiled women in a horse carriage. The man was restrained and the women were forced unveil their faces. Given the eloborate measures taken to hide the women, the soldiers expected to see the famed earthly *houris* but were extremely disappointed.

- **How many American lawyers would it take to a change a lightbulb?**
None because any of them would sue the bulb company first.

- **What happened to the vampire after he bit an American?**
He is fighting a billion-dollar class-action lawsuit for being a pain in the neck.

Americans are the most litigious people in the world.

- **Why did the Malayallee cross the road?**
Simbly.

I heard this joke from someone I knew.

- **Why did the Tamilian cross the road?**

What for you?

- **#CulturalAppropriation**
  In high school, we had to write answers to exercise questions in our own words. One lesson in our English reader was an abridgement of E. R. Braithwaite's *'To Sir, With Love '*. One of the questions for the chapter was "Why was Mr. Braithwaite unemployed for eighteen months?" My innocent answer was "Mr. Braithwaite was unemployed because he was a black for eighteen months".

- **Knock Knock**

  Knock Knock.
  Who is there?
  Who?
  Who who? What?
  Right.
  Who is there?
  Who?
  What is your name?
  What?
  What?
  Who? What?
  What is your name?
  Who?
  Your name?
  Who?
  Your name is 'who'?
  Right.
  How do you spell it?
  H-U.
  Your name is H-U Hu?
  Right.
  What is your last name?
  What?
  What is your last name?
  What?
  [pause] How do you spell your last name?
  W-A-T-T.
  Watt.
  W-A-T-T.
  Watt. I know.
  Right.
  Well, Hu Watt,...
  Right.
  I may regret this but I've come this far so I will risk it. Do you have a

middle name?
Right.
Spelled W–R–I–G–H–T?
Right.
Hu Wright Watt, how can anyone go wrong with it?
Right.

- **What happened to the Irishman after a vampire bit him?**
  The Irishman complained of blood loss but the vampire got a terrible hangover

---

Hangover - Ruskin Bond's column in *The Hindu*

- **What happened to the Russian after a vampire bit him?**
  The Russian complained of two small puncture wounds but the vampire became an alcoholic.

- **What happened to the vampire after he bit an Indian?**
  He became caste-conscious and will only bite ethnic Romanians.

- **What happened to the vampire after he bit an Indian politician?**
  Instead of waking up in the evening every day, he wakes up once in five years or just before election time.

- **What happened to the vampire after he bit an Indian policeman?**
  Now, after he drinks your blood, he demands a bribe to let you go.

- **How did the Canadian leave the outpatient ward so quick?**
  He was a-symptomatic.

Il est a-symptomatique.

- **The Cunningly Clever Chinese**
  Quite a few management books have been devoted to the "inscrutable" Japanese management professionals. In China, Communist Party officials are trained in a somewhat similar way. An Indian computer education company went to China to replicate their success in India. The Chinese invited them because they also wanted to become a software superpower. The officials of the Chinese government and the Indian company decided that it would be good if in the first year at least 500 Chinese-owned computer education franchises were started. When they met Chinese officials for the year-end review, the Indian company officials triumphantly announced that they managed to start over 2500 franchises. The Chinese officials pretended to be unimpressed. Their response was "Only 2500?"

I may have read this in *Businessworld* magazine. I am not sure about the numbers either.

- **A North Korean and a South Korean fought. Who won?**
  None, either or both.

- **Cut from the same cloth**
  A prominent North Korean official defected to the South. The Americans debriefed him and asked the South Koreans to let the Press know him only as Mr. Won. The Americans were worried he was still too much of a Communist

and his opposition was directed only to the current dictator. Two South Korean military psychiatrists, Yen Hee-Wong and Hon Jae-Wong, were assigned to tutor him before he could be showcased to the public as a propaganda coup. But, Won was adamant about his views and his meeting with the press was indefinitely delayed. The *Chosun Ilbo* got the wind of this and let the cat out with the headline "Two Wongs don't make Won right!"

- **What would happen if a Korean was elected mayor?**
  It **woo**ld be **illegal** to **choo** the **fat**.

Lightbulb Jokes

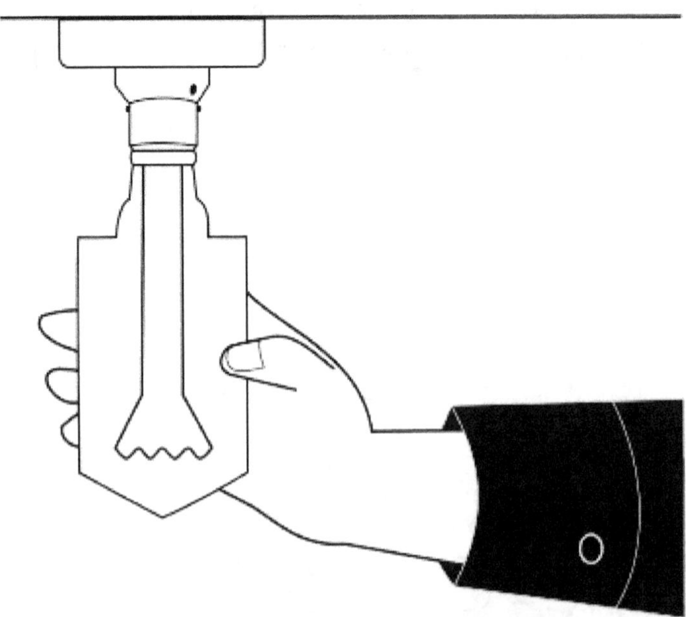

Are you a fan of political correctness? Do you get easily offended? Then, this section is not for you.

TRIGGER WARNING

Contains facts, fiction and opinions.

Symptomatic treatment is recommended.

- **How many Americans does it take to screw a lightbulb?**
  One to screw the lightbulb and 1,00,000 US marines to ensure that it stays that way.

- **How many American politicians does it take to a screw a lightbulb?**
  One to call for an investigation. Several to arrange a fundraiser for the

members of the Lightbulb Committee. One to finally screw the lightbulb because all members of the committee have now been bought by lightbulb industry lobbyists.

- **How many Climate Scientists would it take to a change a lightbulb?**
  Because the science is settled, anyone from the 2% that does not believe in Climate Change will do.

- **How many hypochondriacs does it take to a screw a lightbulb?**
  One but he will suffer all the effects of a burnout.

- **How many Harley-Davidson fans would it take to change a lightbulb?**
  One but he will need the rest of his fan club behind him for support.

- **How many Indian policemen does it take to a screw a lightbulb?**
  None but for a price they will register a false case against the old one.

- **How many Indian policemen does it take to a screw a lightbulb?**
  None but for a price they will make the old one confess.

- **How many Indian policemen does it take to a change a lightbulb?**
  None because they demand bribes in broad daylight.

- **How many Indian politicians does it take to a change a lightbulb?**
  One to demand bribe to screw the lightbulb. Several to allege corruption and demand bribes of their own to remain quiet. None to screw the lightbulb because the party workers have stolen the socket.

- **How many Indian doctors does it take to a change a lightbulb?**
  One to recommend a few routine tests. One to provide a second opinion. Several to perform preventative surgery and declare it a success. None to screw the lightbulb because the new bulb died when it saw the bill.

- **How many mobsters would it take to a change a lightbulb?**
  One but not before he takes the old one out and shoots it.

- **How many psychopath would it take to a change a lightbulb?**
  One but not before he takes the old one out and drowns it in a lake.

- **How many Malayallees would it take to a change a lightbulb?**
  A few to complain about the old bulb. Several to petition the government for a change. A whole town to go in a protest march against the local government's failure to take action. A few to indulge in violence. Many to spread the violence. A few to die in the violence. Many to die in police attempts to quell the violence. All opposition parties to demand the resignation of the state government and call for a bundh. The entire state to come to a stop for a day because of the bundh. One to screw the new bulb. One to steal the new bulb. The whole process repeats endlessly.

- **How many Tamilians would it take to a change a lightbulb?**
  A few to complain about the old bulb. Several to petition the local government for a change. One to screw the new bulb. One to steal the new bulb. The whole process repeats endlessly.

- **How many blonde fathers would it take to a change a lightbulb?**
  None because they would all get electrocuted.

- **How many blonde models would it take to a change a lightbulb?**
  None because lightbulbs don't wear clothes.

- **How many blonde mothers would it take to a change a lightbulb?**

None because lightbulbs don't wear diapers.

- **How many blonde women would it take to a screw a lightbulb?**
  None unless somebody teaches them how to unscrew the old one.

- **How many blonde women would it take to a screw a lightbulb if you teach them to unscrew the old one?**
  You might as well tell them to stop spinning.

- **How many feminists would it take to a change a lightbulb?**
  One but not before she electrocutes a few male volunteers with the task.

- **How many mobile phone addicts does it take to screw a lightbulb?**
  None because there is an app for that.

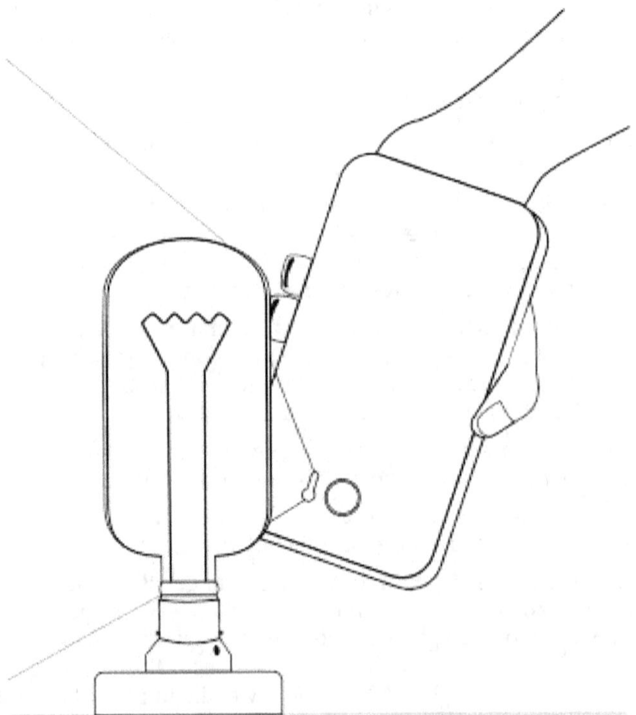

Is there an app for this?

Off-The-Wall Philosophers

Are you a fan of political correctness? Do you get easily offended? Then, this section is not for you.

TRIGGER WARNING

Contains facts, fiction and opinions.

Symptomatic treatment is recommended.

Vandals who deface walls should be punished. However, some of the stuff they write is so profound that it makes you pause for a while to think. These special few are born rebels, confirmed jokers or really desperate people. The jokes in this section are written along those lines but should not be construed as an excuse for vandalism.

- **ACTIONS SPEAK LOUDER THAN WORDS**
  if you are far away.

- **THE AGE OF MIRACLES IS PAST**
  - Welcome to campaign financing
  - *Welcome to the world of stockmarket derivatives*
  - Welcome to offshore tax planning

- **BEGGARS CAN'T BE CHOOSERS**
  - But they have a lot of change
  - *'Financial solicitors', not 'beggars'*
  - They chose to beg

- **BEAUTY IS ONLY SKIN-DEEP.**
  - It should be
  - *Why? Are you a surgeon?*
  - Or a psychopath?

- **A CHAIN IS ONLY AS STRONG AS WEAKEST LINK**
  So what? There will always be one.

- **CLEANLINESS IS NEXT TO GODLINESS**
  Then, clean this godforsaken street!

- **CRIME DOES NOT PAY**
  if you are polite like that

- **THE CUSTOMER IS ALWAYS RIGHT**
  - That's why he left?
  - *Except when he wants to return stuff*

- **DANGEROUS CURVES**
  Unless you are more crooked

- **THE DARKEST HOUR IS BEFORE DAWN**
  Read *The Friday Times* instead.

Dawn (**www.dawn.com**) is Pakistan's leading English daily and was founded by the country's founder Mohammed Ali Jinnah in 1942. *The Friday Times* (**www.thefridaytimes.com**) is a weekly. It has a very funny humour section.

- **DEATH IS THE GREAT LEVELLER**
  - Taxes are the great extractor.
  - *Certainly!*

- **DESPERATE TIMES CALLS FOR DESPERATE MEASURES**
  - Sellout! Traitor! Slave!
  - *Poverty of ideas?*
  - Necessity is the mother of invention.
  - New York or LA?
  - Tape or scale?

- **DIE ON YOUR FEET THAN LIVE ON YOUR KNEES**
  - Pray on your knees and fight on your feet
  - *How about I crouch a little*
  - Smoke on your lips and die on your couch
  - Drink in your hands and ~~pass out on the floor~~
  - die without your liver

- **DO NOT CROSS BRIDGE UNTIL YOU COME TO IT**
  - Another one of those head-scratchers. I hate you!
  - *If you cross the bridge, you fall into water.*

- **DO NOT FEED THE ANIMALS**
  - You make us sick.
  - *You make us fat.*

- **DO NOT ~~PARK~~ IN FRONT OF GATE**
  bark

- **DO NOT ENTER**
  AUTHORIZED PERSONNEL ONLY
  Really the keyhole is not big enough for anyone.

- **DO NOT LITTER**
  - ~~liter~~
  - *litre*
  - imperial units please

- **DO NOT SCRIBBLE**
  Write legibly

- **DO NOT USE MOBILE PHONES**
  - Smash those infernal devices!
  - *Is it okay to pretend? I'm going crazy here!*

- **DON'T DRINK AND DRIVE**
  - Take the peanuts too

- *Pay the tab first*
  - *Don't forget you hat and coat*

- **DONT TAKE MORE THAN YOU GIVE**
  ... unless you get there first

- **DOUBT IS THE BEGINNING, NOT THE END, OF WISDOM**
  I doubt it.

- **EARLY BIRD CATCHES WORM**
  Come late if you have coupons.

- **EVEN A WORM WILL TURN**
  - so do not ~~crawl~~ when you can ~~walk~~
  -               scrawl   talk

- **FACTS ARE STUBBORN THINGS**
  - Is this a fact? I can't rub it off.
  - *Offensive fact!*

- **FEMALE OF THE SPECIES IS DEADLIER THAN THE MALE**
  - How many world wars did we fight?
  - *Wait for World War 3*

- **FORGIVE AND FORGET**
  - Never forget it.
  - *If you just give and forget, I would like to borrow some money.*

- **A FRIEND IS SOMEONE WHO ~~SUPPORTS YOU WHEN YOU ARE IN THE WRONG.~~**
                            rescues you from the wrong

- **A FRIEND IN NEED ~~IS A FRIEND INDEED~~**
                    may want to borrow money

- **GENDER IS A SOCIAL CONSTRUCT**
  - I identify as the owner of your wallet, car, house and bank account.
  - *Gender is an economic construct?*
  - Pay my debts then!
  - I identify as your God. Worship me!
  - If I kill someone, I identify myself as 'not guilty'.
  - This is dangerous and harmful!

- **GOD CREATED MAN IN THE IMAGE OF HIMSELF**
  - And God created Man's opposite, the woman, in the image of...
  - *If it's the devil, I will go to hell*

- **GOD HELPS THOSE WHO HELP THEMSELVES**
  But thou shall not steal

- HASTE MAKES WASTE
  When you squeeze toothpaste.

- HELL HAS NO FURY LIKE WOMAN SCORNED.
  Heaven has no angel like mother to newborn.

- I THINK. THEREFORE, I AM.
  - You are what?
  - You are definitely something.
  - i for incomplete.
  - I can't get it out of the head.
  - My eyes! I hate it when they do that!

- IDLE HANDS ARE DEVIL'S PLAYGROUND
  I was idling here. I don't know what came over me.

- IMITATION IS THE SINCEREST FORM OF FLATTERY
  Imitation is the sincerest form of flattery.

- IT IS BETTER TO GIVE THAN RECEIVE
  - if what you give is punches.
  - Hopefully, it is not a cold
  - Or the coronavirus

- IT IS BETTER TO BE POOR AND HAPPY THAN RICH AND MISERABLE
  - Of course. Ask any poor guy.
  - Or a rich one

- JESUS SAVES
  - Devil charges interest
  - Taxman collects from both

- KNOWLEDGE IS POWER
  Can it light this bulb?

- LAUGHTER IS THE BEST MEDICINE
  Then, don't make me laugh.

- LIVING WELL IS THE BEST REVENGE
  Stop it. You are killing me.

- ~~LOOK BEFORE YOU WALK~~
  ≥ Look up from your phone, dummy. ≤

- LOVE MAKES THE WORLD GO AROUND
  It is all that unwanted talk that makes it spin

- MAN CREATED GOD
  - Try using God as a dependent on your tax returns

- o *Government created God?*

- **MONEY DOES NOT GROW ON TREES**
Of course not. It is made from trees.

- **MISERY LOVES COMPANY**
and pain loves incorporation.

- **NEVER JUDGE A BOOK BY ITS COVER**
Explains why old-paper marts remove the cover when they weigh it.

- **NEVER SAY NEVER**
  - o Better late than NEVER
  - o *It NEVER rains but pours*
  - o Lightning NEVER strikes the same place twice
  - o You are never too old to learn

- **NEVER SPEAK ILL OF THE DEAD**
But they always say what *illness* they died from

- **NO BILLS**
What's the postman doing in the bathroom?

- **NO DOGS**
On the menu?

- **NO HORN**
What if it is a bullock cart?

- **NO FISHING**
  - o What will sharks eat
  - o *Polluted or prohibited?*

- **NO SOLICITATIONS**
  - o We are too broke to buy anything
  - o *MLM salesman lives here*

- **NO SMOKING**
Don't sell cigarettes then.

- **NOBODY IS MORE ENSLAVED THAN THOSE WHO FALSELY BELIEVE THEY ARE FREE**
  - o Damn those 'rule followers'
  - o *And tax payers*
  - o "A little less freedom for a little more security"

- **ONE GOOD TURN DESERVES ANOTHER**
Beware of borrowers.

- **OPEN CONFESSION IS GOOD FOR THE SOUL**
  - o Confess and be hanged.

- ○ *Yeah, never confess to your wife.*
  - ○ Use the confession app and tell Google, NSA, FBI....
  - ○ ... who will save it for eternity

- **THE PARANOID SURVIVE**
  - ○ Conspiracy theorist!
  - ○ *Hater!*

- **A PENNY SAVED IS A PENNY EARNED**
  Don't tell the IRS.

- **PHOTOGRAPHY IS STRICTLY PROHIBITED**
  - ○ God sees everything.
  - ○ *So does Google and the Cloud...*
  - ○ NSA, CIA, FBI...
  - ○ Hackers and identity thieves
  - ○ Credit history bureaus and bounty hunters

- **PRACTICE MAKES PERFECT**
  - ○ perfect what?
  - ○ *Practice writing complete sentences.*

- **REMAIN SILENT AND APPEAR FOOLISH THAN SPEAK AND REMOVE ALL DOUBT**
  Only practice will make you perfect.

- **QUESTION EVERYTHING**
  Who wrote this?

- **SILENCE IS GOLDEN**
  Will they buy it?

- **SLOW CHILDREN**
  - ○ Where are they?
  - ○ *By running them over?*
  - ○ 'Learning Disability', not 'slow'!

- **SLOW COWS**
  - ○ And invisible!
  - ○ *Who can slow cows?*

- **SOCIALISM MADE A ~~MAN~~ OF ME -- GBS**
  - ○ ~~mice~~
  - ○ *mouse*

- **SPEAK SOFTLY AND CARRY A BIG STICK**
  - ○ Use a cell phone for longer distances
  - ○ *Spoken like a pole vaulter*

- SPEED KILLS
  - What do you you care?
  - *They need you for the taxes*
  - Speed does not kill. People kill people.
  - It's not the speed – it's the deceleration!

- STICKS AND STONES MAY BREAK MY BONES BUT WORDS WILL NEVER HURT ME
  - This offends me!
  - *Welcome to the Internet*
  - Never met a SJW or a pressure group?
  - Welcome to offensive journalism "I am offended so ban everything!"
  - Those who say offensive words constitute as violence never received a punch in the face.
  - And deserve one.

- STICK NO BILLS
  That's Hillaryes

- TALK IS CHEAP
  But some expressions are priceless

- TAKE CARE OF THE PENNIES AND THE POUNDS WILL TAKE CARE OF THEMSELVES
  - Do not eat pennies
  - *Still overweight*
  - Pennies? Pounds? This is Merica – U.S. of A!

- TIME AND TIDE WAIT FOR NO MAN
  - Someone signed me up for a Readers' Digest subscription
  - *I use Surf*
  - ~~Gender discrimination~~
  - Matriarchy

- TO BE LIKE CHRIST IS TO BE A CHRISTIAN.
  - HOW MANY ARE LEFT?
  - *You are right.*

- TOUGH TIMES DONT LAST. TOUGH GUYS DO.
  - Discrimination!
  - *On average, women live longer.*
  - Matriarchy!

- TO ERR IS HUMAN. TO FORGIVE IS DIVINE.
  To foment is devilish

- TOMORROW NEVER COMES
  - Don't hire it then
  - *Haste makes waste*

- TRESPASSERS WILL BE SHOT
  Take a selfie

- THERE IS NO SUCH THING AS A FREE LUNCH
  - Can you pay back your parents?
  - *Everything does not need to have a price tag*
  - Best things in life are free

- TWO WRONGS DO NOT MAKE A RIGHT
  Around a block, two lefts will.

- UNITY IS STRENGTH
  Too many cooks spoil the broth

- WASH YOUR HANDS WHEN YOU LEAVE THE BATHROOM
  - The door handle is dirtier than the toilet seat.
  - *I hate you*

- WE TWO. OURS ONE.
  Depopulation!

- WOMEN CAN BE JUST AS GOOD AS MEN
  And just as mistaken.

- YOU ARE NEVER TOO OLD TO LEARN
  You cannot teach an old dog new tricks

- YOU CANNOT WIN THEM ALL
  So defeat them

Political Jokes

Are you a fan of political correctness? Do you get easily offended? Then, this section is not for you.

- **Politically correct reasons not to like political correctness**
  Political correctness is a self-issued get-out-of-jail permit. It is also:
  - Not inclusive.
  - Presumptive guilt.
  - Defamatory.

- o Intolerant.
- o Thought bullying.
- o Meaning appropriation.
- o Weaponised negativity.
- o Toxic subjectivity.
- o Masked prejudice.

- **What is the politically correct name for a ghost?**
Death-involved person.

- **What is the politically correct name for a Fascist?**
Corporate-involved person.

- **What is the politically correct name for a lobbyist?**
Charity-involved person.

- **What is the politically correct name for a Socialist?**
Fantasy-involved person.

- **What is the politically correct name for a Communist?**
Slavery-involved person.

- **What is the politically correct name for a warmonger?**
~~Hillary clone~~… ~~Obamabot~~… Creative-destruction-involved person.

- **What is the politically correct name for a drunk?**
Gravity-involved person.

- **What is the politically correct name for a homeless person?**
Outdoors-involved person.

- **What is the politically correct name for a prisoner?**
Security-involved person.

- **What is the politically correct name for a condemned prisoner?**
Extinction-involved person.

- **What is the politically correct name for a terrorist?**

Risk-involved person.

- **What is the politically correct name for a suicide bomber?**
  Warming-involved person.

- **What is the politically correct name for a hijacker?**
  Direction-involved person.

- **What is the politically correct name for a blackmailer?**
  Literacy-involved person.

- **What is the politically correct name for a thief?**
  Ownership-involved person.

- **What is the politically correct name for a killer?**
  Health-involved person.

- **What is the politically correct name for a psychopath?**
  ~~Derivatives trader~~ Logic-involved person.

- **What is the politically correct name for a bootlegger?**
  Trademark-involved person.

- **What is the politically correct name for a pirate?**
  - Copyright-involved person.
  - Retirement-involved person.

- **What is the politically correct name for a vampire?**
  Donation-involved person.

- **What would happen if Mercury entered politics?**
  - It will be accused of unleashing poisonous propaganda.
  - It will be considered a political hothead.

- **What would happen if Venus entered politics?**
  Feminists would hate it because she is sweet and beautiful, and all men like her.

- **What would happen if Mars entered politics?**
  - Democrats will accuse it of being funded by the glue-gun lobby.
  - Republicans will accuse the red planet of being a commie.

- **What would happen if Jupiter entered politics?**
  - Libertarians will say that it was nothing but hot air.
  - Green Party activists will tell the green planet to take a hike.
  - Rent Is Too Damn High Party will complain that the rent is already too high.

This is a real party in the New York. The leader of the party is a really humorous personality. Anyone would have liked him but he was not very successful at the ballot box.

- **What would happen if Saturn entered politics?**
  Deadweights would run rings around it.

- **What would happen if Uranus entered politics?**
  It would be accused of harbouring extremist views.

Pluto is not farthest planet because it is not considered a planet anymore.

- **What would happen if Pluto entered politics?**

It will be relegated as a has-been.

- **Masculinity and Femininity**
When you say 'feminine charm', are you implying that men do not have charm? When you say 'feminine beauty', are you claiming that men cannot be good-looking? Men are handsome and women are beautiful? Let us not bluff. I am sure you get my drift.

Meaning of *femininity* in English

femininity

the fact or quality of having characteristics that are traditionally thought to be typical of or suitable for a woman:

In recent years, PC propagandists have been pushing the term 'toxic masculinity' to describe abrasive behaviour that men sometimes exhibit towards women. Offended men are saying that masculinity means being there to open jars or teaching kids to use swear words. Both sides are wrong. Here are the correct definitions:

- Masculinity: personal qualities of a man.
- Femininity: personal qualities of a woman.
- Masculine: the nature of a quality found in a man; belonging to men.
- Feminine: the nature of a quality found in a woman; belonging to women.

Any quality found in a woman is a feminine quality. The sum of all feminine qualities in a woman is her femininity. Not necessarily unique or traditional qualities. The strength in a woman is her feminine strength. Just because it is called feminine strength, it does not mean strength is unique to women. The feminine proclivity to like teary-eyed soaps is a uniquely feminine quality. Men would not like to be caught dead with tears in their eyes. These are uniquely feminine and masculine characteristics.

Being a father is not masculinity. Some men abandon their families. They continue to be masculine but not fathers or husbands. Women work in the military as soldiers and also die fighting in wars. They may have adopted a traditionally masculine role but the roles were not masculine or feminine. Nursing used to be an exclusively feminine domain. (I could have said female domain.) After years of struggle against discrimination, some wimps have broken through the glass ceiling imposed by the matriarchy.

How can established lexicographers get it so wrong? This is one of many reasons why you should buy my *Dictionary of Indian English (DIE)* when it is released. Because of PC invading every aspect of life, the lexicon and even grammar will become unrecognisable and not understandable in the next few years. That is when a dictionary like mine will become valuable.

- **The other cheek**
  Many years ago, All India Radio (AIR) FM had leased some of its air time to private broadcasters. These one-hour 'private' programs allowed listeners to call the radio station and take part in a discussion. One of these programs had an anchor whose stylish of speaking was not liked by many listeners including me. One listener took the extraordinary step of calling the show and telling him live that he sounded very annoying and should not be on air. The accused man calmly replied, "Dear Sir, I am aware of the fact that while some people will like me, there will be others who will not. All of us have people whom we like and dislike. I am sure that in your family there are relatives who you like and do not like. And, there are relatives who like you and do not like you. Hence, this is nothing extraordinary. I am not bothered by it. In fact, I like people who hate me more than those who like me because it is from them I will know how to improve myself and make myself more likeable. So, thank you very much." I instantly changed my mind about the guy, and realized how stupid and bigoted we can be over superficial things. Not that I stopped being all that – I just realized it.

- **Is it wrong to claim that Obama was not born in the USA and therefore ineligible for being president?**
  Of course. Obama would not have bombed Africa if he was really a Kenyan.

- **What does Barrack Obama's school yearbook say about him?**
  "Most likely to win the Nobel Prize for nothing."

- **What does George W Bush's school yearbook say about him?**
  "Most unlikely to become US president but, if he does, the dumbest ever!"

During his two terms, "Dubya" Bush was very famous for his 'Bushisms'. A selection of
Bushisms is available in the section Quotations.

- **What does Tony Blair's school yearbook say about him?**
  "Most likely to star as the lead in the film adaptation of Pinocchio."

- **What does M. K. Gandhi's school yearbook say about him?**
  "Most likely to spin a great yarn and bring down the empire!"

- **What does Indira Gandhi's school yearbook say about her?**
  "Most likely to cause a national emergency."

- **What does Narendra Modi's school yearbook say about him?**
  "Most likely to give everyone a run for their money."

- **Top 10 Reasons Why Stalin Slapped Metro Passenger**
  - There was a mosquito on his face. Jayalalitha's metro trains are already a breeding ground for disease-causing insects.
  - Ticket inspector was approaching and Stalin did not have a ticket.
  - Nobody gave Stalin a seat.
  - Stalin missed his stop because this guy had been blocking the window.
  - Stalin ran out of ideas on how to steal the limelight from Jayalalitha, who

had come out of jail just in time for the Metro inauguration.
- o Stalin wanted to show small-time opposition leader Capt. Vijayakanth the proper way of slapping party workers.
- o The guy stepped on Stalin's toe.
- o Stalin wanted to take a selfie with ordinary passengers and this guy was hogging the frame.
- o The guy asked "Stalin Uncle" to gently brush his hand across his cheek. [This was the actual reason given by the passenger.]
- o It was all a conspiracy by Jayalalitha and Jaya TV.

- **What would happen if a bird was elected mayor?**
  - o The city would be declared a bird sanctuary city, and more statues and artificial fountains will be installed.
  - o All public areas of the entire city will be declared as one big cat-free zone. All cat owners will have to register themselves and their pets will not be allowed access to open spaces outside the house. All unlicensed cats (feral cats) will be caught and exterminated.

NO CATS ALLOWED

This cat was very cute in colour. When I turned it into black for this book, it started looking like Hitler! There have been many times when I see a Youtuber who positions himself under a light in a way that his nose tip forms a shadow. It makes him look like Hitler! After I notice it, I cannot un-see it.

- **What would happen if a chicken entered a political debate on TV?**
  It would be ~~tarred and feathered~~ plucked, tarred and feathered.
- **What would happen if a chimp entered a political debate on TV?**
  Nobody will be able to tell the difference.
- **What would happen if a donkey entered a political debate on TV?**
  All that hee-hawing would drive it crazy.
- **What would happen if a monkey entered a political debate on TV?**
  The intellectual quotient of the political discourse would register a jump.
- **What would happen if a brain-eating zombie entered a political debate on TV?**
  It will come back hungry.
- **What would happen if a turkey entered a political debate on TV?**
  It might get roasted.
- **What would happen if an ant was elected mayor?**
  The mayor would march all over town and solve all problems from the ground level.
- **What would happen if an antelope became the mayor?**
  It would beat around the bush and run away from problems.
- **What would happen if a bat was elected mayor?**
  The mayor will always have a **big ear** for citizens' problems.
- **What would happen if a badger was elected mayor?**
  Several trees will be destroyed to build a new toll bridge across the river.
- **What would happen if a bear was elected mayor?**
  If you have a garbage disposal problem, the mayor will be happy to come by and take care of it immediately.
- **What would happen if a bee was elected mayor?**
  Apiary workers will be exposed in a sting operation.
- **What would happen if a camel was elected mayor?**
  It would be illegal to use the last straw.
- **What would happen if a cat was elected mayor?**
  It would be a catastrophe for dogs.
- **What would happen if a caterpillar was elected mayor?**
  If the mayor takes a hiatus from politics, observers may notice a complete transformation.
- **What would happen if a chameleon was elected mayor?**
  - It will be okay to stick your tongue out.
  - Insects will be in a sticky situation.
- **What would happen if a cow was elected mayor?**
  Kids will have to learn that chocolate milk does not come from brown cows.
- **What would happen if a dog was elected mayor?**
  All trees would be clearly marked so that dogs could bark at the right tree.
- **What would happen if a donkey was elected mayor?**
  It would become the laughing **stock** of the entire nation.
- **What would happen if a dragon was elected mayor?**
  Decision-making could **drag on** forever.

- **What would happen if an eel was elected mayor?**
  Councillors on both sides of the political aisle would be shocked.

- **What would happen if an elephant was elected mayor?**
  It would make a lasting impression on the political landscape.

- **What would happen if a fish was elected mayor?**
  It might open a can of worms.

- **What would happen if a fly was elected mayor?**
  Anyone hurting a fly will be S.W.A.T.'d.

- **What would happen if a fox was elected mayor?**
  The mayor will be put himself in charge of the hen house.

- **What would happen if a frog was elected mayor?**
  - If anyone has a problem, he or she would have to jump (not run) from pillar to post.
  - Politicians will hurl all kinds of allegations but nothing will stick.
  - High-school biology teachers will be framed.
  - French restaurants will be shut down.

- **What would happen if a giraffe was elected mayor?**
  The glass ceiling will be definitely broken.

- **What would happen if a goose was elected president?**
  It will be known as the propagander-in-chief.

- **What would happen if a horse was elected mayor?**
  Flogging a dead horse will become a criminal offence. Do not even think about flogging a live horse.

- **What would happen if a lion was elected mayor?**
  - Lion tamers will be made to stand trial.
  - His pride will be brimming with family.

- **What would happen if a llama was elected mayor?**
  The mayor will be accused of surrounding himself with his cronies but he will claim that they were held at spitting distance.

- **What would happen if a llama gets re-elected mayor?**
  Everyone will say that the mayor is the spitting image of his predecessor.

- **What would happen if a mantis was elected mayor?**
  - Prayer will be back in government schools.
  - The stigma associated with women killing their husbands will be gone.

- **What would happen if a mice was elected mayor?**
  It would be like what the cat brought in.

- **What would happen if a narwhal was elected mayor?**
  It should be able handle the ~~tusk~~ task.

- **What would happen if an octopus was elected mayor?**
  It would be a sucker for all kind of scams.

- **What would happen if an otter was elected mayor?**
  Political minnows will have their heads chewed off.

- **What would happen if an ostrich was elected mayor?**
  After a spirited run for the office, the mayor will be bury his head in people's problems.

- **What would happen if an owl was elected mayor?**
  The mayor will burn the midnight oil for his town.

- **What would happen if a parrot was elected mayor?**
  The mayor will be accused of repeating the same mistakes as his predecessor.

- **What would happen if a pelican was elected mayor?**
  Please be aware that his bill doesn't hold much water.

- **What would happen if a pig was elected mayor?**
  - The political arena is already like a pig sty.
  - It will not be the first time pork-barrel budget allocations are made.
  - Anyone accusing the mayor of taking 'ham-handed decisions' will be accused of speciesism. [Speciesism is a real thing with some animal-rights activists. ("Don't kill mosquitoes - let them take blood donation, urges French animal-rights activist"; The Independent)]

- **What would happen if a porcupine was elected mayor?**
  It will definitely be a thorny problem for the city council.

- **What would happen if a possum was elected mayor?**
  It will be easy for the mayor to play dead.

- **What would happen if a puffer fish was elected mayor?**
  Attacks on sharks will register a sharp spike.

- **What would happen if a python became the mayor?**
  Public finances will be stretched and development programs may get suffocated.

- **What would happen if a quail became the mayor?**
  Denying quails their quail identity will attract a huge fine. Remember that before misaddressing a quail as a chicken.

- **What would happen if a raccoon became the mayor?**
  Anyone placing eatables at the bottom of a garbage can will attract a massive fine.

- **What would happen if a rabbit became the mayor?**
  - The city's problems may multiply like the mayor.
  - Instead of history and civics, kids will have to learn about 'political carrotness'.

- **What would happen if a rat became the mayor?**
  - Corrupt humans infesting the system will have to leave. Born professionals will be taking over.
  - High-school biology teachers will be ratted out.

- **What would happen if a rhinoceros became the mayor?**
  Legislators will address him as the 'Hornable Mayor'.

- **What would happen if a salmon was elected mayor?**
  The mayor will be accused of kicking the can down the fiscal road.

- **What would happen if a seal was elected mayor?**
  The mayor will be accused of playing to the gallery.

- **What would happen if a shark was elected mayor?**
  "Read my lips. No new attacks."

- **What would happen if a sheep was elected mayor?**

It would be illegal for politicians to "appropriate sheep culture" in clothing.

- **What would happen if a sloth was elected mayor?**
  The new mayor will be appalled at the slow pace of bureaucracy.

- **What would happen if a snail was elected mayor?**
  The mayor will straddle the razor-thin majority in the council like a pro.

- **What would happen if a snake was elected mayor?**
  - Public finances will continue to be looted like a bottomless pit.
  - Snake charmers will be given powerful positions in the administration.

- **What would happen if a squirrel was elected mayor?**
  Politics is for nuts anyway.

- **What would happen if a stork was elected mayor?**
  Parents who fail to tip will have to pick up future deliveries themselves.

- **What would happen if a swan was elected mayor?**
  Public finances are under water anyway. You might as well elect a swan.

- **What would happen if a termite was elected mayor?**
  Corrupt bureaucrats would be prosecuted for misappropriating termite culture in public offices!

- **What would happen if a tortoise was elected mayor?**
  Decision-making may slow down to a crawl but public will have more time to study official plans and decisions.

- **What would happen if a toad was elected mayor?**
  - More bar licenses will be issued so that watering holes will only be a hop away!
  - It will be time for 'hop and change'.

- **What would happen if a turkey was elected mayor?**
  - Thanksgiving Day and slaughter of turkeys will be banned.
  - Sales of chicken will be tax-exempted.

- **What would happen if a whale was elected mayor?**
  The city will have to float bonds to stay above water.

- **What would happen if a wolf was elected mayor?**
  The council will pass a resolution excoriating the three little pigs for setting a bad precedent and permits for all new brick houses will be denied.

- **What would happen if a zebra was elected mayor?**
  Road crossings will be banned for appropriating zebra culture.

- **What would happen if one was elected mayor?**
  Referring someone as 'one' would become an offence.

- **Why did the white ant couple break up?**
  She finds all white ants as racist and now identifies herself as a termite.

- **What would happen if an ordinary terrorist was elected mayor?**
  He would have a blast.

- **What would happen if a suicide bomber terrorist was elected mayor?**
  He would invite everyone and have a blast.

- **What would happen if a hijacker was elected mayor?**
  The mayor will hold up funds for projects started by his predecessor until his demands are met.

- **What would happen if a pickpocket was elected mayor?**
  He will line his pockets with public money.

- **What happens if a dog comes on the radio?**
  It could sound dogmatic.

- **What would make an opponent's mudslinging worthwhile?**
  A landslide victory.

- **Should you call a spade a spade?**
  No, you should first say hello.

- **Political Freedom Index**
  Russia: In Soviet Russia, the Party has you.
  USA: In America, we have two recognized political parties - Tweedleree and Tweedledumb.
  India: In India, we have numerous thieving gangs that operate under a political banner.

- **The blonde and her political awakening**
  Teacher: Who wrote the book 'How to win friends and influence people'?
  Blonde: Most likely a lobbyist.

- **What is the technical term for the irrational fear/hatred usually exhibited by Leftists?**
  Cherophobia [fear of happiness]

- **How many Socialists does it take to change a lightbulb?**
  One to write a flyer on the Socialist Theory of Production. Several to strike work at the lightbulb factory. None to screw the bulb because the production and supply of lightbulbs has stopped.

- **How many Communists does it take to change a lightbulb?**
  One to denounce the bourgeois Capitalist System of Production. Several to burn down the lightbulb factory. None to screw the bulb because the production and supply of lightbulbs has stopped.

In the Soviet Union, workers had no right to strike and also had to work for several months without pay. This surprised Indian Communists when they visited the USSR just before it broke up.

- **Why would it be wrong to adopt a turkey as a pet?**
  Because a pet turkey can be easily misinterpreted as patriarchy and 'trigger' someone.

- **Confucius say joke: What is politically incorrect name for a walking talking 3-dimensional clickbait?**
  Confucius say honourable gentleman who go by initials S.J.W.

- **Confucius say joke: Why SJW couple break up?**
  Confucius say a case of mistaken identity.

- **Confucius say joke: What films honourable gentleman like to see?**
  Block comedy.

- **Confucius say joke: What difference between blonde and honourable gentleman?**
  If you explain the joke, the blonde may like it.

- **Confucius say joke: How you transport vampire in a train?**

With reservations.

- **Confucius say joke: How you transport honourable gentleman in a train?**
  With high stakes.

- **Confucius say joke: What films Socialists like to see?**
  Fairy tales

- **Confucius say joke: What films Communists like to see?**
  Historical fantasies

- **Confucius say joke: What live entertainment Fascists like to see?**
  Puppetry

- **Confucius say joke: What films austerity economist like to see?**
  Slasher

- **Confucius say joke: What films fat people like to see?**
  - Mealodrama
  - Satirical

- **Confucius say joke: What films thin people like to see?**
  - Lighthearted
  - Ghost

- **Confucius say joke: What computer game fit people like to play?**
  Mass Effect

- **Confucius say joke: What films non-vegetarians like to see?**
  - Creature feature
  - Hard-boiled

- **Confucius say joke: What computer game hijacker like to play?**
  Grand Theft Auto

- **Confucius say joke: What computer game Fascists like to play?**
  - Resident Evil
  - Warcraft
  - Hitman

- **Confucius say joke: What computer game Socialists like to play?**
  Call Off Duty

- **Confucius say joke: What computer game Communists like to play?**
  Counter-Strike

- **Confucius say joke: What computer game nationalists like to play?**
  Borderlands

- **Confucius say joke: What films vegetarians like to see?**
  ~~Sad~~ Salad movies.

- **Confucius say joke: What films vegans like to see?**
  Survivalist drama

- **Confucius say joke: What fiction raw-food enthusiasts like to read?**
  Mango

- **Confucius say joke: What films climate activists like to see?**
  Apocalyptic

- **Confucius say joke: What computer game climate activists like to play?**
  Unreal Tournament

- **Confucius say joke:** What magazine do SJWs like to read?
  Consumer Reports

- **Confucius say joke:** What fiction PC militia like to read?
  Oh... guilt literature

- **Confucius say joke:** What you get when cross *PC Magazine* with honourable gentleman?
  Confucius say: *PC Magazine*. But, 'PC' mean 'Political Correctness', not 'Personal Computer'.

- **Confucius say joke:** What did honourable gentleman tell Devil when honourable gentleman went to hell?
  Confucius say honourable gentleman say, "Totally unnecessary. I boil at room temperature."

- **Late dawning**
  He who laughs last... Confucius say honourable gentleman not very bright.

- **Confucius say joke:** What films do climate alarmists like to see?
  Post-apocalyptic

- **Confucius say joke:** What computer game climate alarmists like to play?
  Doom

- **Confucius say joke: What fiction globalists like to read?**
  Utopian

- **Confucius say joke: What fiction conspiracy theorists like to read?**
  Dystopian fiction

- **Confucius say joke: What computer game creationists like to play?**
  Pro Evolution Sucker.

- **Confucius say joke: What computer game evolutionists like to play?**
  Monkey Kong.

- **Confucius say joke: What happen if crocodile encounter honourable gentleman?**
  Confucius say: Crocodile shed real tears.

- **Confucius say joke: What happen if honourable gentleman meet Chuck Norris?**
  Confucius say: Honourable gentleman politically correct himself.

- **Confucius say joke: Why honourable gentleman cross road?**
  Confucius say: To be in safe space.

- **Confucius say joke: Why honourable gentleman hate sports?**
  Confucius say: Race is trigger.

- **Confucius say joke: What happen if zombie bite honourable gentleman?**
  Confucius say: Zombie get offended.

- **Confucius say joke: What happen if Count Dracula bite honourable gentleman?**
  Confucius say Count Dracula finally die of food poisoning.

- **Confucius say joke: What technical term for irrational fear/hatred by honourable gentleman encountering original thought**
  Confucius say: Isolophobia.

Isolophobia - Fear of being alone

- **Honourable gentleman is offended easily**
  A little learning is dangerous thing. Confucius say honourable gentleman offended easily.

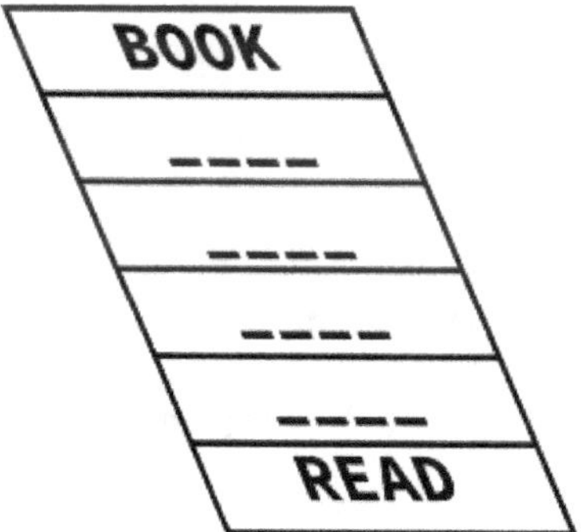

One and only one letter needs to change in each rung of the ladder. No acronyms, proper nouns or loan words.

- **Why did the Mac couple break up?**
  Her comments were non-PC.

- **What is a politically incorrect name for a strong box?**
  Safe space.

- **What is a politically incorrect name for a sign maker?**
  ~~Man~~ Person of letters.

- **What is a politically incorrect name for a busted neon sign?**
  ~~Empty~~ Differently abled words.

- **What is a politically incorrect name for a car mechanic who specializes in removing dents?**
  Dentist.

- **What is a politically incorrect name for someone who specializes in repairing fans?**
  Fanatic.

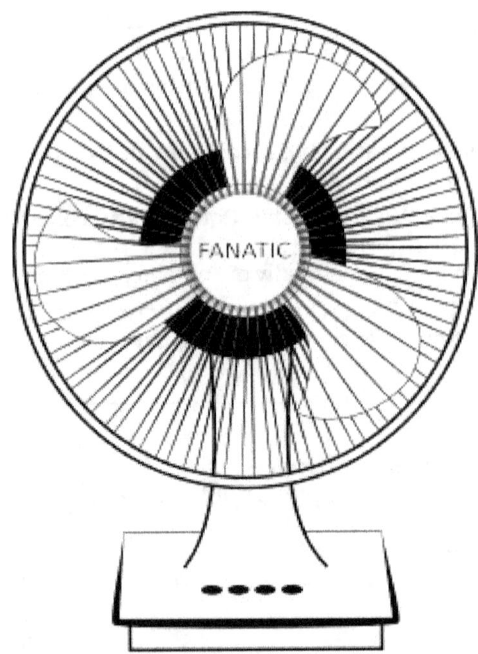

- **What is a politically incorrect name for a painter?**
  Person of colour.

- **What is a politically incorrect name for a Modern Art painter?**
  Visually handicapped person.

- **What is a politically incorrect name for a person who buys Modern Art paintings?**
  Mentally handicapped person.

- **What is a politically incorrect name for a person who steals Modern Art paintings?**
  Psychopath.

- **What is a politically incorrect name for an alien from outer space?**
Undocumented pilot.

- **What is a politically incorrect name for a human abducted by an alien from outer space?**
Undocumented emigrant.

- **What is a politically incorrect name for a flying saucer?**
Undocumented Flying Object (UFO).

- **What is a politically incorrect name for a lizard that crawls upside down on the roof to catch a bug?**
Paranormal investigator.

- **What is a politically incorrect name for damage caused by a rioter?**
Commercial break.

- **What is a politically incorrect name for a parent who calms a screaming kid with candy?**
Exorcist.

- **What is a politically incorrect name for a cat owner who drives the animal crazy with a remote-controlled car?**
Poltergiest.

- **What is a politically incorrect name for a cat owner who drives the animal crazy with a laser pointer?**
Raycist.

- **What kind of computer games do honourable gentlemen hate to play?**
Racing.

- **What kind of fiction do feminists hate to read?**
Romantic (not just because there is a man in it).

- **What is a politically incorrect name for a chicken thief?**
Poulterhiest.

- **What is a politically incorrect name for a terrorist bomb-maker?**
Time killer.

- **What is a politically incorrect name for a weightlifter?**
Weight supremacist.

- **What is a politically incorrect name for a person with a selfie stick?**
Extremist.

- **What is a politically incorrect name for a person with a selfie stick after he/she has fallen of a cliff?**
Martyred extremist.

- **What is a politically incorrect name for a liar?**
Imaginative.

- **What is a politically incorrect name for a person who cannot tell a decent lie?**
Developmentally challenged.

- **What is a politically incorrect name for a person who can successfully defend their lies?**
Chronologically advantaged.

- **What is a politically incorrect name for a stamp collector?**

Nationalist.

- **What is a politically incorrect name for a stamp collector who steals them?**
  Jingoist.

- **What is a politically incorrect name for a dog breeder?**
  Traitor.

- **What is the politically incorrect term for the study of apes?**
  Apology.

- **What is the politically incorrect term for the study of lightbulbs?**
  Ideology.

- **What is a politically incorrect name for a junk caller?**
  Televangelist.

- **What is a politically incorrect name for a bald person?**
  Globalist.

- **What is a politically incorrect name for a kid who tries to explain his poor report card?**
  Activist.

- **What is a politically incorrect name for a parent who hides the tin with sweets on the top shelf?**
  Elitist.

- **What is a politically incorrect name for a kid who eats the sweets in the top shelf and then gets caught?**
  Pacifist.

- **What is a politically incorrect name for a sibling who finds the sweets in the top shelf before you can?**
  Thought criminal.

- **What is a politically incorrect name for a sibling who can reach the sweets in the top shelf?**
  Height criminal.

- **What is a politically incorrect name for an older sibling who prevents you from reaching the sweets in the top shelf?**
  Obstructionist.

- **What is a politically incorrect name that a parent calls you when you get caught and your story changes each time you tell it?**
  Revisionist.

- **What is a politically incorrect name for a sibling who is too chicken to get into trouble or does not get caught often enough?**
  Conformist.

- **What is a politically incorrect name for a sibling who always has a backup plan?**
  Survivalist.

- **What is a politically incorrect name for a sibling who does get caught but does not get punished as often as you do?**
  Expert.

- **What is a politically incorrect name for a sibling who manages eliminate his tracks before you bring it to your parents' attention?**

Futurologist.

- **What is a politically incorrect name for a sibling whose problem-escaping skills have improved from pacifist to escapologist really quickly?**
Evolutionist.

- **What is a politically incorrect name for an older sibling who steals stuff from you and gives them to his friends for free?**
Socialist.

- **What is a politically incorrect name for an older sibling who always promises to return the stuff he has stolen from you but never does?**
Escapologist.

- **What is a politically incorrect name for a sibling who is too chicken to get into trouble and when you get into trouble he is there to tell you 'I told you so'?**
Moralist.

- **What is a politically incorrect name for a sibling who comes up with a plausible excuse for any situation?**
Innovator or child prodigy.

- **What is a politically incorrect name for a sibling who get in and out of trouble without the slightest damage whatsoever?**
Constitutionalist.

- **What is a politically incorrect name for a sibling who backs up your version of the story?**
Loyalist.

- **What is a politically incorrect name for a sibling who rats on you?**
Populist.

- **What is a politically incorrect name for a sibling who rats on you and also correctly explains the motive?**
Conspiracy theorist.

- **What is a politically incorrect name for a sibling who rats on you, explains the motive and backs it up with proof?**
Crazy conspiracy theorist.

- **What is a politically incorrect name for a sibling who rats on you with extreme attention to detail?**
Archeologist.

- **What is a politically incorrect name for a sibling who tells your parent the exact differences between what you promised and what you actually did?**
Perfectionist.

- **What is a politically incorrect name for a sibling who rats on you with exaggerated detail?**
Inflationist.

- **What is a politically incorrect name for a sibling who pokes holes in your 'cover' story?**
Acupuncturist.

- **What is a politically incorrect name for a sibling who ratted on you and failed but made your parents not trust you anymore?**
Controversialist.

- What is a politically incorrect name for a sibling who threatens to rat on you but is ready to offer you a deal?
  Mercantilist.

- What is a politically incorrect name for a sibling who offered you a deal and then ratted on you?
  Dichotomist.

- What is a politically incorrect name for a sibling who does not believe in the statute of limitations and continues to extort stuff citing crimes committed long ago?
  Imperialist.

- What is a politically incorrect name for a sibling who threatens to rat on you and refuses to cut a deal?
  Antimaterialist.

- What is a politically incorrect name for a sibling who does not just rat on you but also tells about your threats to use force?
  Antimilitarist.

- What is a politically incorrect name for a sibling who does not just rat on you but also tells about your use of force?
  Victimologist.

- What is a politically incorrect name for a sibling who whittles down the crime despite your best efforts to exaggerate it?
  Abstractionist.

- What is a politically incorrect name for an older sibling who forces you into his crime when you threaten to rat on him?
  Neocolonialist.

- What is a politically incorrect name for a sibling who rats on your attempts to subjugate him?
  Abolitionist.

- What is a politically incorrect name for a sibling who threatens to rat on another sibling who threatened to rat on you?
  Salvationist.

- What is a politically incorrect name for a parent who refuses to believe your spin of the story?
  Subjectivist.

- What is a politically incorrect name for a parent who does not want to hear your legitimate excuses?
  Russophobe.

- What is a politically incorrect name for a parent who refuses to believe your 'act of God' story?
  Rationalist.

- What is a politically incorrect name for a parent who grounds the kid and banishes him to his room?
  Isolationist.

- What is a politically incorrect name for a parent who remembers the exact number of times you made the same mistake before?
  Numerologist.

- What is a politically incorrect name for a sibling who rats on you and suggests punishment options?
  Lobbyist.

- What is a politically incorrect name for a sibling who takes what you have and then makes you earn it?
  Communist.

- What is a politically incorrect name for a younger sibling who is still nibbling at the top of her chocolate bar when you have finished yours eons ago?
  Chauvinist.

- What is a politically incorrect name for an older sibling who grabs your chocolate bar when you are still nibbling the top of it?
  Hijacker.

- What is a politically incorrect name for a younger sibling who is still nibbling at the top of her chocolate bar when you have finished yours eons ago and refuses to share hers with you?
  Exclusivist.

- What is a politically incorrect name your younger sibling calls you when you try to explain what may have happened to the remainder of the chocolate bar she placed in the chiller?
  Fantasist.

- What is a politically incorrect name for your older sibling who eats your chocolate bar and then begs you not to tell your parents?
  Apologist.

- What is a politically incorrect name for your older sibling who thinks he can get away with it?
  Optimist.

- What is a politically incorrect name for your younger sibling who thinks you cannot get away with it?
  Pessimist.

- What is a politically incorrect name for a younger sibling who takes the window seat while you bring in the luggage?
  Opportunist.

- What is a politically incorrect name for a younger sibling when he explains to the horrified parent how you hit him?
  Dramatist.

- What is a politically incorrect name for a younger sibling who walks in and ruins everything?
  Anarchist.

- What is a politically incorrect name for a younger sibling who walks in, ruins everything and then threatens to rat on you?
  Terrorist.

- What is a politically incorrect name for a younger sibling who walks in, ruins everything, threatens to rat on you and then offers to cut you a deal?
  Humanist.

- What is a politically incorrect name for a younger sibling who walks in, sees

everything and then ignores it?
Solidarist.

- **What is a politically incorrect name for a younger sibling who gets everything simply by asking while you have to beg and/or scream?**
  Welfarist.

- **What is a politically incorrect name for a friend who listens to your joke and then tells others as if he invented it?**
  Plagiarist.

- **What is a politically incorrect name for a kid who refuses to take baths?**
  Conscientious objector.

- **What is a politically incorrect name for a miser?**
  Economist.

- **What is a politically incorrect name for a plastic surgeon?**
  Feminist.

- **What is a politically incorrect name for a plastic surgeon when the surgery goes bad?**
  Misogynist.

- **What is a politically incorrect name for a politician who climbs the greasy pole and refuses to back down?**
  Columnist.

- **What is a politically incorrect name for a politician who climbs the greasy pole and then immediately back down under criticism?**
  Scenophobe.

- **What is a politically incorrect name for a pressure cooker?**
  Whistleblower.

- **What is a politically incorrect name for stealing?**
  Quantitative easing.

- **What is a politically incorrect name for a butcher?**
  Piecemaker.

- **What is a politically incorrect name for vegetarians?**
  Plant killers.

- **What is a politically incorrect name for non-vegetarians?**
  Animal lovers.

- **What is a politically incorrect name for vegan?**
  Invasive species of the cow ecosystem.

- **What is a politically incorrect name for a designated driver?**
  Plunge-protection team.

- **What are politically incorrect names for alcohol?**
  - Toxic assets.
  - Bio-fuel.
  - Socialized Medicine.
  - Chemotherapy.

- **What are politically incorrect name for a drunk?**
  - Unstable ~~man~~ person.
  - The Man-Bird Hybrid system, a top-secret military research programme

[*per* a drunk].
  - ~~Man~~ Person in high spirits.
  - Spiritual ~~man~~ person.
  - Extrovert; free-speech activist; and non-conventional philosopher.
  - Green-fuel activist.
- **What is a politically incorrect name for a sober person?**
  - Introvert.
  - Anti-social element.
  - Loner.
- **What is a politically incorrect name for a drunk who is driving on the right side of the road in a country where everyone else drives on the left?**
  Alt Right.
- **What is a politically incorrect name for a drunk who has driven his vehicle into the gutter?**
  Far Right.
- **What is a politically incorrect name for a drunk who takes three steps backwards for every one step forward?**
  Retard.
- **What is a politically incorrect name for a drunk who leaves without paying?**
  Leftist.
- **What is a politically incorrect name for a drunk who buys drinks for everyone without any money?**
  Liberal.
- **What is a politically incorrect name for a drunk who buys drinks for everyone, cheers, drinks and falls backwards from his stool?**
  Libtard.
- **What is a politically incorrect name for a drunk who is afraid of leaving his stool because he knows he will end up like the libtard?**
  Protectionist.
- **What is a politically incorrect name for a drunk who buys drinks for everyone, cheers, writes an IOU, drinks, and falls backwards from his stool?**
  Socialist.
- **What is a politically incorrect name for a drunk who has no idea where he is?**
  Internationalist.
- **What is a politically incorrect name for a drunk who is desperately trying to see clearly but cannot?**
  Reform-oriented.
- **What is a politically incorrect name for a drunk who is trying various ways to stand up but is unable to?**
  Technocrat.
- **What is a politically incorrect name for a drunk who thinks the world is spinning around him?**
  Revolutionary.
- **What is a politically incorrect name for a drunk who is holding his head because he thinks the world is spinning around him?**

Counter-revolutionary.

- **What is a politically incorrect name for a bartender who will not provide one milliliter over the limit?**
  Millitant.

- **What is a politically incorrect name for a drunk who gives the same shocked expression each time the bartender tells him he is over the limit?**
  Reactionary.

- **What is a politically incorrect name for a drunk who is trying to get more out of the bottle?**
  Illusionist.

- **What is a politically incorrect name for a bartender who will kick you out if it is time to shutter the place?**
  Maoist.

- **Why did the tiger couple break up?**
  As a born Meowist, she constantly accused him of being a reactionary paper tiger.

- **What is a politically incorrect name for a security guard or bouncer who will not let you in to get a drink?**
  Stallinist.

- **What is a politically incorrect name for a bartender who says no to everything?**
  Nazi.

- **What is a politically incorrect name for a new bartender who seems to say no to everything?**
  Neo-Nazi.

- **What is a politically incorrect name for a drunk who beckons to a Nazi to listen to him?**
  Commie.

- **What is a politically incorrect name for a security guard who will sell you a drink for a marked-up price?**
  Lenienist.

- **What is a politically incorrect name for a drunk who does not have all the answers?**
  Conservative.

- **What is a politically incorrect name for a drunk who has just banged his head on the lamp post?**
  Confrontationist.

- **What is a politically incorrect name for a drunk who has banged his head on a lamp post and is now engaged in an animated conversation with it?**
  Conversationalist.

- **What is a politically incorrect name for a drunk who is holding on to the lamp post for dear life?**
  Fundamentalist.

- **What is a politically incorrect name for a drunk who climbs the lamp post and gets electrocuted?**
  Shock-therapist.

- **What is a politically incorrect name for a drunk who refuses to leave the bar?**
Institutionalist.

- **What is a politically incorrect name for a drunk who tries to hide under the umbrella in his glass?**
Austrian economist.

- **What is a politically incorrect name for a drunk who is trapped in the revolving door?**
Undecided.

- **What is a politically incorrect name for a drunk who is spinning inside the revolving door?**
Centrist.

- **What is a politically incorrect name for a drunk who has passed out on the floor?**
Unaffiliated.

- **What is a politically incorrect name for a drunk who crosses the road at the wrong time and gets run over immediately?**
Fatalist.

- **What is a politically incorrect name for a drunk who gets bumped by a vehicle and then gestures to the driver to run him over from the other side?**
Multilateralist.

- **What is a politically incorrect name for a drunk who drives a vehicle and runs over somebody?**
Cellist.

- **What did the clown say to his psychiatrist after he joined politics?**
"I feel like I am surrounded by buffoons."

- **Freedom of the Press**
India political parties put a lot of pressure on the owners of newspapers and editorial independence is a precarious bird. The editors of *The Times of India* were no exception. After several changes at the helm of the newspaper, someone (probably Khushwant Singh) suggested that the paper place an ad for "Editor Wanted: Journalists need not apply".

- **How did Gandhi become bald?**
Gandhi went to the forest and did *tapas* (meditate/penance) without a break. But, even after two days, God failed to appear before him. Gandhi became very angry and broke his *tapas*. As he was just about to leave, God appeared and said "Gandhi, what do you want? Ask me anything." But, Gandhi was still angry and said "I don't need a single hair from you!"

- **TN Seshan**
Seshan was a feared Chief Election Commisioner. He cleaned up elections in

India. For the first time since Indira Gandhi's Emergency, politicians and government employees were afraid of someone. Before one election, he was inspecting preparations in Chennai. One journalist asked him about reports that a political party (MDMK, I think) was distributing spinning tops to children to secure votes. Seshan did not say if it would be considered for disqualification but he said that it was a good thing they did not have an elephant for their party symbol.

- **Under the influence**
  A student of biology or chemistry knows that alcohol cannot be considered as a regular food item. Even though its breakdown releases energy, acetaldehyde is also generated. Acetaldehyde is a toxic substance and not typical of a food item. I do not drink alcohol or smoke tobacco but some of my friends do. In these matters, I have been lucky. I used to be addicted to cricket but got cured after the betting scandal in the 90s. Believe it or not, I have never watched cricket in the new 20/20 format. For a long time, I thought Virat Kohli was a male model. I did not know his name but was seeing him everywhere except where he was playing cricket. When cricket is on TV, the roads are empty. I am happy that something in our country makes our roads less crowded. Back to alcohol. Yesterday, there was news that a drunk guy climbed a zoo fence and took an impromptu ride on a giraffe. How can this happen? People do all kinds of unimaginable things when they are drunk. When I see them passed out on the pavement (always with their heads sticking out into the traffic), I wonder what drives them to go to such extremes on a routine basis. One day, many years ago, some of my friends told me that they were planning to drink alcohol. They were old enough to drink but few families tolerate the habit. Next day during lunch, I asked one of them how their date with drinking went. He said it was fine for him but the other guys who went with him had created a mess. When the 'other guys' joined the lunch, I asked them what happened. They said the first guy was the one who created the mess. Not only did he spill his guts after one glass, he also slapped a police constable.

- **SJW Anthem**

  Everything is RACISM!
  Everyone is BIGOTED, according to the outrage mob!
  Everything is RACISM!
  When you BELIEVE IN THE CURRENT THING!

  Pretending like a MARTYR 'cos you've NO SELF-ESTEEM.
  Opinions are SCARY. Divide 'n' Rule brainwashing is better.
  Common Core education forever!
  Yell at strangers. Live with cats. And, talk to nobody.

  Everything is RACISM!
  Everyone is BIGOTED, according to the outrage mob!
  Everything is RACISM!
  When you BELIEVE IN THE CURRENT THING!

  Set to the tune of the *Lego* movie song *Everything is awesome!*

Unclassified Jokes

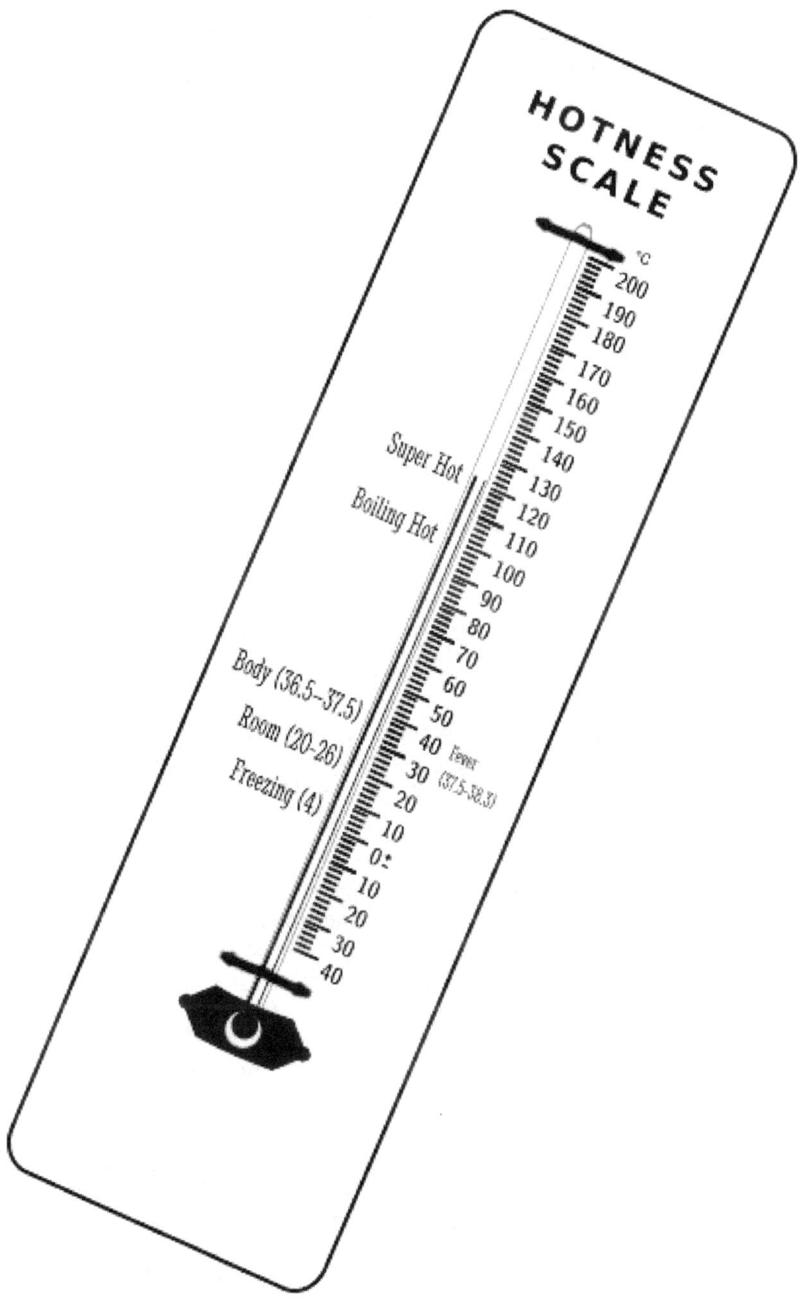

Are you a fan of political correctness? Do you get easily offended? Then, this section is not for you.

These jokes are either rants or too big for George Costanza. I saved the rants for the last because few people like them.

- **Clean tech is the future, not green tech**
  Most of the 'green' [something] universe are oxymorons. The use-and-throw culture is the main problem. If you want to help the environment, consume less. Waste not. Want not. 'Recyclable' products are not a solution. They are just another problem. A lot of the 'recyclable' wastes are too expensive to recycle and are not recycled at all. A huge amount of 'recyclables' are dumped in Third-World countries.
  - When you buy something, buy a good quality product and use it for its maximum designed life and beyond, if possible and safe. Do not discard your phone in the trash just because a new model is on the market. Avoid wireless networks. Their power consumption is mostly wasted. They are slow and a security risk. Use a wired Gigabit Ethernet LAN whenever you can. Turn off the wireless option in the router configuration. Do you suspect planned obsolescence? Your computer does not have an Ethernet port? Then, do not buy that company's products. Do not buy products that are inherently wasteful or polluting.
  - Do not turn off the remote and go away. Turn the switch off.
  - Green tourism is not green. Animals do not need humans. You have invaded their territory. You can put lipstick on a pig but it is still a pig. No offence to pigs. They are wonderful beautiful creatures. Why did God create them? Probably for this proverb.
  - Electric cars are not the future. Hydrogen cars are the future. A safe/economical hydrogen fuel and combustion engine is what we need. Battery manufacture and disposal causes pollution. If something leaves behind wastes to be cleaned up, it is not green.
  - Carbon fuel burning is not so much of a problem, as is plastic (a downstream product of petroleum refining). CO_2 and other exhaust gases will eventually be absorbed by oceans and land. But, discarded plastics remain unavailable to the carbon cycle, even when they disintegrate. (Poisonous chemicals are pumped into the ground to bring out shale oil. It pollutes land and ground water. It is supported by politicians of all hues. Traditional crude oil drilling is many times cleaner but still gets a bad rap.) Avoid plastic-wrapped products as much as possible. Do not buy use-and-

throw plastic items. Use a fountain pen, instead of a ball-point pen. Do not crib over plastic straws and paper straws. They are both bad. Are you a baby? For heaven's sake, use a spoon or drink straight from the glass. Stainless steel, glass and porcelain should be the options in homes and eateries.

- o Before you decide to throw something away, try to find an alternative use for it.

- o Always have an interest in science and decide for yourself. Do not follow the herd. Be sceptical about all hype and propaganda, whatever be the intentions. Ask for data and analyse the claims.

- **Dena Bank – A Government of India Undertaking**
  In the news: "Dena Bank's NPAs (Non-Performing Assets) are at 22–23%." Many many years ago, I took an education loan from them. I spent most of my salary from my first few jobs repaying that loan. One day, some months after I thought I had paid off the loan, they sent a legal notices to me and my loan guarantor. It was not an ordinary notice; it was a *japthi* notice. They threatened to attach our properties to recover the loan. By the time, I paid the last instalment, the loan had borne a further Rs. 50 as interest. The cost of the legal notice was Rs. 500. I took another trip the bank to close the loan by paying Rs. 550. And, this time I asked for a letter stating that the loan had been repaid in full. When minnows fail to pay, they send a *japthi* notice. When big fish default, they declare an NPA. So, kids, remember this passage from *Hamlet* by Shakespeare.

    Neither a borrower nor a lender be.
    Do not forget:
    Stay out of debt.
    Think twice and take this good advice from me:
    Guard that old solvency!

Only the first line is from Hamlet. For a tune of this   *Carmen* song, see the episode
Producer of the TV show   *Gilligan's Island*.

- **Fascism**

    Lucky Refaeli lives in a trailer
    He forgot to clear $8 in dues
    Michigan state foreclosed on his house
    And denied him the remainder of the sales

• Set to the tune of 'Lucy Locket lost her pocket'.
• "PLF's Campaign to End Home Equity Theft"; Scott Barton;
https://pacificlegal.org/plfs-campaign-to-end-home-equity-theft/]

- **Fascism and systematic racism in Flint, Michigan**

    Lead from Flint river waters
    Exempted for General Motors
    Obama pretended to drink it and said it's fine
    He also sent the military for an urban warfare exercise
    To reinforce the investors of the new pipeline

• Set to the tune of 'Hey diddle diddle'.

- **World's Shortest Man**

I do not think the Guinness Book of World Records accepts deformed individuals for this recognition. If it does, then a guy from the city of Chennai will get that honour. I am not sure if he is still alive or what became of him. When I was working there, I sometimes saw him disembarking from an suburban EMU train. He was a beggar and he used stand/sit outside the Moore Market Complex (MMC) in Central Station. He was about a foot high. He had a normal-shaped head. The rest of the body was deformed and was not even half-a-feet high. His hands and legs were deformed as well but he somehow used them transport himself. His head was permanently inclined. This meant that he could not have been more than a feet tall.

He was a tough guy for tough guys. In summer, I would cover my face with my lunch bag when I came out of the MMC. This man did the opposite. He would position himself under the bright sun if he could. If the shadow of the MMC came closer, he would move away from it. His presence in the hot sun would break any heart and people were generous to him. I saw him for several years. On recent visits, though, he did not seem to be there. The parking lot where he used to be is not there anymore because of a redesign. Maybe he has retired. I wish him well.

This man is not the joke. The handicapped people or the homeless people who go about their lives without recourse or complaint are not the joke. Women in war-torn drought-affected countries who have to trudge for miles over landmines to fetch water are not the joke. But, when a celebrity posts a bizarre photo on the Internet and gets everyone to applaud her for overcoming 'adversity' and being an 'inspiration', does it not strike you as a joke? Or, when a man-baby has an online meltdown over some stupid word or some joker? Can the Yazidis who survived Saddam Hussein but were subject to unspeakable crimes by ISIS terrorists (supported by military allies of Western countries) sit on their chairs and complain about lack of 'safe spaces'? Some people have no idea what real problems are yet they get all the support. That, my friend, is a real joke, albeit sad.

- **What is a politically incorrect name for a glutton who gatecrashes weddings?**
Communalist.

- **Clickbait Journalism and Political Correctness**

Not On The Moon: As the paper of record, NYT knows that men are first choice for government experiments but letting 'snowflakes' make judgements without a historical perspective brings in the much-needed clicks.

What happened to the time when journalists were tough-as-nails ladies and gentlemen you looked up to?

In the West, newspapers are dying. Whatever that remains (online news) survives by clickbait journalism. So, journalists are ranked by how much Internet traffic they can drive to their website. As a result, journalists descend to the cheapest form of clickbait.

The cheapest form of clickbait is political correctness. The more offended you are, the more clicks. Political correctness is a fickle business so you need to constantly push the limits of incredulity. The more outlandish your claims are, the more 'viral' it is.

However, the political correctness madness that has been unleashed is an uncontrollable monster of epic proportions. Its influence has spread beyond news media. So, everyone is offended or is seeking something to be offended about. Nobody seems to have real ideas or emotions anymore. People are taking selfies next to their deceased relatives, and when they upload it, their worthless friends go 'Like', 'Like', 'Like, 'Like'...

My unsolicited advice to anyone is do not become a real-life zombie. Unshackle yourself from the Internet. Get rid of your smartphone. Use an old-style phone-and-SMS feature phone if you have to.

Read a real newspaper. By supporting a real newspaper, you are supporting journalism and democracy. Clickbait journalism is just another stop on the road to ruin.

- **Where the mind is without fear**
When an armed policeman is brought in to question a kid studying in third standard for some name-calling, you know that country has hit rock-bottom. ("Student's brownie comment highlights school policing dispute"; CBS News) As I write this, the city of Berkeley, California, has banned the humble word 'manhole' because it has been oppressing women! In Canada, the premier corrected a woman for using the word 'mankind'. "It is 'peoplekind'", he demurred.

Did I use the word 'he'? HE???!!! According to one honourable gentleman, even 'he', 'she' and 'it' are oppressive. Ban them, ~~he~~ 'they' said (It's Time for 'They'; New York Times). What are they teaching these kids? It must be stupefying them.

The West won the Cold War but they have adopted the Communist philosophy. Fear of offending someone has reached such paranoia levels that churches in Europe have been asked to remove crosses even though immigrants who were to be temporarily housed there made no such demand. I am not a Christian but I am offended. Even India has not escaped this blight. They are everywhere. As Thomas Fuller said, a fool's paradise is wise man's hell. Only God can save us now. So, let us all pray to Him for a better future. I wish everyone the best of health, happiness and fortune, and finish this book with a poem by the man who wrote our national anthem.

> Where the mind is without fear and the head is held high;
> Where knowledge is free;
> Where the world has not been broken up into fragments by narrow domestic walls;
> Where words come out from the depth of truth;
> Where tireless striving stretches its arms towards perfection;
> Where the clear stream of reason has not lost its way into the dreary desert sand of dead habit;
> Where the mind is led forward by thee into ever-widening thought and action;
> Into that heaven of freedom, my Father, let my country awake.

Well, you have finished the book. If you give it a good review or rating (☆ ☆ ☆ ☆ ☆) online, it would be much appreciated. If you have any corrections or suggestions, write to me at **Info@VSubhash.Com**.

Some of my titles are available for FREE on several ebook stores and library apps. Give them a try. I have written more than two dozen non-fiction books on a wide range of subjects. I have also written ONE fiction title(s)! Check the backlist for more details or visit: **www.VSubhash.IN/books.html**

Annexures

Before you close the book, learn something about the the main inspiration behind it — vintage American radio shows.

Vintage Radio Shows

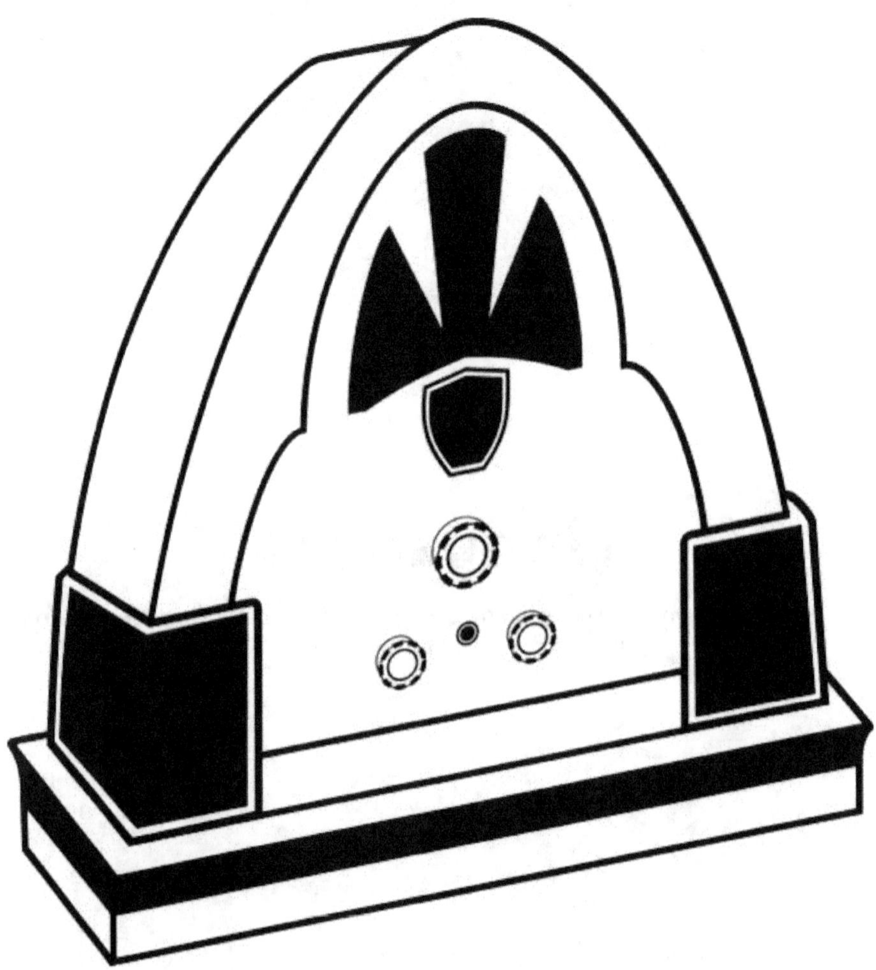

The first radio broadcast was made by a Canadian named Reginald Fessenden on Christmas Eve in 1906. He was also the first one to transmit human voice over radio in 1900. Until then radio transmissions were Morse code messages.♣ His wife Helen♧ wrote:

On Christmas Eve and New Year's Eve of 1906 the first Broadcasting occurred. Three days in advance Reg had his operators notify the ships of the U.S. Navy and of the United Fruit Co. that were equipped with the Fessenden apparatus that it was the intention of the Brant Rock Station to broadcast speech, music and singing on those two evenings.

Describing this, Fessenden wrote:

> The program on Christmas Eve was as follows: first a short speech by me saying what we were going to do, then some phonograph music. The music on the phonograph being Handel's 'Largo'. Then came a violin solo by me, being a composition of Gounod called 'O, Holy Night', and ending up with the words 'Adore and be still' of which I sang one verse, in addition to playing on the violin, though the singing of course was not very good. Then came the Bible text, 'Glory to God in the highest and on earth peace to men of good will', and finally we wound up by wishing them a Merry Christmas and then saying that we proposed to broadcast again New Year's Eve.

By the 1920s, ◇ commercial radio networks run by the National Broadcasting Corporation (NBC) became popular. Television was invented in the 1930s but it languished due to World War II. Consequently, radio lasted as the popular medium for news and entertainment for over two decades. This time is known as the "golden age of radio"♬ in America. After World War II, radio slowly lost the crown to television.

In the age of the Internet, networks such as NBC, ABC and CBS have turned over their vast radio archives to the US Library of Congress and other institutions. The process of archiving radio shows from that age has been slow but the Internet has taken the lead. Vintage radio enthusiasts have networked over the Internet and recovered radio shows from "transcription disks" (such as those given to the US Armed Forces Radio) and from personal collections. These radio shows are now freely available to the public as MP3 audio files that can be played on a computer, phone or portable music player. According to a leading radio archivist group,♪ most of these radio shows were broadcast without a copyright declaration and are hence not covered by US copyright law. A non-profit organization named Archive.org (home of the Internet Archive and the WayBackMachine) is now hosting many of these radio shows. This radio archive covers several popular genres including crime/detective, mystery, science fiction, comedy and horror.

Some popular radio shows

I like humour so I began with comedy shows. Here are some of the best that I found.

Mel Blanc Show (1946-47)

https://archive.org/details/TheMelBlancShow

Mel Blanc was the voice behind popular cartoon characters such as Daffy Duck, Bugs Bunny, Porky Pig, Foghorn Leghorn, Yosemite Sam and Speedy Gonzales. Mel Blanc also hosted an eponymous "Mel Blanc Show". In this show,

Mel speaks in his usual voice (that of Sylvester The Cat) and plays the role of a fix-it shop owner. Mel also voices the role of his assistant Zookie (who speaks like Porky Pig but with more stutter). Mel's unsuccessful attempts to impress the rich father of his fiancée Betty forms the crux of most storylines.

- **Mel:** "Betty, we will elope... No, that's terrible. I just remembered his new shotgun.
  Betty: Mel, stop worrying. You know father shoots nothing but blanks.
  Mel: That's what I am worried about. [He used his real name in the show.]

Also in the cast is one Mr. Cushing who married for money but greatly regrets it. Whenever he meets Mel, he lets loose a litany of unbelievable and outrageous complaints about his wife.

- The other day, we had an argument and she said, "John, you are driving me to my grave." I got the car out of the garage in two minutes.

- Yesterday, we were in a shooting gallery. As I picked up the gun, she stuck her face in front of me and says, "John, shoot the bull's eye. John, shoot the old duck." Damn! What a temptation!

- Yesterday, I was spraying 10 gallons of DDT in the garden and she says, "John, spray the bugs. Kill the ants. Poison the old gopher." Damn! What a temptation!

- I loaded the rifle. I was aiming it when the wife says, "Oh, John, I wanna use the rifle. John, let me have it. Come on, John. Let me have it." Damn! What a temptation.

Then, there is a vain Beau Brummel named Hartley Benson. He talks like a radio commercial and cannot be adequately described in words. Every interlude with Hartley Benson is radio gold. This role was played by Jim Backus, better known as *Mr. Thurston Howell III* from the TV show *Gilligan's Island*.

- **Mel:** Oh, it's you, Benson. I can't talk now.
  Hartley: I know how you feel, Mel. Everyone is struck speechless by the beauty of *The Great Big Adorable Me* .

- **Mel:** Hello, Hartley. Is it drizzling out?
  Hartley: No, Mel, it's merely the tears of thousands of women crying because they can't get *The Great Big Adorable Me* .

- **Hartley:** I am the prettiest thing in my life. Someday, I am going to make myself my wife.

- **Hartley:** In the words of the immortal John Keats, "A thing of beauty is a Hartley Benson."

- **Mel:** What kind of line do you give women?
  Hartley: Mel, I take her hands in mine and say, "Has anyone ever told you how beautiful I am?"

- **Hartley:** I covered myself with suntan lotion but got an awful sunburn anyway.
  Mel: That's odd.
  Hartley: No, it isn't, Mel. My body is so beautiful the Sun fought its way through.

- **Hartley:** I am so lovely as can be that perfume smells me.

Duffy's Tavern (1941-1951)

Duffy's Tavern was set in a rundown Brooklyn, New York bar. The main character is the manager Archie, played by Ed Gardner. Archie is obsessed with get-rich-quick schemes and rich/beautiful/famous women. The regular cast includes his screw-loose friend Finnegan, a wise-cracking waiter Eddie, the bar owner's daughter Miss Duffy and a colourful Russian émigré Yasha Panyaslovnik. (It seems that Finnegan had been using "Daaaaaah" much before Homer Simpson made his "Duh" famous. Moe Szyslak, the owner of *Moe's Tavern*, is definitely Archie-inspired.) In one episode, Archie attempts to patent electricity on the advice of his crooked friend Slippery Joe. The dialogues of Slippery, voiced by Alan Reed of *Fred Flintstone* fame, should not to be missed by anyone. Ditto for episodes with singer/actress Shelley Winters and boxer Maxie Rosenbloom. The main attraction though was Archie – his many pretensions, the unintentionally self-deprecating humour and the constant stream of malapropisms, mixed metaphors and misunderstood fact/fiction. There are over a hundred episodes online that you can listen to. Archie recycled many of his scripts but the new ones are funnier than the original. (The mistakes in the following dialogues are not misprints.)

- **Archie:** Radio? Miss Duffy, I see you are still living in the Middle Evil Ages.

- **Archie [to actress Joan Bennett]:** Joan, tell me my ears just heard a mirage!

- **Archie:** Perish forbid! [An Archie combination of 'perish the thought' and 'God forbid'.]

- **Eddie:** Hey, Mr. Archie. Your friend Slippery McGuire is here.
  Archie: How do you know?
  Eddie: I reached into my pockets and found myself shaking hands with him.

- **Slippery:** Hello, Washington? Patent Office? Clever Ideas Department, please.

- **Slippery:** Arch, the warden up at Sing-Sing [a well-known prison] wants to know if it's okay for them to use a little extra current tonight [not mentioned as for an electric chair execution].
  Archie: Hmmm... for how long?
  Slippery: For about 30 seconds.
  Archie: Tell 'em it's okay.
  Slippery: Warden, throw the switch.... Arch, that was sweet.
  Archie: Oh, you know, you got live and let live.

- **Eddie:** Here is one letter that I am thinking you will find extremely interesting.

Archie: A billet-doux from a female admirer?
Eddie: No, a bill-overdue from the gas company.

- **Archie**: Miss Duffy, did you send me a Valentine?
  Miss Duffy: Isn't there a name on it?
  Archie: No. No signature. Just unanimous.

- **Finnegan**: What good is happiness? Can I buy money with it?

- **Archie**: I wonder if they still remember me out there. I once starred in a picture for Paramount.
  Shelley Winters: Oh, yes, they are still talking about you.
  Archie: Yeah? What were they saying?
  Shelley Winters: I don't know. I am a lady. I always leave the room.

- **Archie**: Well, I ain't exactly saying I am filthy rich but I ain't exactly saying I am filthy poor.
  Yasha: No, he is just filthy.
  Archie: Thank you... You see, Shelley, if I wasn't rich do you think this pheasant would insult me?
  Shelley Winters: Well, if you had so much money, why are working in a place like this?
  Archie: Look, Shelley, this tavern is just a hobby with me. ... Yasha, take the Rolls Royce down to one of me oil wells and fill it up with diesels.

- **Shelley Winters**: How about your background... Your family.
  Archie: Oh, them. My grandpater was also a millionaire, you know. In fact, I shouldn't really talk about my family fortune without giving him credit. You know, he was the original flounder. Started out as a poor boy until he *Mayflower*'d it over here with my grandmumma and they were able to pick up Pennsylvania at the right price. So, I grew up on the estate and went to college.
  Shelley Winters: So, what college did you go to?
  Archie: Well, Dad wanted me to go to Harvard and mother wanted me to go to Yale.
  Shelley Winters: What happened?
  Archie: They compromised. That's when Dad built Princeton.

- **Yasha**: In love, he says. This is what he is telling all his wives...
  Archie: No, Panya... Slovnik, stay away from this.
  Yasha: Miss Winters, did he tell you he has four wives and 48 children.
  Shelley Winters: 48 children?
  Yasha: One for every state in the Union.
  Shelley Winters: Oh, this is terrible. Where are the wives?
  Yasha: Standing by for Alaska and Hawaii!

- **Archie**: By the way, if we are gonna get any publicity on our show tonight, I better call up the fashion magazines. What's the name of the famous one again?
  Eddie: Harper's Bazaar.
  Archie: Hello, is Harp over there?... Well, I would like to talk to somebody about a style show at Duffy's Tavern.... Oh, let me talk to her. Hello, Mrs. Bizarre?

- **Miss Duffy**: Archie, did you see my Dostoevsky?
  Archie: Your what?
  Miss Duffy: My Dostoevsky?
  Archie: Is it animal, vegetable or mineral?

- **Miss Duffy:** Wait a minute, Archie. Maybe we are not talking about the same Shakespeare. What was the first name of yours?
  Archie: William.
  Miss Duffy: That's the one, all right.
  Archie: Of course, William Randolph Shakespeare. [The most famous William Randolph was the newspaper baron Hearst.]

- **Archie:** Your own lecture? Look, Fadiman. Suppose you were in my spot. Would you let every Tom, Dick and Harry come in off the street and read his own stuff? How do I know it's clean? How do I know it makes sense?
  Clifton Fadiman: Well, I was going to talk about the rudimentary forms of the iambic pentameter.
  Archie: You see. In this business, we got to protect ourselves.
  Clifton Fadiman: All right. I will read your speech. If I get fired from *Information Please*, can I eat here?
  Archie: That, I wouldn't advise.

- **Archie:** Ladies, I introduce a man who needs no introduction so without further introducing him I present you Mr. Clifton Fadiman. [Applause] The lecture, Mr. Fadiman.
  Clifton Fadiman: [Groans] Thank yous, one and all. Ladies of the Lord Byron Ladies Literary Society, my subject for tonight is 'Contemptuary Litrachor'. I will discuss 'Contemptuary Litrachor' from litrachor from the Middle Ages to books for children. Litrachor is divided into three parts – Fiction, non-fiction and... Archie, where is the third part?
  Archie: I couldn't think of it. I went nuts. Go on.
  Clifton Fadiman: Litrachor was started by the cavemen who used to chop out stories in stone with an axe. Hence, the term 'hack writer'. This however was very hard on the circulating liberries as people got tired carrying home them stone books. Besides, many times the stones would fall on the author crushing him. Hence, the expression 'pulp writer'. This lead to the invention of sheepskin, which up till then had only been used for diplomas. Litrachor has gave birth to more writers than any other profession. Namely, among whom are Shakespeare, Bacon, Dickens and Sir Walter Lipton. Among the French writers are Boltaire, Charlemagne and [...] Archie, you left out Madamoiselle [...] here.
  Archie: That's a different kind of literature.
  Clifton Fadiman: Now, among the American writers is also a great assortment of literary authors. Just as music has its three Bs – Back, Bach and Bookhoven, American litrachor has it three Os – O'Neill, Odets, and O'Toole [the resident forger]. [Groans] Next, come the Russian writers. Among who is Tolstoy, Rimsky-Korsakov? Dostoevsky and the great Russian of them... Oh, oh, no, I can't! I can't, Archie.
  Archie: Go on, Fadiman.
  Clifton Fadiman: Ivanhoe. Archie... Archie, I can't go on with it. My reputation will be ruined. Ladies, the lecture is over. Bye. Thank you.

- **Archie:** I will start with Dinah Shore.
  Eddie: Maybe your start will be her finish. How do you gonna be able to get her to do it?
  Archie: Very simple, Eddie. Personal maggotism.

- **Dinah Shore:** Well... I had no idea you were so musical, Archie.
  Archie: Music...? Mercy me! I played the piano when I was three years old.

Dinah Shore: Three years old?

Archie: It was a little piano... what they call a pianissimo.

Dinah Shore: So, you were a child prodigy?

Archie: Yeah... yeah. It was a curse, you know. Day after day my father used to say to me, "Archie, why don't you go out and play baseball with the other boys?" You know? And, I would say, "No, Dad, I have to go upstairs and practised my chamber music." Day and night I practiced, and so finally they sent me to the observatory.

Dinah Shore: Archie. Which teacher did you study under?

Archie: They call them maestro. Very conservatory observatory. Anyway, that's where I studied the old masters. You know? I loved them. Chachikovich and Dave Babuski. Puccini. Batch. Tichicowsky.

Dinah Shore: Archie, that's Tchaikovsky.

Archie: So, I mispronounced one of them.

Red Skelton shows (1938-1953)

https://archive.org/details/AvalonTimeRedSkelton
https://archive.org/details/RaleighCigaretteProgramStarringRedSkelton

If you had seen the movie "A Southern Yankee", then you would know Red Skelton. The Red Skelton radio shows were initially sponsored by cigarette companies. The shows start with a monologue by Red and then moves on to situational comedy sketches by his team. Famous characters he played include the cowboy *DeadEye*, the village idiot *Clem Kadiddlehopper* and the *Mean Widdle Kid* (of the "I dood it" fame).

Fibber McGee & Molly (1935-1956)

https://archive.org/details/FibberMcgeeMolly1930s
https://archive.org/details/FibberMcGeeandMolly1943

This 30-minute sitcom was one of the longest running shows in the golden age of radio. It featured real-life married couple Jim and Marion Jones as Fibber & Molly McGee. The adventures of bumbling Fibber and the exasperated Molly along with their colourful friends and acquaintances form the storyline. Bill Thompson, who is best known for voicing the cartoon character Droopy, played several roles including that of the battered husband Wallace Wimple. There are hundreds of episodes for this show on Archive.org.

- **Molly:** Are you really the inventor of this pavement, Mr. Wimple? [Fibber is stuck in a new pavement.]
  Gildersleeve: My God, it is Wallace Wimple.
  Wallace Wimple: Yes, I am, and I am dreadfully sorry that your husband got stuck, Mrs. McGee. Just makes me miserable, to say the least.
  Fibber: What do you mean it makes you miserable? What do you think of me?
  Wallace Wimple: I'd rather not say, in front of all these people.
  Molly: Well, how do we get him out of there, Mr. Wimple?
  Wallace Wimple: Well, Mrs. McGee, as I see it, the whole thing depends on a chemical analysis of the material. Maybe we can dissolve some of it around his feet.
  Fibber: That's the first sensible remark that's been made today. What is the chemical formula, Wimple?
  Wallace Wimple: Oh, that's a secret [sings it], Mr. McGee.
  Molly: What do you mean it is a secret?
  Wallace Wimple: That's what I mean. It's a secret.
  Gildersleeve: Well, you know what the secret is, don't you?
  Wallace Wimple: No, my wife does.
  Fibber: Your wife? What's she got to do with your invention?
  Wallace Wimple: Well, she is really the inventor. I'm only the one who saw the possibilities in it for paving material.
  Molly: Well, what was it in the first place?
  Wallace Wimple: Her recipe for chocolate pudding. [Audience applause and laughter] The minute I tasted it I said to her... I said, "Cornelia," I said, "this would make wonderful paving material."
  Gildersleeve: And, what did she say?
  Wallace Wimple: I don't know. Everything went blank.

- **Molly:** Have you protested Mr. Wimple?
  Wallace Wimple: Oh, many times, Mrs. McGee. I often say to her, "Cornelia," I'd say, "Why don't you give up those drums and go back to your other hobby?"
  Fibber: What was her other hobby?
  Wallace Wimple: Lion taming.
  Molly: Heavenly days! Lion taming?
  Wallace Wimple: Yes, she uses her kitchen chairs too. They are all scarred up with teeth marks. Believe me, that varnish tastes terrible.

- **Fibber:** Hey, is your wife still teaching wrestling and jiu jitsu to the police force?
  Wallace Wimple: Oh, yes. She takes her police work very seriously, Mr. McGee. Too seriously, I sometimes think.
  Molly: Too seriously, Mr. Wimple?
  Wallace Wimple: I told her it was ridiculous to have a siren in front of her vacuum cleaner.
  Fibber: And, what did she say?
  Wallace Wimple: Oh, she just gave me one of those mischievous little smile and kicked my teeth out from under it.

Vintage Radio Commercials

Old radio shows are interesting for another reason - the commercials. The golden age of radio was also a time when many household staples, such as toothpaste (as opposed to tooth powder) and detergents (instead of soaps), were promoted to the public. One tobacco company, which sponsored Red Skelton shows, claimed that "medical science" had provided "proof positive" that their brand was the best for smokers' health than other cigarettes! Product placement was exceptional and the radio medium was tailor-made for it. Commercial messages were written into the dialogs and entire characters built around them.

We also get to hear casual references to politics, war, famine and suffering. In one unusual episode, Duffy's Tavern replaced its regular programming with a serious drama (by a different cast of characters) about the famine in India - to urge Americans to contribute money for Indian famine relief. Thank you, Mr. Gardner.

We can also note how the political correctness epidemic was going on even then. In one episode, Red Skelton tells how "newsboys" (at that time) wanted to be called as "newspaper boys"!

History of radio

According to the Library of Congress, commercial radio broadcasting began in 1926 when the Radio Corporation of America (RCA), a subsidiary of Westinghouse, bought a New York City radio station operated by AT&T (since 1922) and amalgamated it with its own Newark station (started in 1921) to form the National Broadcasting Corporation (NBC). By 1927, NBC had two networks, Red and Blue, with a total of 25 stations. In the same year, another network named Columbia Phonograph Broadcasting System came into being. It later changed its name to Columbia Broadcasting System (CBS). The original investors which included a phonograph company were bought off by the new owner, a tobacco magnate. The US Federal Communications Communication (FCC) forced a split of NBC and its "Blue" network was bought by a candy company. That became the American Broadcasting Corporation (ABC) in 1943.

Regular radio shows required serious production effort including radio actors, writers, props, and orchestra. Many shows were recorded in front of a live audience. Some of these were recorded on disks and played back by other stations by 'transcription'. Thus, comedy shows had the laugh track as part of the original live broadcast. When these shows were not on air, music, news and interviews with local notables filled the gaps. World War 2 added to the popularity of radio.

Initially, Hollywood was not interested in radio. But, as radio stars moved to Hollywood, Hollywood started producing radio shows based on their old and new movies - it was good publicity. A good example is the Lux Radio Theater. Advertising seems to have been largely provided by tobacco companies and makers of soaps and cosmetics.

In 1928, television made its first appearance. In 1935, the German government started the first regular TV transmissions with 90-minute broadcasts three times a week. In the UK, the BBC started television broadcasts in 1936. In the USA, NBC started with two hours of TV broadcasting per week from 1939. At that time, RCA began selling television sets whose screens were 12x5 inches. World War II disrupted television manufacturing and broadcasting, as factories were diverted for war effort. Only six TV stations with limited programming was left to cater to 10,000 "TV receivers" or TV sets. Hence, radio continued to rule the air waves in the 40s. When the restrictions were lifted in 1946, television sales grew exponentially. Initially, TV broadcasts were mostly seen in bars and restaurants but by the end of the decade the number TV sets in use was in the millions. Many radio stars had moved to TV and they made their old radio shows even bigger hits on the small screen. There was a *Duffy's Tavern* movie and a *Duffy's Tavern* TV show too. The movie was noted for the huge cast of famous stars who had earlier appeared on the radio show but it did not do well at the box office. The TV version also did not last long. Apparently, ♪ Duffy's Tavern's main strength lay in the clever use of dialogue written by Gardner and it was mostly lost on the screen. Red Skelton had no such problems. He was a great pantomime artist and his histrionics extended to physical comedy. So, he had a much longer run on TV. From the 60s onwards, radio programming catered to Americans commuting in their cars. (This change can be observed in newer shows such as that of Sears.) By then, the golden age of radio had ended.

Vintage radio shows live forever

For today's listener, the payoff is in the richness of the content, as radio shows by the nature of the medium had to have consistently sharp writing. An ordinary TV sitcom fan will find that old radio comedies have more jokes per dialogue than today's TV shows. Like other forms of audio entertainment, you can listen to vintage radio shows when you are doing some other activity.

References

♣ Radio's First Voice...Canadian!;
http://www.ieee.ca/millennium/radio/radio_birth.html

♣ Helen Fessenden; Fessenden: Builder of Tomorrows; 1940;
https://archive.org/details/fessendenbuilderoofessrich

◇ National Broadcasting Company history files;
https://www.loc.gov/item/2002660093/

♬ Golden Age of American radio;
https://www.britannica.com/topic/Golden-Age-of-American-radio

♪ OTRR policy on copyrights;
http://otrrlibrary.org/copyright.html

♪ Duffy's Tavern: A History of Ed Gardner's Radio Program;
http://martingrams.biz/duffys-tavern/

Some Aanayum-Urumbum Jokes

These are some real elephant-and-ant jokes popular in my state of Kerala.

- Aana and Urumbu were playing hide-and-seek near a temple. Aana told the Urumbu that the temple was out of bounds for hiding. When they began playing, Aana had to seek and Urumbu could hide. Aana searched everywhere but could not find Urumbu. Aana became suspicious and decided to check the temple. It blocked the entrance and when the Urumbu sneaked back to capture the post, Aana caught him. How did Aana know that Urumbu was hiding in the temple? Urumbu's shoes were outside.

- An aana was travelling on the road when it met with an accident. The ambulance took him to the hospital. An urumbu was seen following the ambulance on a motorcycle. What was the reason? To give blood for his injured friend, of course.

- One day, Aana and Urumbu went on a pilgrimage. When evening came, they decided to sleep under a tree. Aana could not sleep. What was the reason? Urumbu was snoring.

- Aana and Urumbu were travelling on a bike. They met with an accident. Aana died but Urumbu survived. How did that happen? Urumbu was wearing a helmet.

Disclaimer, Acknowledgements & Thanks

- All trademarks and copyrights are properties of their respective owners.

- Use of trademarked and copyrighted names and works are permitted under fair-use terms of copyright and freedom of expression statutes. Parody and reporting rights of the writer are also covered under case law, such as the Barbie Girl lawsuit (Mattel, Inc. v. MCA Records, Inc.).

- The "fresh" part of this book's title is a mere assumption. The author wrote these jokes over four months. Some jokes are what the author had heard from friends and acquaintances, which had to be paraphrased from memory or embellished to suit the section title or the joke type. In some instances, a published joke has been used to set the stage for one or more jokes that follow the same setup. Some are published quotes (not published jokes). It is possible that the author's memory of reading of some published joke had faded and the author was under the false impression that he came up with it first. A person's memory and imagination can play tricks with each other and nobody (including the author) is immune from the consequences. An excess of 2020 jokes are available in this book to adjust for the intentional/unintentional inclusion of old jokes.

- Many maps in this book are based on outlines provided for free by NASA on their website.

- The sad cartoon illustration in the 'Jokes You Love to Hate' section is based on an episode of *The Road Runner Show* (Warner Bros.) in which the coyote finally catches the road runner.

- The illustration of a water anole in the *Biology Jokes* section was created from a video taken by biologist Lindsey Swierk.

- The illustration for the *Blonde Jokes* section is based on *Broadway Babes* found in *Dizzy Dames* comic published by American Comics Group.

- The White House CCTV still in the *Journalism Jokes* section is based on a photo published by several news organizations about Hillary Clinton on a hike. A low-quality manipulated version of the photo from one of the news websites has been used under fair-use terms.

- The photos of the snoops are official photos funded by US taxpayers' money.

- I would like to thank:
  - the people and organisations behind open-source software: Richard Stallman (Free Software Foundation), Linus Torvalds (Linux) and those behind Mate desktop environment, LibreOffice, GIMP, Inkscape, gcc, python, perl...
  - makers of several typefaces used in this book.
  - old radio show artists, producers and archivists: Ed Gardner (Duffy's Tavern), Jim and Marion Jones (Fibber & Molly), Mel Blanc and many others, Archive.org, Old Time Radio Researchers (OTRR.org), NBC, ABC, CBS,...

- And, I would like to thank you, the reader, for buying the book.

More From *World of Word Ladders*

There are two books in this series for children, each with 100 word ladder puzzles. In a word ladder, you need to change one letter in each rung and transform the first word into the last word. Conditions are that none of the words be a proper name, foreign (non-English) word or abbreviation.

BEE
___
___
DIN

BET
___
___
WIN

BOB
___
___
PIN

CAT
___
___
DOG

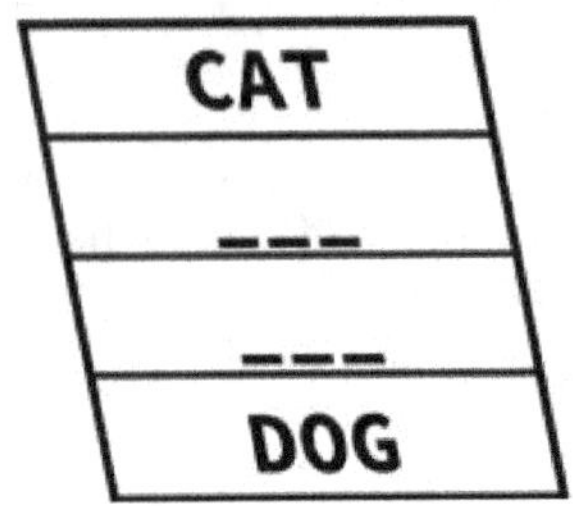

BOAR
_ _ _ _
_ _ _ _
_ _ _ _
_ _ _ _
PORK

BOWL
_ _ _ _
_ _ _ _
_ _ _ _
BEAT

BITE
_ _ _ _
_ _ _ _
_ _ _ _
_ _ _ _
TOPS

COIN
_ _ _ _
_ _ _ _
_ _ _ _
_ _ _ _
DIME

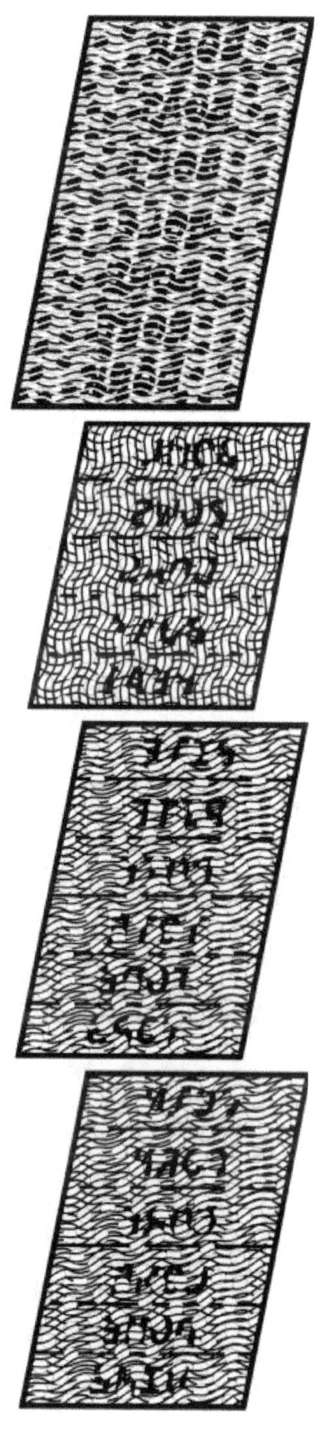

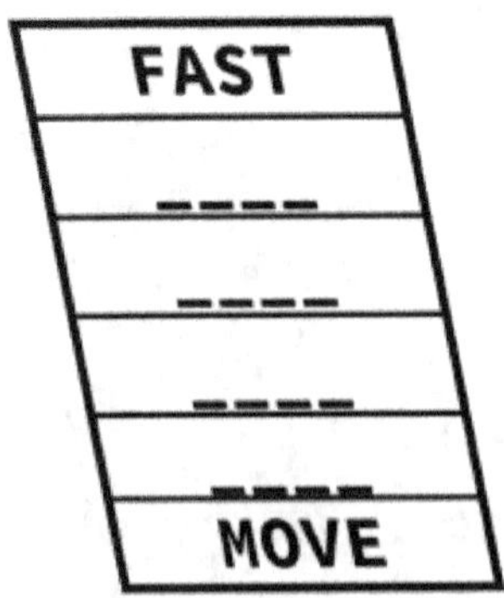

EASY
_ _ _ _
_ _ _ _
TASK

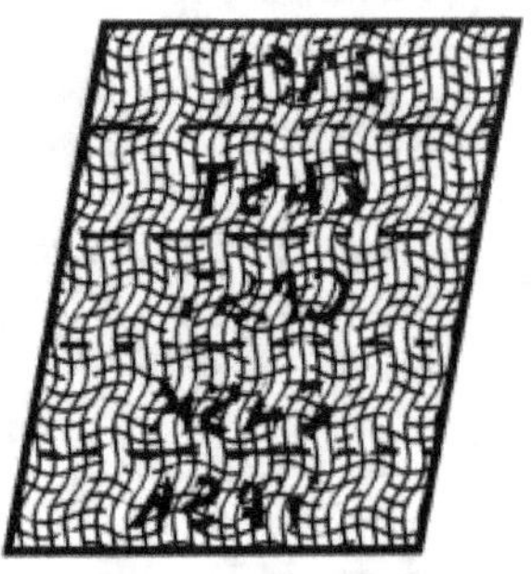

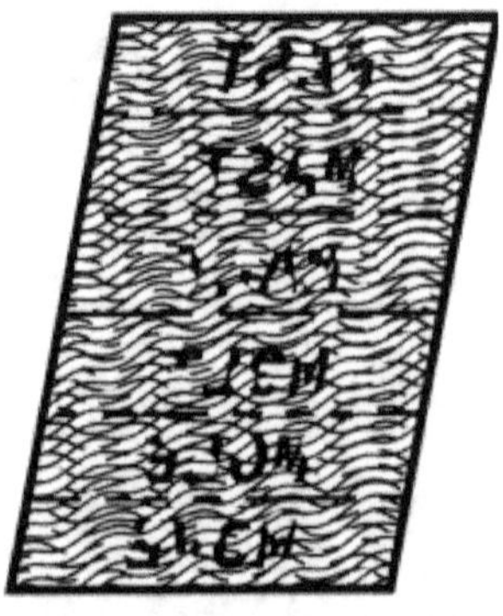

FAST
_ _ _ _
_ _ _ _
_ _ _ _
MOVE

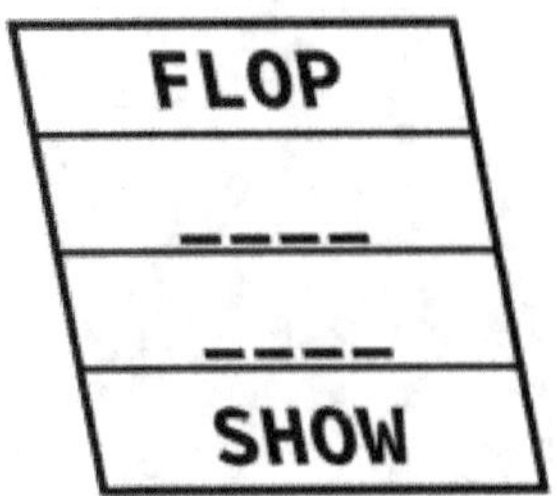

FLOP
_ _ _ _
_ _ _ _
SHOW

GOOD
_ _ _ _
_ _ _ _
_ _ _ _
MILE

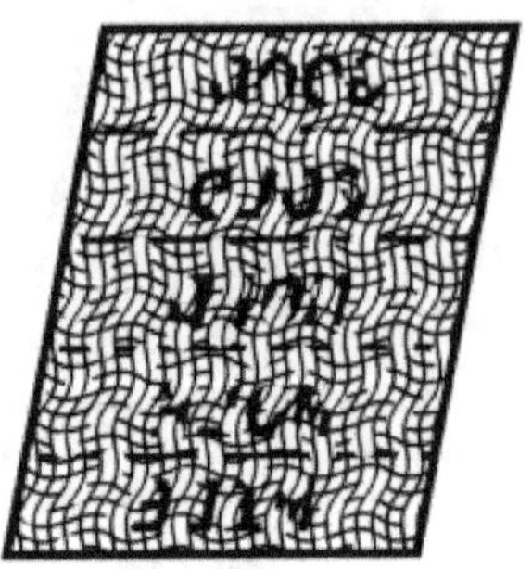

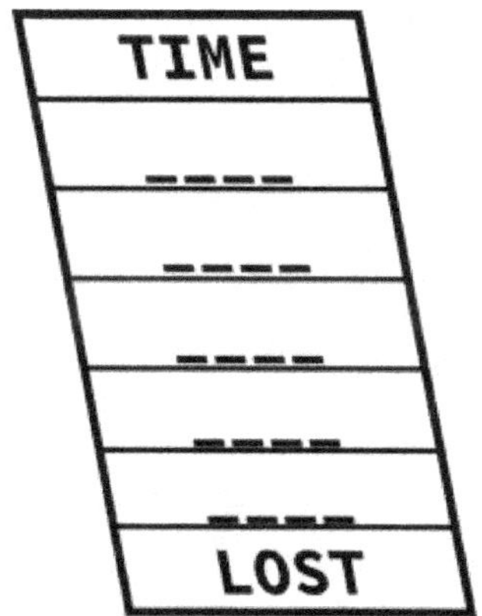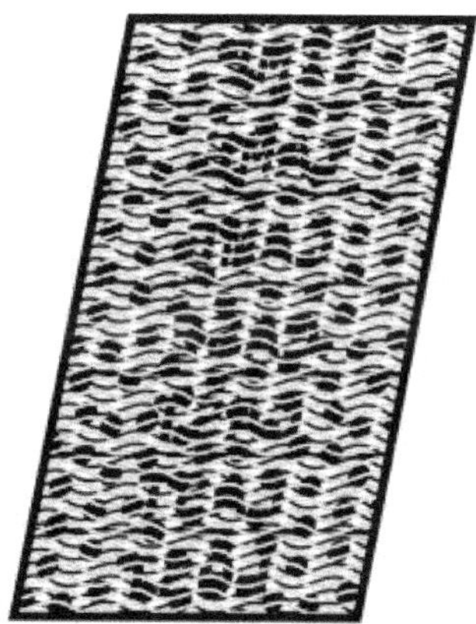

TIME

_ _ _ _

_ _ _ _

_ _ _ _

_ _ _ _

_ _ _ _

LOST

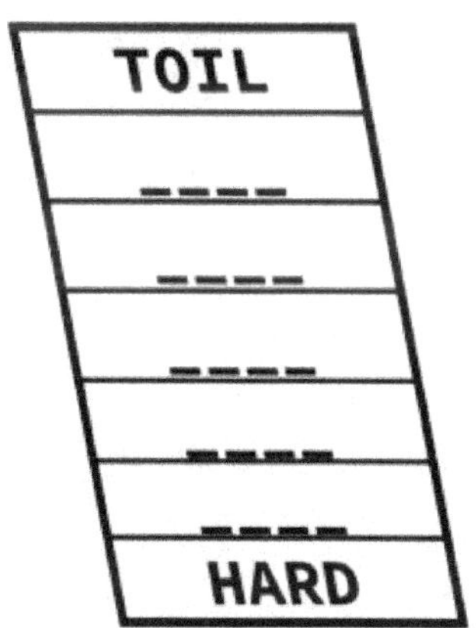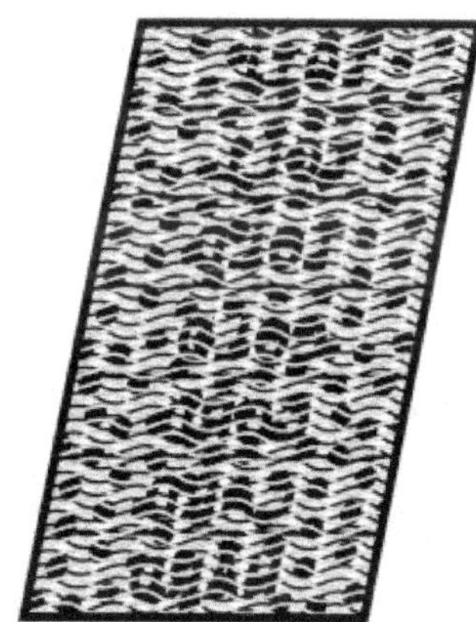

TOIL

_ _ _ _

_ _ _ _

_ _ _ _

_ _ _ _

_ _ _ _

HARD

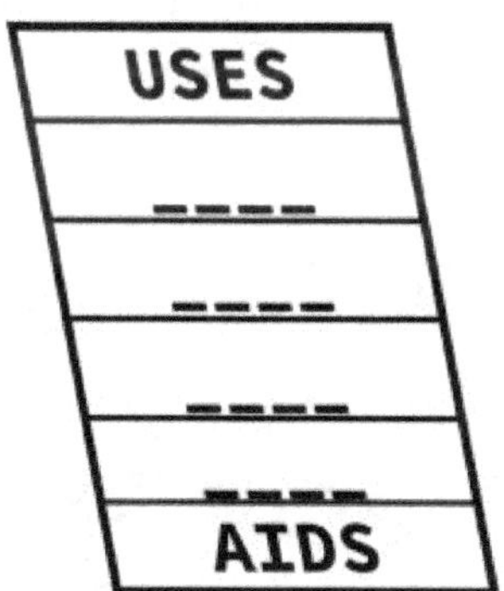

USES

_ _ _ _

_ _ _ _

_ _ _ _

_ _ _ _

AIDS

Books By V. Subhash

I invite you to visit my site **WWW.VSUBHASH.IN**, and check out my other books, special discounts, sample PDFs and full ebooks. In 2020, I started publishing books. For two decades before that, I have been publishing feature articles, free ebooks (old editions still available), software (server/desktop/mobile), reviews (books, films, music and travel), funny memes and cartoons. You can follow these adventures on my blog: **http://www.vsubhash.in/blogs/blog/index.html**

My books for children are under the pseudonym **Ólafía L. Óla** (because it has laugh and LOL).

2020 Fresh Clean Jokes For Everyone

This is one of the biggest jokebooks ever written - over 3200 jokes spread over:

- *Part 1 — For Learning* (computer jokes, programming jokes, physics jokes, chemistry jokes, biology jokes, medical jokes, financial jokes, geography jokes, pun jokes and THREE CHAPTERS DEVOTED TO FOREIGN LANGUAGES)
- *Part 2 — For Fun* (bar jokes, blonde jokes, cross-the-road jokes, knock-knock jokes, lightbulb jokes, knock-knock jokes, romantic (breakup) jokes)
- *Part 3 — Only For Intellectuals* (jokes about philosophy, advertising, news and politics)

It has lots of jokes purely for the hedonist consumption of humour, content to improve vocabulary and general knowledge, thought-provoking poems (mostly as financial/political limericks set to the tune of popular nursery rhymes) AND some of the best one-liners EVER written in English. Absolutely no (_x_) humour.

• Pages: 292   • Paperback: $10   • Ebook: An older subset with 420 jokes is available FOR FREE

2020 Fresh Clean Jokes For Kids

This 'for kids' subset of the 2020 jokebook has over 2200 jokes. It has all of *Part 1 (For Learning)* and some non-political jokes from *Part 2 (For Fun)* & *Part 3 (Only For Intellectuals)*. Joke types include computer jokes, programming jokes, cross-the-road jokes, physics jokes, chemistry jokes, biology jokes, medical jokes, financial jokes, geography jokes, knock-knock jokes, breakup jokes...). Special chapters include *Elephant & Ant Jokes* , *Off-The-Wall Philosophers*, *Useful French Phrases* , *Useful Latin Phrases*, *Other Useful Foreign Phrases* , *Jokes You Love To Hate* , *Jokes In Advertising* , and *Fancy Creature Jokes* . No political or controversial jokes. Absolutely no (_x_) humour.

• Pages: 166   • Paperback: ₹550 or $7.70   • Ebook: Will never be published

Ólafía L. Óla's Favourite Traditional Nursery Rhymes (Illustrated)

The political correctness pandemic has caused many nursery rhymes to be rewritten or eliminated altogether. This illustrated children's book has **50 popular English nursery rhymes in their traditional form**. The selected rhymes have stood the test of time and this **large-print paperback with edge-to-edge colour** makes it easy for kids to read them.

• Pages: 44 (39 with real content)   • Colour Paperback: $9

Animalia Humorosum

This is an illustrated children's storybook based on Aesop's Fables. The stories have been made more believable by changing the ending with a humorous twist. **The book is a large-print paperback with edge-to-edge colour.**

• Pages: 30 (26 with real content)   • Colour Paperback: $9   • Ebook (for parental review): ₹70 or FREE

World of Word Ladders

A word ladder has a diagram of a ladder with a word on both the first and last rungs. You need to change only one letter in the blank middle rungs so that the first word is transformed into the last word. Your words CANNOT be proper nouns, abbreviations, or loan or slang words.

Word ladders are a wonderful pastime. These puzzles are neither tough nor easy. They have the right balance between exercising the brain and having fun.

• Puzzles: 100 • Paperback: $6 (per volume)

Vastu Shastra Explained

Vastu Shastra Explained is a plain-English Vástu Śastra building-architecture guide for those who wish to draw their own Vastu-compliant house plans. The book does not upsell Vaastu as a panacea for all ills nor does it portray Vastu as the Indian Feng Shui. Instead, it presents Vastu as a collection of time-tested best-practices in Indian building architecture.

• Pages: 40 (30 with real content)   • Colour Paperback: $7.77   • Ebook: ₹100

Learn To Ride A Motorcycle In Five Minutes

Yes, you can! For most of my life, I did not know how to ride a motorbike. But, when I had to do, it took me only five minutes. On my first ride on my first bike, I travelled nearly 100 kilometres, across two cities and one national highway. Acquiring the skill takes less than five minutes and honing it will require a few weeks.

• Pages: 40 (30 with real content)
• Paperback: $7.70   • Ebook: ₹100

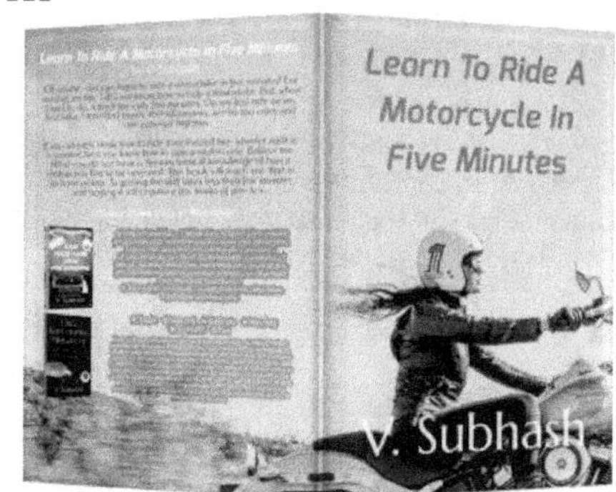

How To Invest In Stocks, 2nd Edition

The first edition book was written in 2003 for the Indian stockmarket. It was popular around the world because it was a plain-English guide to investing in the stockmarket. The 2020 completely revised second edition maintains the original premise but has a global focus, updated information and new chapters. **It has some useful 'extra' information that you will not find in any investment book and no business school will teach you.** Mere book knowledge about stockmarkets will not help you understand the markets. Markets are influenced by news and information (there is a difference).

• Pages: 94   • Paperback: $9.90   • Ebook: ₹100 or FREE

Email Newsletter Strategies For Profit

An organically grown mailing list is an invaluable resource for your business. It is your own social network. You need to nurture it like a baby. This book not only explains how to create user-friendly email newsletters but also helps you improve email deliverability, organically grow your mailing list, implement industry-standard best-practices and apply practical troubleshooting tips and tricks.

• Pages: 40 (33 with real content)   • Paperback: $7.70   • Ebook: ₹100

How To Cure Common Cold

Non-allergic rhinitis or common cold is an ailment that usually resolves on its own. It can be very disruptive and make you feel miserable. *How To Cure Common Cold* **describes several palliative measures** (not curative options) that can be used to treat the symptoms while the body fights off the infection. Because this is a thin topic, **bonus content** on natural weight-loss techniques, an easy-to-cook vegetarian food recipe, dental care tips, skincare tips, and some family-planning advice are included in this book. **DISCLAIMER**: The author is not a medical professional. Despite seeking medical treatment for common cold, his deviated nasal septum made the episodes very difficult to go through. Over several years, he tried and tested several palliative measures to treat the symptoms. In this book, he describes what measures might work for young healthy individuals like him. These recommendations are not intended for kids, adolescents, convalescents, seniors or in people where the cold symptoms are part of a larger ailment. **This book is not sponsored by any drug firm or commercial entity.**

• Pages: 31 (8 with real content)   • Paperback: $4.99   • Ebook: ₹99 or FREE

The Devil's Dictionary

The Devil's Dictionary by Ambrose Bierce from 1911 is a great repository of brutally frank and unusually cynical descriptions for popular words and phrases in English. In my 2020 remake, the original text has been illustrated with contemporary caricatures (of Alexandria Ocasio Cortez, Bill Gates, Don Lemon, Elon Musk, Joe Biden...). It has the **neat easy-on-the-eye look of any new dictionary (modern fonts, two-column pages, starting/ending words on every page)**. If you consider yourself as a woke, liberal, Leftie, Progressive, Socialist, Communist, Feminist... then this book is not for you. This book by Bierce is a product of its time and may not match your unrealistic expectations. Maybe, you could gift it to your (fr)enemies. They might like it.

• Pages: 160   • Paperback: $9   • Ebook: ₹100

Quick Start Guide to FFmpeg

FFmpeg is THE BEST software to easily create, edit, enhance and convert audio and video files. It is a FREE and open-source command-utility available **for Linux, Mac and Windows**. And, *Quick Start Guide to FFmpeg* is THE BEST book for an extensive FFmpeg tutorial, hack collection and quick reference. It is richly illustrated with color screenshots, code examples and tables to help you work with audio, video, images, animations, fonts, subtitles and metadata like a PRO. NOTE: In 2023, the old self-published book *FFmpeg Quick Hacks* was withdrawn.

• Pages: 280   • Colour Paperback: $44.99   • PDF Ebook: $29.99 (from Apress/SpringerNature)

CommonMark Ready Reference

MarkDown is an easy human-readable text format that can serve as the common base for exporting to multiple document formats such as HTML, ODF, DOC/DOCX, PDF and ebook (EPUB, MOBI...). It is a great tool for authors, technical writers and content developers to create books, manuals, web pages and other rich-text content. CommonMark is a new well-formed standard for the old MarkDown spec. **CommonMark was one of the reasons I was able to write and design 21 books in one year.** Incidentally, this is the first-ever book on CommonMark. You will be buying a piece of history! The paperback's covers are designed like a quick reference card.

• Pages: 56 (39 with real content, 6 with bonus content)   • Paperback: $6   • Ebook: ₹100 or FREE

Linux Command-Line Tips & Tricks

This is a tips-and-tricks collection for Linux command-line warriors. It is also at an advanced level. It assumes that you already know how to use the terminal and are adept at shell programming. It does not teach you the basics or try to be a comprehensive reference. It trusts your intuition and focuses on things you are most likely to forget. Because of its ancient history, BASH scripting has some odd programming constructs that are difficult to memorize. This book tries to provide a ready-reference for such archaic but crucial details. It pays special attention to coding mistakes or unusual circumstances in which your script or command will fail. The paperback has screenshots and syntax-highlighted code examples, all in full-colour.

• Pages: 100   • Colour Paperback: $9.99   • Ebook: ₹100 or FREE

PC Hardware Explained

You can build a PC in 30 minutes with just a screwdriver. Knowing which computer components will work together is not so easy. This full-colour paperback will explain computer hardware using **simple terms, illustrations, photographs and tables**. Before **buying a new laptop from the store** or **assembling a new desktop from parts**, get this book. You will be able to read the technical specifications of a PC and understand what it can and cannot do. The mumbo-jumbo accompanying the sales pitch of a new computer will not be so alien.

• Pages: 30 (22 with real content)   • Colour paperback: $7   • Ebook: ₹100

Cool Electronic Projects

If you are learning electronics or thinking of it as a future hobby, this FULL-COLOUR book has some fun projects to begin with. They will not waste your time or money, will be extremely useful (particularly in emergencies) and are quite easy to make. Just one of these projects uses AC (alternating current). The rest work on DC (direct current) and are safe for kids (if you think soldering is safe). These projects are good for the environment too, as they reuse electronic parts that would have been discarded. If you are a survivalist, then you will be happy that all the projects will run off-the-grid, as they can consume renewable energy. For the tinkerer, there are projects that add MORE POWER than what the manufacturer had provided. For the parent of lazy children, there are annoying alarms that can wake up the dead.

• Pages: 40 (33 with real content)   • Paperback: $9.90   • Ebook: ₹100

How To Install Solar

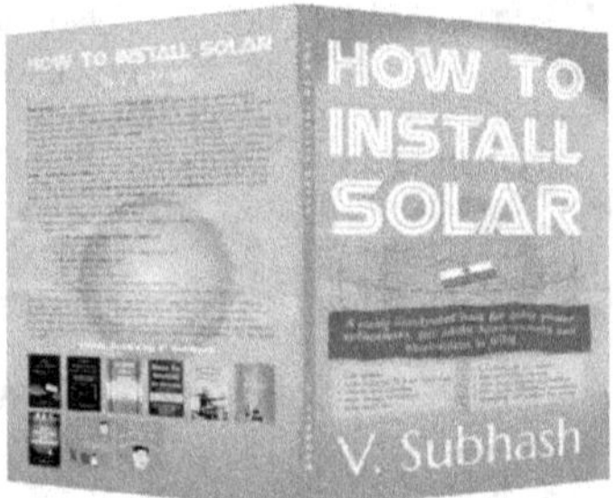

This is a heavily illustrated guidebook for **INDIAN** solar power enthusiasts, DIY hacks, home-owners and electricians about solar panels, batteries, inverters, charge controllers, installation procedures and costs. It starts with a simple introduction to home electrical systems, proceeds on to describe various aspects of solar power and options available for home owners, and then provides step-by-step instructions for installing a low-cost DC-only solar charge controller system for ₹6000 and a solar inverter system providing AC power backup for ₹30,000. Also included is an extensive FAQs section based on questions and reviews published by solar power users online.

• Pages: 76   • Colour paperback: $7.70   • Ebook: ₹100

Unlikely Stories

This is an anthology of horror and comedy stories **based on real incidents**. After writing so many non-fiction books, I was **forced by governments of several nations** to name this book as '*Unlikely Stories*' and release it only as a fiction title (!) with this rather quaint description (verbatim copy):

> *Boy meets girl. Both fall in love. Boy proposes marriage. Girl postpones decision for one month. Girl's gonna leave next day. Until then, boy tries to impress girl by telling stories — funny stories… scary stories… and all kinds in between. No worries. Everything ends well.*
>
> *The stories were tough to come by. Having given up on fiction years ago, the young man had to marshal some old personal anecdotes, wild tales told by strangers, and even some vividly detailed nightmares for his first novel. Like a male Scheherazade, he somehow wove those yarns together. They also just about helped him bag his babe.*

As a result, the stories are mostly **supernatural/paranormal fantasies with ample doses of action, horror, humour and sci-fi**. The entire book is in first person and everything happens very fast. There is never a dull moment.

- **The trip**: The lead is invited by his friend to spend the weekend at a resort. There, he meets the first heroine **Vampira**. That is not her real name.
- **The swim**: The lead decides that *Vampira* is the soul mate he has been waiting for all his life. He tells several stories to entertain his friend's kids and also impress Vampira.
- **The exorcist**: The second lead is an Indian scamster who escapes to the US to start a new life. He attempts to go legit but finds competition from a professional medium operating under the trade name of **Mademoiselle Zuma**. (She is dangerous because she is secretly a mind-reader.) He is forced to try his hand at performing an exorcism that the Church has given up on.
- **Alien encounter**: After the successful exorcism, this lead is asked to help a teenager who has been repeatedly 'abducted' by an 'alien'. This story also includes a scientifically accurate discussion that convincingly proves the impossibility of alien presence on Earth and the 100% likelihood of all UFOs and alien abductions being staged by governments. Hopefully, this story will help victims of these frauds achieve some sort of explanation or closure to their harrowing experiences.
- **The lift**: A recently deceased security guard haunts a lift where he had died and seeks revenge.
- **Femme fatale**: The second lead has a showdown with a female animal spirit.
- **The seance**: A young woman in the city is troubled by nightmares involving a hooded skeleton. A newly married nurse in a rural area blanks out every night. She is also troubled by bizarre nightmares. Mademoiselle Zuma solves both cases.
- **The haunting**: An old mansion is haunted by a presence. Every new buyer and his family gets driven to such desperation that they eventually sell. The current owner wants the paranormal activities investigated. The second lead tries and almost gets killed.
- **Family planning**: The first lead and Vampira plan their life together. In the first ending, they get married. In the second ending (written by the lead after their first night), **Stone Age Man (SAM)** and **Stone Age Woman (SAW)** discover some truths about the mystery of life. (This is an over-the-top parody of the **controversy about *MEN WRITING WOMEN*** .) Other than these intimate events implied in comic fashion, there is no physical contact between the sexes in the entire book. Not even a kiss. It is clean throughout. (The attractive elf on the cover is on the lines of James Hadley Chase covers but nothing more. She does exist in one of the stories as a scary animal spirit.) No corny mushy dialogue. No degeneracy. No weirdness. Just no low-hanging fruit (that seems to be the staple fare today).

WARNING: The 1st edition has content toxic (… lots of unrestrained *mansplaining* that is very *triggering*) to woke individuals. If you are one, do not read it and be disappointed. Get the 2nd edition instead. It may be available in 2023. The woke-toxic content has been mostly removed to make room for new content. 'Mostly' because I do not care or believe in *THE CURRENT THING* .

Second-edition stories are mostly written from the perspective of Zuma.

- **Shadows in the night**: A young woman is troubled by a ghostly intruder at night.
- **Zuma vs. Cutie**: Zuma finds competition from an unlikely friend. She and her husband are asked to help rescue a kidnapped boy.
- **The evil twin**: A rich heiress is driven to desperation by a deceased twin who wants her to die too.
- **The alien invasion**: A huge bolide crashes down in the Atlantic. The site becomes an alien platform for launching attacks on USA, Canada, Australia and New Zealand. The aliens do not attack any other nation. The US government and military collapse after a few days. The strangest thing about the invasion is that the alien's primary objective is not humans but cows.

  While this story will describe the alien invasion in plain English, it will also provide a viable economic model for a successful alien invasion.

• 1st edition paperback (140 small grayscale pages): $9   • 2nd edition paperback (150 bigger colour pages): $20   • 1st edition ebook: ₹100   • 2nd edition ebook: Will not be published

About the author

V. Subhash is an invisible Indian writer, programmer and cartoonist. In 2020, he published one of the biggest jokebooks of all time and then followed it up with a tech book on FFmpeg and a 400-page volume of 149 political cartoons. Although he had published a few ebooks as early as 2003, Subhash did not publish books in the traditional sense until 2020. For over two decades, Subhash had used his website **www.VSubhash.com** as the main outlet for his writing. During this time, he had accumulated a lot of published and unpublished material. This content and the automated book-production process that he had developed helped him publish 21 books in his first year. In February 2023, Apress (SpringerNature) published his rewritten and updated FFmpeg book as *QUICK START GUIDE TO FFMPEG*. Thus, by early 2023, Subhash had published 30 books! In 2022, Subhash ran out of non-fiction material and tried his hand at fiction. The result was *UNLIKELY STORIES*, a collection of horror and comedy short stories. After adding new stories to this fiction title (for its second edition), Subhash plans to pause his writing and move on to other things. Subhash pursues numerous hobbies and interests, several of which have become the subject of his books such as *COOL ELECTRONIC PROJECTS*, *HOW TO INSTALL SOLAR* and *HOW TO INVEST IN STOCKS*. He was inspired to write his gigantic jokebook after years of listening to vintage American radio shows such as *Fibber & Molly* and *Duffy's Tavern*.